THE WORLD'S GREATEST AIR MYSTERIES

Michael Hardwick

SAPERE
BOOKS

THE WORLD'S
GREATEST AIR
MYSTERIES

Published by Sapere Books.

20 Windermere Drive, Leeds, England, LS17 7UZ,
United Kingdom

saperebooks.com

ISBN: 978-1-80055-607-2.

TABLE OF CONTENTS

PREFACE 7
1: THE GREATEST MYSTERY OF THEM ALL 10
2: THE DISASTER TO R101 39
3: FLIGHT INTO MYSTERY 61
4: TWO STARS FALL 69
5: A 27-YEAR MYSTERY SOLVED 87
6: THE DEATHS OF ULM AND KINGSFORD SMITH 101
7: BALLOON OVER THE NORTH POLE 123
8: A ROYAL TRAGEDY AT EAGLE'S ROCK 136
9: THE DISASTER OF MOUNT TORMENT 145
10: THE COLORADO JIGSAW 154
11: FIRST ACROSS THE TASMAN? 163
12: "A RED EAGLE FALLING" 180
13: THE ACE WHO FLEW TOO HIGH 188
14: THE MYSTERY OF THE *ITALIA* 194
15: THE LESSON OF *YOKE PETER* 207
16: THE LOST TYCOON 220
17: DISASTER ON "RED 19" 232
18: EXIT A HEROINE 244
19: SUICIDE BEHIND SCHEDULE 256
20: THE ECCENTRIC AVIATOR OF WOBURN ABBEY 265
21: COLLISION COURSE 274
ACKNOWLEDGEMENTS 292
BIBLIOGRAPHY 293
A NOTE TO THE READER 294

PREFACE

Some two hundred years have passed since people first went up in a balloon: the first flights by heavier-than-air machines were made only within our own century; yet mankind has been sailing the seas since time immemorial. By comparison, our conquest of the air was achieved only yesterday.

That is, our scientific conquest; for there is reason to believe that the art of levitation, by which human beings could take-off, hover and fly without mechanical aid, was instinctive to certain communities many centuries ago. The chapter here dealing with "flying saucers" makes mention of quite accredited accounts of levitation, as well as of legendary ones. "In the old days," says the Galway legend, "everybody danced in the air like leaves in the autumn wind ... people made a song to a plate." "They hit a plate and made a song, and the song said where they wanted to go — and so they went," adds a Caribbean tale; and there are other such from different parts of the world but quite similar in detail and phraseology.

An American experimenter, J. W. Keely, seems to have harnessed some such sonic force in the 1890s when he was able, by sounding a certain note, to make a small metal model of an airship rise and fly. No one wished to encourage him. He destroyed his papers and died. Yet it is quite on the cards that some day the application of sonic and mental vibrations, like other forces as yet unharnessed or unconceived by us, will be commonplace and people will again walk on air.

Until then we must rely upon aircraft and the coming spacecraft to get us off the ground. With the exception of the chapter on flying saucers and a couple of accounts concerning the now discredited airship, this book deals with mysteries surrounding aircraft flights. Too often, alas, these involve disaster, despite the often-repeated truism that the most dangerous part of a journey by air is the drive to the airport. But there is something tributary in this: as many chapters show — and especially that dealing with the Comet tragedies — the aircraft industry has plumbed its mysteries, distilled fact from supposition, and used the knowledge so painfully gained to further the safety, comfort and convenience of flying.

An aircraft that goes up must come down in a matter of hours. There can be no possibility in the following pages of stories to parallel some of the greatest sea mysteries: no *Mary Celeste* or *Joyita* of the air, mysteriously abandoned yet flying on; no *Marlborough*, manned only by skeletons; no *Waratah*, seen again after many years' disappearance, only to vanish once more.[1] (There has been some equivalent of the latter case, though, in the experience of air travellers who have cancelled a flight due to apprehension of danger, thereby escaping death, like Mr Sawyer of the *Waratah*.) If there are any really good tales of ghostly aircraft or flying apparitions I am sorry not to have come across them for inclusion. The First World War, which produced its Angel of Mons, ghostly bagpiper, and so on, threw up one or two vague stories of invincible fighter aircraft flown by spectral figures, but I have been able to find no substantial account of them.

"The world is big enough for us. No ghosts need apply," said the ever-wise Sherlock Holmes; and the following stories, if not, by their essential nature, "down to earth", come from factual sources, with supposition intervening. There have been other aerial mysteries, a number of which are recounted in

---

[1] For accounts of all these see *The World's Greatest Sea Mysteries* by Michael and Mollie Hardwick (Sapere Books, 2022).

some of the books listed in the Bibliography. A selection had to be made, and this is mine.

Michael Hardwick

1970

1: THE GREATEST MYSTERY OF THEM ALL

Most of the mysteries recounted in this book have either been solved or are insoluble. The few others may yet be explained in detail owed to more than conjecture; but there is one of them which, capable of future explanation though it must surely be, one might prefer to see remain on the unsolved list for the time being. Mankind has more than enough problems to occupy it just now. When it comes to flying saucers, some of us regard them much as Sherlock Holmes did the giant rat of Sumatra — "a story for which the world is not yet prepared".

What are flying saucers, anyway? It is much easier to say what they are not — saucers, to some extent, included. Records of sightings refer in many instances to objects that have been ovaloid, discoid, star-like, cigar-shaped, diamond-shaped. American scientists were probably wise, if somewhat prosaic, to be the first to classify them as "Unidentified Flying Objects", or, for short, UFOs.

People have been seeing things in the sky for thousands of years: from Heavenly Hosts, to angels, to dread portents, to warring armies, to chariots of fire, to "flying wheels of light". The sky being where Heaven was reckoned to be somewhat vaguely situated, humans of centuries before ours tended to glance upward a great deal, quite prepared to find some symbol of approval or displeasure on display. Any considerable event (generally disastrous) on earth was preceded by its quota of sky-borne omens, and it was no doubt accepted that objects of no particular import that happened to be noticed nipping about in space were ramifications of celestial mechanics.

Nowadays we think we know rather more. If we have not quite managed to take a true bearing on Heaven itself, we have pinpointed the planets and stars and demonstrated to such as may have life on them that Unidentified Flying Objects — which, if they only knew it, are satellites and spacecraft from a mixed-up globe known locally as Earth — do exist. Also (inconceivable as it may seem at times) we have learned much from our forefathers' example of human gullibility. It has taught us, in the presence of any phenomenon that is not immediately explicable, to doubt first and work cautiously towards reasoned belief, rather than the other way round. A section of a report on Unidentified Flying Objects which has been two years and 500,000 U.S. dollars in the making seems to characterize our attitude when it ends, "Although conventional or natural explanations certainly cannot be ruled out, the probability of such seems low in this case and the probability that at least one genuine UFO was involved appears to be fairly high."

Though the report as a whole is summarized by its compilers as proving nothing that has added to scientific knowledge, the existence of even one such phrase as that quoted above is enough to nourish those who prefer to believe in the existence of "flying saucers". The remark that nine out of ten sightings "prove to be quite plausibly related to ordinary objects such as aircraft, satellites, balloons, street lights, clouds or other natural phenomena", while it may satisfy the wishes of those who do not believe, leaves the way right open for the rest to cry triumphantly, "What about the *tenth* case?"

Let us consider the tenth case. It comprises many strange tales, of which the following is but one of the more recent examples.

On the evening of Saturday, 2 September 1967, a number of adults and children saw an UFO (or UFOs) on the Bentilee estate in the English Midlands city of Stoke-on-Trent. They were later interviewed keenly by two amateur astronomers, Roger H. Stanway and Anthony R. Pace, who published the results together with accounts of other British sightings under the title *Flying Saucer Report*.

Between 9.10 and 9.15 p.m. on that Saturday, the account goes, a group of children who lived near Beverley Drive on the Bentilee estate were playing hide-and-seek when they saw a strange object which flew above the roof tops and was, according to one young witness, Kenneth Harrington, "like a bright red light with a dull yellow glowing on the side".

One of the adult witnesses was a Mrs Stevenson who lived nearby at Wendling Close. She told the investigators, "It was a clear sky and a mild evening at around 9 p.m. This object came straight over the roofs. It wasn't low, but pretty high and it was whirling — going round and round like a spinning top. It went over towards the fields." She then heard children shouting that the object had made a landing. She also described the UFO as being "bright red, like a great big sun, the colour of the sun setting". When the six children who had first seen it began to walk towards what they believed to be its landing-place they were followed by Mrs Stevenson and a Mrs Bowen who had also seen the UFO. Mrs Bowen testified, "We were frightened for the safety of the children, but at the same time we were curious." The object apparently rose again, hung suspended in space for a few seconds, then moved over a hedge. Mrs Stevenson said: "When it came down, the field looked as though it was on fire — like a bonfire. I could see the leaves on the trees lit up by the red glow."

Two of the boys, David McCue and Kenneth Harrington, told the investigators that once the object had landed its bright dome was extinguished, but the orange section remained illuminated for about three minutes longer and then seemed to take on a yellow hue. Then it went out. The two boys ran to where they had seen the UFO and felt about with their hands in the darkness. They found nothing. The "thing", whatever it was, had vanished.

By now Mrs Stevenson had telephoned the police at Hanley nearby. The sergeant and two constables who arrived at Bentilee were inclined at first to cast a good-natured doubt on the whole affair. Then they, too, suddenly noticed a bright light coming into view above the low hills, a "big white glow" which rose steadily and seemed to be ascending on a slanting path. When it had reached a height of two or three hundred feet above a hill it became stationary for a moment, before disappearing instantaneously, in the words of one witness, "Just as a television picture does when you turn the set off."

Another group of boys, between the ages of 15 and 16 years, were playing in the fields at about 9.45 p.m. that evening when one of them, Terry Bagnall, spotted what he described as a bright white cigar-shaped object pass over the houses. It was seen by a number of adults, one of whom described it as being as big as the top of the roof of the average semi-detached house. When questioned by Messrs Stanway and Pace, the police who had seen the white light were non-committal but admitted they had seen the light "take off". They said it could have been a car's headlights. The most they could do was to set up a 24-hour patrol on the estate.

Clearly, something was seen over the Bentilee estate that September evening; something totally unlike a conventional aircraft in appearance and manner of flight. Witnesses'

13

descriptions tallied to quite an extent, although the mention of a cigar-shaped object in addition seemed perhaps to suggest that more than one UFO had been involved.

It might be interesting to compare this present-day example of a sighting with one of long ago, travelling back in time and setting from 1967 on a housing-estate, bristling with TV aerials, to the quiet of Byland Abbey, Yorkshire, in the thirteenth century. In the book *Flying Saucers Have Landed* Mr Desmond Leslie quotes from an ancient manuscript in the possession of the Benedictine monks at Ampleforth Abbey:

"Took the sheep from Wilfred and roasted them on the feast of SS. Simon and Jude. But when Henry the Abbott was about to say grace, John, one of the brethren, came in and said there was a great portent outside. Then they all ran out, and Lo! *a large round silver thing like a disk flew slowly over them* and excited the greatest terror. Whereat Henry the Abbott immediately cried that Wilfred was an adulterer, wherefore it was impious to…"

The rest of the manuscript is lost to us and so, alas, is the connection between this event and the waywardness of Wilfred. It is the shape and colour of the disc that interest us with their pre-echo of more recent phenomena.

A good deal later, in 1704, people in Devon gazed skywards one day at a neat, V-shaped formation of dark elliptical objects with fins or streaming exhausts. An old print shows them as dark, solid objects flying in formation in broad daylight. The logs of old ships are worth scanning for records of strange craft that winged their ways across the sky long before the days of the Wright brothers. Sailors are, of course, notoriously superstitious and it might be argued that they are more liable than most to see strange portents — the impression is that when not watching UFOs they were pretty fully occupied with

14

the gambols of mermaids and sea-serpents. On 22 March 1870 Captain Banner and the crew of the *Lady of the Lake*, at Latitude 50° 47' N., Longitude 27° 52' W., saw an amazing circular object which flew below the clouds. Its trailing edge was surrounded by a fuzz or luminous band, divided into four equal sectors and from its centre extended a long curved tail. It seemed to be flying against the wind and was visible for quite a time before the clouds obscured it; the Captain was able to make a drawing. We are indebted to the Admiralty for a report on 15 May 1879 which came from H.M.S. *Vulture* in the Persian Gulf and referred to two colossal rotating luminous wheels which sank slowly down from just above the surface till they disappeared into the depths.

Reports of UFOs came thick and fast from the latter part of the nineteenth century. Communications were getting better, and more accurate accounts survive. What are we to make of the closely documented reports of an airship over Kansas City in April 1897? The obvious answer is that nothing should be made of it, since there were certainly no airships to put in the air anywhere at that time. But *something* was seen over Kansas, Chicago and Benton, Texas. It was said to have green and red tail-lights and to be cigar-shaped, with enormous projections. In Sistersville, Virginia, it was described as "a huge conical ship, 180 feet long, with fins on either side".

Supposing that one out of ten Unidentified Flying Objects down the centuries really has been a "flying saucer", where did they come from? An inhabited planet, most of us would suspect; and Mars has long been the popular fictional source of little green men with television aerials sprouting from their heads. Yet not without basis, for many scientists believe that Mars tops the list of likely locations of "human" life. Some years ago a Harvard astronomer named Lowell studied maps of

Mars and came to the conclusion that indentations on its surface were a network of canals. He stated, "These canals must have been in existence for many thousands of years. I do not believe this would be possible without some intelligence capable of irrigating them." Greenish patches on the surface have been taken as vegetation by some scientists and by others as merely due to chemical changes. Those who believe in life on Mars point out that vegetable life must be partnered by animal life — though not necessarily human life. According to Dr Gerard P. Kuiper, a Chicago astronomer, "No form of life as we know it could exist on Mars but insect life." Perish the thought that we should embrace the likelihood of insects controlling flying saucers; but there have been wilder theories.

In *Flying Saucers Have Landed* Mr Leslie reminds us that it is possible for all of us, by switching a knob in our living-rooms, to pick up pictures or sounds from most parts of the world. Supposing, he hazards, there existed a race of beings who could project images or objects? It's a thought.

It has been suggested that UFOs could be attributable to an accomplished use of levitation. Certainly, levitation — the ability to raise oneself and objects from the ground and to "float on air" — is an accredited phenomenon to which men and women down the centuries have been strangely subject and have often been able to practise at will. South American legends speak of "the olden days when the wise old people could fly quite easily… Anybody could dance in the air like leaves in a storm. Everything was so light." The lives of the saints abound with instances of levitation. St Joseph of Cupertino (1603–63) seems by all accounts to have spent as much time off the ground as on it, to the embarrassment of his superiors who had to exclude him from certain processions and gatherings — even the communal meals in the refectory

— because of the disturbance he would cause by suddenly floating off. Once, taking pity on ten workmen who were finding it impossible to move a heavy cross, he leapt astride it and, as if it were a hobby-horse, coolly flew it to its destination. The famous St Teresa of Ávila (1515–82) was another whose rapture often manifested itself in levitation, which she found it impossible, and exhausting, to resist. And, nearer to our own time, the feats of that most reputable medium, Daniel Douglas Home (1833–1886), were scrutinized and pronounced genuine beyond doubt by most distinguished witnesses. He once floated out of a window 70 feet above a London street and in at another.

This is not to suggest that UFOs will some day be shown to be nothing more than levitationally-minded individuals commuting through the skies without need of public transport; but it might well be that levitation provides the effortless, silent means of propulsion which UFOs almost always seem to possess. It has, in addition, been cited often as the solution to the mystery of the building of the central chamber of the Great Pyramid, whose stones are estimated to weigh 70 tons each and date back to the dawn of time. Machinery equal to the task of lifting them did not exist. Were they simply slipped through the air by the application of levitation; and is this how "flying saucers" are powered?

The absence from most UFOs of sound, smoke or vapour has puzzled many laymen and enabled many "experts" to clinch their arguments in favour of the sightings being put down to tricks of light, and so forth. Yet who knows what sources of energy may be available to other intelligences than ours? We on earth have in the past few decades harnessed forces the possibility of whose existence would have been derided a century or two ago, and there are undoubtedly many more phenomena to be discovered, investigated and at length controlled. It were surely arrogant to maintain that because we could not achieve something with our present resources, no one else could with theirs; as arrogant as it is to suggest that life as we comprehend it on Earth is the only life form in the whole of the universe.

There are various other leading theories about the power source of UFOs, largely to do with gravity, a controllable "G-field", and so on, and they have been discussed in great and intriguing detail by a number of authors. But if we are not to crowd out all the other chapters from this book in favour of this one greatest mystery alone, we must get back from theory to fact.

A sceptical scientist once commented, "The trouble with most of the so-called sightings of UFOs is that they are American." He was perhaps recalling, rather unfairly, how credulous many American radio listeners had once shown themselves to be when startled by the possibility of invasion from space in a dramatization of H. G. Wells's *The War of the Worlds* which caused widespread hysteria. The truth is that sightings have not been predominantly American. The first post-war report was; but it was not made by someone prone to hysteria.

In June 1947 an American businessman, Kenneth Arnold, was piloting his own aircraft over the Cascade Range of mountains near the northwest Pacific coast. Near Mount Rainier he suddenly spotted nine very bright disc-shaped objects, spinning through the sky like "saucers tripping over water". Arnold calculated their speed to be 1,700 miles per hour. Newspapers headlined the story and dealt with the rush of reported sightings that followed. One of these was to lead to tragedy.

In mid-afternoon on 7 January 1948 the Kentucky State Police came excitedly on the line to the control tower of Goodman Air Force base near Louisville. They had been inundated with calls from the towns of Owensboro and Irvington, reporting "strange circular aircraft" measuring perhaps 300 feet across. This news was greeted with irreverently expressed scepticism by the control tower — until the police managed to add that the objects were moving westward at high speed and would soon reach Goodman. Then followed reports of a strange object hurtling through the sky, resembling a giant cannonball, although subsequent witnesses likened it to an enormous dinner plate. Instructions were given hastily. Contact was made with a flight of four F-51 interceptors coming in from the south. They were ordered to investigate. The flight leader, Captain Mantell, took his aircraft smartly ahead of the others. His voice reached the Flight Operations Room: "I've spotted something above and ahead of me. I'm at 10,000 feet and still climbing." Then, "I have the thing in my sights. It's above me and I'm gaining on it. Going up to 20,000 feet."

Nowadays, such an intention would cause no comment. But this was 1948 and the aircraft had no pressurized cockpit, only oxygen cylinders for the pilot's use. Mantell and his planes had been on a low routine flight, not one anticipating a sudden switch in altitude to 20,000 feet. When the tower called Mantell again they got no response. The aircraft were recalled. The other three obeyed — but not Mantell.

His aircraft had been climbing steadily. It could be assumed that he had been overcome by dizziness and blacked out. All that was known was that his F-51 had gone out of control, diving so steeply that a wing had broken away. Later came the public announcement that Captain Mantell had crashed to his death.

No one has ever discovered what this UFO was and there has been no official verdict upon it. Some people believed it was a "Skyhook" weather-balloon from Clinton County Air Force Base. If so, one might wonder why this was not admitted, and why the debris of the crashed plane was scattered over so wide an area — almost as though it had disintegrated in flight, rather than on impact with the ground. Many prefer to believe that the U.S. Air Force chose to keep silent about an attack on the aircraft by some object unknown either to aviation or science, perhaps controlled by an alien intelligence. If the experience of U.S.A.F. Lieutenant H. G. Combs at Andrews Field, Washington D.C., is to be believed, the latter would seem to be not impossible.

On 18 November 1948 Combs, flying with a Lieutenant Jackson, was about to land his T-6 at 9.45 a.m. when a strange object loomed up near him. It had the appearance of a greyish globe and gave off an eerie, subdued light. On impulse, Combs decided to follow it. "I chased it for over ten minutes," he stated later. "It evaded every move I made. It was either piloted or controlled remotely. Of that I haven't the slightest doubt." His reports were turned over to the Pentagon, whence a statement eventually emanated: "The mystery was cleared up when the object was identified positively as a cluster of cosmic-ray research balloons." This easy explanation was contested vigorously by Combs who insisted: "If there had been more than one balloon I wouldn't have survived to tell the tale. This wasn't a radar-responder gadget. It dodged me too cunningly. An intelligent mind was directing every turn."

Life is considerably more exciting these days for the Spanish Air Force who, when they get the Spanish equivalent of the order "Scramble!", realize that there is a good chance that a search for flying saucers is under way. For at the end of 1968 Spain became inflicted with what can only be described as UFO fever. Her Air Ministry is known to be taking extremely seriously the question why so many mystery flying objects have been reported. Instructions have been issued that any such reports should be made immediately to the nearest Air Force station. This interest in flying saucers began in November 1968 when a chemist, Antonio Sanz, claimed that a flying object followed his car as he drove home to Duenas, 150 miles north of Madrid. Ten years earlier, in September 1958, thousands of people in Madrid saw a bright object passing through the sky. Air Force jet fighters set off in pursuit. One pilot climbed to 50,000 feet, but reported that the mystery object was still above him. His fuel was running low and he returned to base. The "flying saucer" got away. The Spanish Government has made no enlightening statement about the details of the incident. But then, official reticence has been a characteristic of the whole saga of flying saucers, as a letter to *The Times* on 22 January 1966 observed. It was prompted by one of the most sensational sightings in the whole history of flying saucers.

On 26 December 1965 Miss Jacqueline Wingfield, research assistant to the well-known aviation historian Mr Charles Gibbs-Smith, was driving a young Danish friend, Miss Mortensen, along a road near Cappoquin, Ireland. The weather conditions were just about perfect with a clear blue sky. Miss Mortensen's attention was suddenly engaged by a strange object moving steadily across the sky in front of them. Miss Wingfield immediately stopped the car (and engine) and both got out their cameras. Miss Mortensen had time to take one shot of what they described later as a solid-looking, rounded object flying in complete silence with a trailing plume of flame-like brightness at its stern, but no trail of smoke or vapour. Mr Gibbs-Smith subsequently took the precaution of having the roll of film processed in circumstances which would guard against any accusations of faking. Then he sent it to *The Times* which published it together with an account of the sighting and an implied invitation to defence experts to comment. They did not respond, despite Mr Gibbs-Smith's challenge that top intelligence authorities in America and England must have much more information about phenomena of this and other kinds, and of the potential capabilities of other civilizations with perhaps 70,000 or 700,000 years of experience behind them compared with our mere 6,000–7,000, than they will disclose or discuss with speculative Press and other inquirers.

Mr Gibbs-Smith's letter to *The Times* had been provoked by an article in that newspaper two days earlier by Dr Allen Hynek, an American astronomer and "adviser to the U.S. Air Force on reports of unidentified objects". In general, Dr Hynek had discounted the idea that UFOs are vehicles from outer space, producing several examples of the seemingly bizarre turning out to be the mundane. Even a UFO sighted simultaneously from the ground and from a helicopter broadcasting reports of traffic conditions — an apparently strong combination of evidence — had proved to be an advertising aircraft whose flashing lights spelt out "Learn to Fly at Palwaukee", an injunction clearly owing nothing to Mars. But Dr Hynek conceded that "for each truly but temporarily mysterious case there remain one or two equally mysterious unsolved cases", and instanced one of them.

An anthropology student of the University of Wisconsin was driving his wife, her mother and young sister one night in a quiet country road when they saw a horrifying spectacle. A blaze of lights, tearing towards them head-on, seemed to be a crashing airliner that was going to hit them. The young sister was so terrified that she flung herself on to the floor in the back of the car. But there came no impact. The approaching lights suddenly slowed and halted, taking up a hovering position almost alongside the car. They seemed to mark the four corners of a huge rectangular structure which continued to hover without a sound until it moved to the rear of the car and glided silently away. The now-recovered student gave chase at top speed, but his car was no match for the receding lights.

Had it been some form of helicopter? Dr Hynek pointed to its lack of sound, and to the folly of any helicopter pilot who would descend into pitch-dark terrain, strewn with potential obstacles. There was no evidence that the occupants of the car had suffered a delusion due to mass hysteria. There was, in short, no explanation.

Dr Hynek revealed that he was accustomed to receive an average of a report a day on UFO sightings, and that most came from "solid citizens and technically trained men". All the more disappointing, then, that he should conclude his article: "I have recommended to the Air Force that a panel, including sociologists and psychologists, should examine the growth of rumour. Possibly the study of some of the people who report the sighting of UFOs would be more rewarding than the investigation of what they saw."

The United States Air Force began treating UFO reports seriously when in September 1947 the Chief of the Air Technical Intelligence Centre (A.T.I.C.) informed the Air Force commanding general that A.T.I.C. firmly believed that UFOs were worth scientific investigation. To this end there was set up at the Wright-Patterson air base the official "Project Sign", after which a flood of sightings were reported by and to the Air Force. Most of them contributed little to a real understanding of what had been seen.

Then, in 1966, the U.S. Air Force gave a grant of £107,000 to a team of scientists under a distinguished physicist, Professor Edward Condon, to carry out independent inquiry. British scientists were invited to help Professor Condon with his work at the University of Colorado. The fevered itch to keep up with the Joneses being a characteristic of nations as well as individuals, the Russians were determined to show the world that they had as fine a claim to UFOs as anyone else, and on 12 November 1967 Moscow announced that Air Force General A. Stolyerov would lead a commission to investigate the large number of reported Russian sightings. The next country to get smartly into the act was Canada. The Royal Canadian Air Force intensified its inquiry into more than a hundred reports of UFO sightings over the city of Calgary, Alberta. At a Press conference, Squadron-Leader E. B. Chase of Calgary claimed that the R.C.A.F. possessed one of the best photographs ever taken of an Unidentified Flying Object.

In America, at least, UFOs are deemed officially to exist and to be worth serious scientific investigation. The Inspector General of the U.S. Air Force, in an Operations and Training Order to Base Commanders on 24 December 1959, commanded: "Unidentified Flying Objects — sometimes treated by the Press and referred to as flying saucers — must be rapidly and accurately identified as serious Air Force business in ZI (Interior Zone)."

Professor Condon's report was published in January 1969, the original grant of £107,000 for its compilation having grown into an actual expenditure of £208,000. The result is anticlimax — nothing, the report concludes, has been added to scientific knowledge by the study of UFOs. There is "no direct evidence whatever of a convincing nature for the claim that any UFOs represent spacecraft visiting earth from another civilization". Further extensive study "probably cannot be justified". It is a curious summing-up of a report which includes amongst its voluminous data the following case, upon which it comments, "Although conventional or natural explanations certainly cannot be ruled out, the probability of such seems low in this case and the probability that at least one genuine UFO was involved appears to be fairly high."

The incident involved a R.A.F. Venom jet fighter which in 1956 was put up to intercept an unidentifiable object travelling at some 4,000 miles per hour over the highly important strategic bomber bases of Lakenheath and Sculthorpe, in East Anglia. The Venom, one of two, was guided by radar to within half a mile of the UFO, when the pilot reported, "Roger. I've got my guns locked on him," the electronic equivalent of having the "enemy" dead in his sights. A moment passed, and then the pilot was heard asking, "Where did he go?" He soon found out. With an unbelievably swift manoeuvre the UFO had turned the tables on the fighter and was sitting on its tail. For the next ten minutes that pilot tried every trick he knew to shake it off. It acted, in the American phraseology of the report, "like it was glued right behind him. Always the same distance, very close ... he was getting worried, excited and also pretty scared". Running short of fuel the Venom returned unmolested to base.

As noted earlier, it is the one case in ten, or even in a hundred, that presents the substance for belief in "flying saucers", and the Condon Report's negative conclusions have by no means ended the debate. Dr David Saunders, formerly joint principal investigator on the project, has written a book criticizing Dr Condon's approach and his criteria, arguing that psychological considerations were allowed to outweigh scientific ones. A panel of the American National Academy of Sciences has endorsed the report. But the director of the 12,000-member National Investigations Committee on Aerial Phenomena has declared, "We are publicly challenging the attempt to dismiss UFOs. Dr Condon started off as a non-believer and made his findings fit his beliefs."

Needless to say, no one in Britain has undertaken so elaborate an investigation. Indeed, if the experiences of the energetic Roger Stanway and Anthony Pace are to be believed, the Ministry of Defence does very little about Unidentified Flying Objects. In *Flying Saucer Report* they relate a visit they paid to the Ministry in Whitehall on Friday, 29 September 1967. After an interview with a junior civil servant in which they described the Stoke-on-Trent sighting and others of which they had recorded particulars in compiling their reports, they were told that the Ministry's interest was limited solely to possible military and defence implications of UFOs. There was no department, scientist or other person in the Ministry solely concerned with them.

Their thirst for information unsatisfied, Stanway and Pace continued to press the somewhat reticent Ministry for rather more precise details of UFO sightings in Britain and learnt eventually that up to the start of 1967 there had been a total of 625 British sightings. Those not decisively attributable to natural or man-made phenomena amounted to some 10 per cent. Our own more recent approach to the Ministry produced the figures for 1967 — 362 sightings investigated, of which some seven were still the subject of speculation and fourteen "not capable of rational explanation", the main reason for this being that witnesses had given incomplete descriptions. The investigation procedure is to find out from the nearest R.A.F.

radar establishment whether or not a bleep was registered on its screens at the time. Civil-airline flights and weather reports are checked. There may be discreet questioning of witnesses. This would seem to suggest a serious attitude by the Ministry towards UFOs, but, plainly, Britain is far from being as "saucer-orientated" as America where a flight of supersonic aircraft is kept permanently ready to follow up sightings.

On 19 July 1966 Sir J. Langford-Holt, M.P. asked Mr Harold Wilson, the Prime Minister, at Question Time in the House of Commons:

"In view of the fact that the Secretary of State for Defence is responsible only for the air defence implications of the reports of unidentified flying objects, will the Prime Minister allocate to a Department the duty of assessing the wider implications of these reports?"

Mr Wilson replied: "No, sir."

The authors of *Flying Saucer Report* condemn this reply as "unrealistic and dangerous". They make the point:

"If in fact the phenomenon does exist, and the British Government is unaware of this fact, then there is always the frightening possibility that a UFO, or formation of UFOs may be misidentified as hostile high-altitude bombers, or intercontinental ballistic missiles, or even an artificial satellite bearing a hydrogen bomb. In order to avoid such a potentially catastrophic error, it would appear necessary to fully brief defence personnel and programme computers with the known characteristics of the UFO phenomenon. How can this be done if the British Government has not scientifically investigated the phenomenon? General L. M. Chassin, former General Air Defence Co-ordinator, Allied Air Force, Central Europe (NATO), drew the world's attention to this horrifying possibility nearly a decade ago, and since then, his words appear to have remained unheeded for a disturbingly long time."

Flying Saucer Report gives details of 70 Unidentified Flying Objects investigated within a radius of approximately 20 miles of the Midlands town of Stoke-on-Trent during 1967 — a year which saw a spurt of unprecedented UFO activity. With the co-operation of the British Unidentified Flying Object Research Association, witnesses were questioned within hours of sightings. The Bentilee estate sighting, which we have already described, was the most spectacular. But there were others that seem equally impressive.

At 8.30 a.m. on 30 August 1967 two newsboys, Peter Hollander, 12, and David Anthony Jones, 13, both of Nantwich, were cycling along Middlewich Road in the direction of Crewe and were approaching a road bridge. The weather was dull, dry with a light breeze and plenty of cloud. They were riding in single file, when suddenly David who was in the lead spotted an object in the sky to the left, about a mile away. He called out to Peter who related how he looked up to his left and behind him, and saw the object move rapidly towards them at an angle approximately 45° to the road. They both thought at first it was a private aircraft, until it came nearer and they noticed its peculiar shape. "A few seconds more and we realized it could be a flying saucer," said Peter. The strange craft must have slowed down quickly, for moments later it was at a standstill, hanging almost motionless directly above them. Not looking where he was going, David rode into the kerb and Peter collided with his rear mudguard. A car travelling in the same direction behind them sounded its horn as they stumbled from their bicycles, but carried on along the road apparently unaware of the object in the sky. The boys forgot their bicycles. "We were scared," said David, "and dived under a hedge and looked up. We noticed its underside, and just stared for a few moments. We got up and looked at it for a few moments — about 30 seconds, then it flew away so fast, we could not keep track of it. We were a bit shaken up about it, but soon recovered."

On 4 September 1967 Stanway and Pace interviewed Peter and David who described their dramatic encounter with an Unidentified Flying Object. The shape which appeared from the south-south-west had been oval and coloured silver, they said. Above it was a small transparent dome and beneath the oval structure a dark grey ridge, somewhat longer than the base of the dome. The dome's transparency became apparent when dark clouds were visible through it. Peter recalled that the dome had what appeared to be a cross on the side and from a point near the top rose what looked like an antenna. As it came towards them, Peter noticed a small yellow light at the front, but could not be sure whether this was on the oval part or the dome. David saw what he thought were two small openings at the rear of the craft which he presumed to be "exhaust outlets". From the ground the "undercarriage" of the craft appeared about as large as a half-crown piece held at arm's length. David estimated the object's true height at approximately 100 feet. They could see the underneath quite plainly and described this as having a silver-coloured outer perimeter with an inner oval of what appeared to be millions of black tubes or wires on a silver background. Along the centre ran a silver rectangular section containing three identical solid black circles, one towards each end, and one at the centre. The craft was completely silent, and as they watched it seemed to be moving silently to and fro. It is probable that the rectangular section was in fact the underside of the dark grey ridge, observed beneath the oval structure.

When he had dived for cover David scratched his face on a hawthorn bush and the interviewers noticed the scar when they interviewed him. Peter stated that the UFO, hardly surprisingly, visited him in his dreams. Both boys described how, after half a minute, the craft began to move forward, horizontally at first; then it climbed and was gone in a few seconds. They gathered their bicycles and continued their journey discussing a fantastic adventure. The interviewers have testified to the calmness of the two boys and give it as their opinion that here had been a sighting of an aerial craft of unknown origin.

Perhaps it is natural to wonder why the passing car had carried on, evidently unaware of the UFO. It may be that the occupants would not have seen something so near, yet almost above them in the sky, due to the restricted view from the windows. What else can be gathered from the accounts of the two boys? The strange craft had a deliberate motion — an intelligence in control, and a considerable intelligence at that. The craft hovered directly above the two boys, as if observing their actions and perhaps also their reactions to its presence. Stanway and Pace pose the question: "Could it be that this aerial vehicle, completely unfamiliar in appearance, was in fact a remotely controlled surveillance craft, which had detected the boys as they moved along the road, and had come down for a closer look?"

A man who saw another UFO seems to have had an impression of being "watched". At about 6 p.m. on Tuesday, 17 October 1967, Mr J. D. Stotter of Doxey, Stafford, was driving his lorry on the M6 motorway travelling south. The sky was clear with some scattered cloud when he approached the turn-off to Holmes Chapel. He was to recall later that it was still reasonably light, although some vehicles had switched on their lights. He was conscious of the glow of the setting sun to his right, in the west. All at once he had the feeling "as though someone was looking at me". He glanced up and in some astonishment saw through the top left-hand corner of the windscreen a strange craft moving in the same direction along the left-hand side of the motorway. It was fairly low in the sky, and Mr Stotter compared the size and height to a Boeing Stratocruiser on its first circuit over an airfield, before reducing height and coming in to land. He had seen many large aircraft circling before landing at Manchester Ringway Airport from the cab of his lorry while travelling on the motorway.

But as he travelled alongside the object at 35–40 miles per hour he was able to see that here was no aircraft. In his own words, "It looked like a large apple pie in a dish and there was no real colour to the main structure — it was just like a dark mass." He had the impression that there was no paint on the hull and he remembered thinking, "it could do with a coat of paint". He noticed a rounded underneath section, with a group of circular lights or portholes towards the front. Above the rounded section there seemed to be some kind of rim, from the rear of which came three continuous mauve-blue flames, possibly exhausts. These were equally spaced at the rear end and seemed to point backwards and downwards. Above the rim was a taller structure narrowing off to a flat top.

Mr Stotter was able to confirm later that from when he first sighted the UFO till he finally pulled his lorry on to the hard shoulder and stopped, he had travelled 5½ miles — he measured it next day on the lorry's milometer. He climbed out of his cab for a clearer view and watched the object for a full ten minutes, hearing a noise like a jet aircraft, only much higher in pitch "like a whining sound and rushing air, not unlike the noise of air issuing from the pinched neck of a balloon".

Suddenly the UFO veered to the left and forward and came almost to a standstill, before sweeping sideways across the motorway. It dropped, turned, accelerated away back the way it had come, and in a few seconds had disappeared. As it swung across in front of him, Mr Stotter could see that there were three mauve-blue coloured flames on the other side of the vehicle, identical to the first. As it gained speed, these increased in intensity and appeared to pivot backwards until they were one continuous horizontal line.

Stanway and Pace's request for sightings for *Flying Saucer Report* brought Mr Stotter's strange experience to light. He stated that he had been in the R.A.F. and had received routine training in aircraft identification and he was sure that what he had seen on the motorway had not been an aeroplane.

None of this, of course, proves that UFOs are interplanetary. Equally, there is no evidence that they are man-made here on the earth and operated by foreign powers who wish to keep themselves informed about what our paperboys and lorry drivers are up to. Perhaps we shall never be fully convinced until one has landed in Whitehall and its occupants interviewed. Yet there is a man who has claimed in a book that he has actually met and communicated with a crewman from an extra-terrestrial craft:

"It was about 12.30 in the noon hour on Thursday, 20th November 1952, that I first made personal contact with a man from another world. He came to Earth in his space craft, a flying saucer. He called it a Scout Ship.

"This took place on the California desert 10.2 miles from Desert Center toward Parker, Arizona."

Mr George Adamski, co-author of *Flying Saucers Have Landed*, who makes this astonishing claim has stated in a letter to a colleague of this author that he met the man from Venus on other occasions and that "he can speak our language as well as any other language on this earth". Adamski who is of Polish extraction and describes himself as "philosopher, student, teacher, saucer researcher", lives on Mount Palomar, California, 11 miles from the Hale Observatory, home of the giant 200-inch telescope. He himself has two telescopes and until 1946 confined his studies to the stars, entertaining no particular feelings either way for "flying saucers". Then on 9 October 1946, he claims, he saw with his naked eyes "a gigantic space craft hovering high above the mountain ridge to the south of Mount Palomar, towards San Diego". Adamski describes it as similar to a gigantic airship. It hovered motionless. It appeared to have no cabin compartment or external appendages.

From then on the amateur astronomer kept his eyes open for further sightings, and in 1952 paid one of many visits with some enthusiastic friends, Mr and Mrs A. C. Bailey, of Winslow, Arizona, and Dr and Mrs George H. Williamson, of Prescott, Arizona, and some others to Desert Center, a remote part of Arizona from where several reports of UFOs had emanated. The ground there, on each side of the highway leading to the town of Parker, was strewn with sharp and jagged rocks. A strong wind blew over the eerie, deserted landscape when, at 11 a.m. on 20 November, Adamski and his friends saw nothing more unusual than a two-engined aircraft, apparently on a routine flight. A few minutes later, however, looking towards a mountain ridge, they spotted "riding high and without sound ... a gigantic cigar-shaped silvery ship, without wings or appendages of any kind". Everyone had set out with the idea of being scientific and detached, and taking photographs and films. But they could only stand motionless, except occasionally to pass binoculars to each other in a daze.

Adamski later recalled Dr Williamson commenting on a dark marking on the side of the craft, plainly some form of insignia. Meanwhile, according to Adamski, cars continued to pass down the highway, but their occupants seemed preoccupied with the tortured landscape.

George Adamski testified later to a sudden feeling that this sighting was for him alone and that the craft would disappear never to return if too many people saw it. He beckoned his companions into their cars and they drove down the highway, looking for a quiet turning well off the road where observations could be continued without the risk of disturbance. Eventually, they discovered a spot some half a mile from the road at the base of a low, flat-topped incline. All the while, Adamski claims, the spacecraft followed them, hovering at times directly above the car. Adamski unpacked his telescope and photographic equipment. Then he bade his companions drive farther away and leave him for an hour.

Then the spell was broken as a number of "conventional" aircraft made a sudden appearance as if to circle the stranger. It turned its nose upwards and shot out into space, leaving the planes circling nothing. It was then that Adamski's attention was attracted by a flash, "and almost instantly a beautiful small craft appeared to be drifting between two of the mountain peaks and settling silently into one of the coves about half a mile from me". He lined up his telescope, with its attached camera, and quickly exposed seven films (frames?), not taking time to focus in his excitement. Then, as he attempted to snap the saucer with his hand-held Brownie, Adamski noticed it flash brightly and disappear over the hillock from which it had appeared. Hardly daring to hope that his pictures would be successful, he stood for a few moments lost in thought, staring at the spot where the second saucer — child of the big mother ship, perhaps — had vanished.

It was then, Adamski says, that he saw the man standing at the entrance of a ravine between two low hills, some quarter of a mile away. Adamski approached him and has described him as being about twenty-eight, with long sandy hair reaching to his shoulders and blowing in the wind. He was about five feet six inches tall, weighing about 135 pounds. He was a magnificent specimen. Adamski describes the man in considerable detail — from his clothing, a uniform of chocolate-brown colour not unlike that worn by modern astronauts, to his ox-blood shoes made of some woven material that was soft and flexible.

Adamski's first question was predictable, "Where do you come from?" The man evidently did not understand. Adamski, desperate to will him into some sort of response, began using signs and forming mental pictures in his mind which he strained to transmit to his companion. He thought of a planet, pointing at the same time to the sun, high in the sky. Eventually, his strange companion smiled, pointing to the sun, making one orbit with his arm, then another. He touched himself with his left hand, gesturing several times with his right index finger towards the second orbit. The second planet! With sudden inspiration, Adamski asked, "You mean you came from Venus?" The visitor replied with the single word, "Venus".

Largely through signs, gestures and mental pictures — an elementary form of telepathy — the visitor, Adamski claims, told him of the concern felt in outer space about the explosions on earth of bombs that created radioactive clouds, which were affecting outer space. Adamski claims that this would be possible because "it has long been known by scientists of earth that the cosmic ray, as it is called, is more powerful in outer space than it is in the Earth's atmosphere. And if this be true, is it not just as logical to assume that the radioactive force from the bombs being tested by nations of Earth could also become more powerful in space, once leaving the Earth's atmosphere? Logical deduction supports the statement of this spaceman."

Adamski also received the information that the small craft — hovering just above the earth during the exchanges of astronomer and spaceman — had been brought to earth by a larger one, the original saucer he and his companions had seen. They were operated by some form of magnetic force. The Venusian picked up a little pebble and dropped it, while the astronomer picked up two pebbles and placed them close to each other as though one were magnetic. George Adamski does not elaborate further on this rather vague account of saucer control, although he adds that the smaller discs were remotely controlled and not piloted. The Venusian also told him that all the other planets were inhabited and that men like he had come to earth in the past and were inhabiting it as mortal men.

The Venusian was not, evidently, sufficiently obliging to permit photographs to be taken but he allowed Adamski to view his craft which is described as small and beautiful, shaped more like a heavy glass-bell than a saucer and as translucent, and of exquisite colour. It had at its top a round ball like a heavy lens which Adamski took to be one end of a magnetic pole to draw the power from space as the object moved through it. In the side wall were round portholes. Adamski was not permitted inside the craft to observe more about its construction. Eventually the Venusian stepped on to the lower outside portion of the saucer which was like a flange, or ring. It had a small aperture through which the spaceman entered. The craft began to move and Adamski spotted two rings under the flange and a third around a centre disc. The inner ring and the outer seemed to be revolving clockwise while the ring between these two moved counter-clockwise. The Scout Ship — for so the Venusian had described it — glided silently above the uneven ground and vanished into space.

Adamski's story of an encounter with a man from space was backed by his companions who had, from a discreet distance, watched what had happened. Casts were taken of the Venusian's footprints by Dr Williamson. The meaning of the patterns of these prints, said by Adamski to have been interpreted by the use of astronomical charts and ancient mythology, has never been revealed. Neither, as far as we are aware, has there been published any reaction from the pilots of the aircraft which had circled the mother ship. George Adamski states that none of the photographs taken of the footprints "turned out good enough". Only drawings have survived. As for the other pictures, he claims that the power of the ship had "neutralized" them.

He also states that the Venusian had requested one of the films and that he had handed it to him, having received a promise that it would be returned. On 13 December that year he was alert at his telescope at home and getting an unobstructed view over a great distance including an expanse of ocean, when at 9 a.m. he saw a flash in the sky and there appeared an iridescent glass-like craft. It lost height, eventually hovering over a valley at 500 feet. It approached within a mere 100 feet of Adamski. One of the portholes was opened slightly and the folder of film dropped to the ground. The man from Venus had kept his promise.

What was on that film? All we are told in *Flying Saucers Have Landed* is that "there were indications of the original photo —

which I had taken before the space visitor took the holder — being washed off; and this was replaced by a strange photograph and a symbolic message, which to this day has not been fully deciphered. Several scientists are working on it."

Adamski's story was seized upon by the *Phoenix Gazette* and splashed to such effect that the presses could not cope with the demand. The Oceanside, California, *Blade Tribune* made Adamski a household name throughout the State. All the witnesses to the encounter with the Venusian swore affidavits supporting his story before Notaries Public in the States of Arizona and California.

In his letter to our colleague, in 1954, Adamski stated:

"Since that first meeting I have met this man again on a couple of times and he can speak our language as well as any other on earth. Let me make it very definite, this man was no more spirit than you or I. He was not materialization, he was a physical being the same as you or I, and there is nothing mysterious about him. I swear to my God that the experience I have told in my book is every word true. Whether people believe me or not, does not alter the truth."

It seems to us, to sum up the story, either you believe, or you don't. Either you accept that undemolished tenth of the evidence, or you echo the boy who was shown a giraffe for the first time and commented, "There's no such animal". The case is like that for and against ghosts. It is more than an air mystery, but one of the greatest and most intriguing mysteries of them all.

2: THE DISASTER TO R101

The spacious, bleak airfield at Cardington just outside Bedford had become the most talked-about place in England. All day, crowds had been arriving in their hundreds and the road leading to the airfield itself was one solid mass of traffic — something of a phenomenon in 1930. As they stepped from cars and charabancs the arrivals found themselves accosted by men proffering picture postcards depicting the thing everyone had come to see — His Majesty's Airship R101 (R for Rigid), due to leave on this late afternoon of 4 October on her maiden voyage to Egypt and India. In the early darkness the airship herself, a gigantic silver torpedo moored by the nose to her tall tower, shone magically in the blaze of searchlights. She had been six years under construction; this, at last, was *her* day.

Forty years ago, many aeronautical enthusiasts saw the future less in terms of conventional aircraft than of airships; magnificent, mammoth metal skeletons, encased in fabric skin enclosing envelopes of gas. Airships, their champions claimed, were unquestionably the air transport of the future. In the 1920s, aeroplanes were small and unreliable, limited in carrying capacity, and certainly not at such a stage of development where they could have been employed in an international commercial service. The First World War, with its demonstration of the long-distance capabilities of the Zeppelins, had scarcely been over four years before plans were going ahead in England for an Imperial airship service.

Commander Dennistoun Burney, who during the war had invented that ingenious device for countering nautical mines, the paravane, was one of those most convinced that the airship had a big role to play in improving communications, particularly from England to corners of the Empire like India and Australia. He approached Vickers and Shell Petroleum for backing and took advice from Dr Hugo Eckener, the German airship expert.

The Admiralty showed interest in Burney's proposals, because they felt that airships could be of use in some future defence role. Money was short and the Services could not afford to build these craft themselves. However, if they could be made with private backing, then there would be a ready-made fleet, should they ever be needed in war. Burney was convinced that airships could be built more cheaply than battleships. Naturally enough, he encountered opposition from the R.A.F., jealous of any schemes that could diminish the future role of conventional aircraft.

Already designers were looking forward to the 1930s which, as it turned out, saw the first flowering of commercially viable aviation. One early official report on airships contained a sentence which epitomized the general view: "It is felt that we stand to gain nothing by forcing a means of warfare which tends to reduce the value of our insular position and the protection of our sea power."

Despite the doubts and jealousies, airships were built in Britain. By 1928 the Government had spent £2,315,000 on seven airships, though all had either met disaster or been scrapped. Yet enthusiasm prevailed. Even before the war the Germans had shown that airships could carry passengers in great comfort over long distances, and had done so many times without a single disaster. America, Italy and France were conducting airship-building programmes. The British R34 had crossed the Atlantic and back in 1919. Commander Burney and others maintained that what the country needed was a fleet of really giant airships, carrying passengers, goods and mail on regular services from London to the main points of the Empire. He spoke of the possibility of an airship which could fly to India by way of Egypt in 74 hours, an enormous improvement upon the 17 days of a sea voyage, and would carry between 130 and 150 passengers twice weekly. The fare was envisaged at between £70 and £80, thus slightly undercutting the cost of a liner passage.

In order that both the State and private enterprise should be given a fair chance, the Cabinet agreed that two airships should be built: the Royal Airship Works at Cardington would produce the State-dirigible R101; the Airship Guarantee Company Ltd would build the R100.

Today, we are accustomed to watching Governments cancelling visionary projects of the aircraft industry, at a waste of enormous sums of money and invaluable experience. In the 1920s, much of the criticism of the airship programme stemmed from public resentment at the cost involved.

However, Sir Samuel Hoare, Secretary of State for Air, succeeded in firing the enthusiasm of politicians and people at home and in the Dominions. He was assisted by a well-conducted public relations campaign, designed to ensure that the whole country was going to be "airship-conscious". Hardly a newspaper in the late twenties did not carry several stories of the R101's building and the man responsible, its chief designer Colonel V. C. Richmond. An ex-dock builder who had invented an experimental glider in 1917, he had, before he evolved the R101, no practical experience of airship building, but collectively he and his colleagues represented an extremely able design team. Richmond, tireless as a propagandist, lectured widely about the type of craft being produced at Cardington. It would have five engines, capable of producing

2,400hp, and would be 724 feet long — twice the size of the largest airship already in existence. Inside, it would be a tasteful mixture of first-class hotel and exclusive club, with an all-electric kitchen — a notable luxury in the 1920s. Newspaper columnists, primed with excellent lunches, were delighted to write about the blue-and-gold panelled smoking-room and the main lounge, 60 feet by 32 feet, fitted with green cane settees. Prospective passengers who might be anxious about practical comforts were soothed to read of electric fans which would draw air through radiators to provide heat in cold conditions, or could suck in cooling draughts during tropical flying. Where safety was concerned, the smoking-room was being given an aluminium floor to lessen the danger of fire. Fifty passengers could be accommodated in cabins inside the hull. The chartroom would also be enclosed, situated over the control cabin which would protrude under the great structure. There would be 48 crew.

Behind the scenes, all was by no means well with the building of R101. She would certainly not be ready for preliminary tests in the early spring of 1927, as planned. A total expenditure of £1,350,000 had been allocated for the building of both R100, by private enterprise, and R101 by the State: estimates of expenditure at Cardington alone, between 1926 and 1927, reached £770,000 and completion was nowhere in view. Serious difficulties were being encountered at the Royal Airship Works. The propellers of R101 would not work satisfactorily on the giant Beardmore engines. The foreman engineer, Mr H. J. Leech, carried out experiments by rigging one of the engines at the far side of the hangar, complete with propeller, sensibly erecting safety screens of steel netting. If he had not done so, he and his staff would have been cut to pieces as soon as the engine rejected the blades, sending them spinning into the nets like flying scimitars. Mr Leech commented later, "The metal blades couldn't stand up to the strain. They suffered metal fatigue at the roots. The engine flung them out on the net and raced away on its own." If more time had been available for experiments, variable-pitch propellers — ones whose blades could be adjusted to correspond with the speed of the engines — would undoubtedly have been used, or at least considered. Wooden propellers were fixed as a substitute for metal, but at first the engine made short work of these. Eventually, the propellers were secured by clamping sheets of emery cloth between the boss at the centre of each propeller and the hub nave plate, the central block. After that, each propeller was secured in place by high-tensile steel bolts.

Parliamentary and public pressure upon the project grew. The Government changed in 1929. Lord Thomson succeeded Sir Samuel Hoare as Air Secretary. He shared his predecessor's enthusiasm and also found it his duty to speed progress. He refused to urge speed at the cost of thoroughness; yet many who were connected with the work — and many more who were not — were to insist later that impatience had been a prime cause in R101's fate.

Engine trouble prevailed during early test flights. The engines were "pushers", with propellers at the rear. So that they would not throw too great a strain on the supports holding each car, a heavy steel rope ran back from the centre of each propeller to the side of the airship. This had the effect of taking up part of the engine's jerky thrust and spreading it. It was effective, but crude. Many experts felt that if the R101 had not been chronically behind schedule and above her budget, further research might have produced a refinement less in keeping with the spirit of Heath Robinson.

On one occasion a party of Members of Parliament was taken on a short demonstration flight in R101. A sudden lurch caused crockery to fall from the tables. It was explained to the visiting dignitaries that this had been due to poor distribution of the water ballast: the airship had too big a lift at the bow. In his book *The Millionth Chance: The Story of the R101*, Mr James Leasor reveals that Lieutenant N. G. Atherstone, A.F.C., First Officer on the final flight of R101, had earlier commented to the Captain, Flight-Lieutenant H. Carmichael Irwin, A.F.C.: "The ballast tanks are not satisfactory. A simple form of contents indicator is required for *all* tanks so that the level of fuel can be *seen*." There was to be no record in Atherstone's logbook that such gauges had ever been fitted.

At Cardington on 12 October 1929 R101 had been taken from her 812-foot shed and moored to the towering mooring mast, dwarfing the buildings around. She looked, indeed, a Queen of the Air, majestic and beautiful. But her shape was soon to be changed. After an endurance trial of nearly thirty hours it was plain that she was not providing enough lift in relation to what she weighed and would carry when loaded. The solution was to add more gasbags to increase the hydrogen capacity, which in turn meant lengthening and heightening the entire structure in order to accommodate them. R101 went back to the shed, to be cut in half and be lengthened by some 50 feet, to 777 feet overall, enabling her gas capacity to grow half a million cubic feet to 5½ million, giving a gross lift of 165 tons.

An Imperial Conference to discuss all forms of modern transport was due to be held on 20 October 1930. Lord Thomson was keen to report the unqualified success of R101. Wing-Commander R. B. Colemore, O.B.E., Director of Airship Development at Cardington, stated flatly to a friend,

"If R101 doesn't get back in time for that conference, there will be no money for further airship work. It just won't be asked for."

The days and weeks spent on trials seemed to speed by until there was only a fortnight left before the conference. This would be sufficient to accomplish the maiden voyage to India, but there was no margin for further delay.

Men may labour over drawing boards, urge technicians to work all hours of the clock on construction, and an unprecedented number of trials may be initiated; but the one thing no one can fabricate is the weather. A bad spell at the crucial moment can be the greatest timewaster of them all, as was to prove in the case of R101. On 27 September 1930 she was ready to leave her shed again for a week of trials which would culminate, it was confidently expected, in the granting of her Certificate of Airworthiness. As it turned out, the weather was unfavourable even for bringing her out of the shed. It was not until 1 October that this could be done.

On 1 October the weather was just about perfect. Like a cigar being drawn out of its case, the great silver airship was hauled forth at 6.30 a.m. and raised to be moored by her nose to the tower. Preparations for departure went on all day, passengers went aboard during the afternoon, and soon after four o'clock the great ship was cast off and set course for London, Southend, and the east coast. Having spent the night off Yarmouth, she returned to Cardington in the morning. This final test flight had lasted well under the twenty-four hours originally planned and there had been some engine trouble in the course of it; but, all in all, everyone was satisfied, not to say relieved, that the way was now clear for the proving flight to India, with its implications of national prestige. R101 was English — *ours*, the invincible airship: her success the needed tonic at a time of depression. If anyone at the time recalled the supreme confidence which, in 1912, had been voiced for the *Titanic*, no one would have cared to mention it now.

R101 remained at her Cardington mast until her departure day, 4 October. Lord Thomson arrived early, his official car immediately surrounded by reporters and photographers. While his valet busied himself with baggage, the Air Minister, in ebullient mood, posed for pictures and endeared himself to everyone by referring to R101 as "the old bus".

Sir Sefton Brancker, the Director of Civil Aviation, who was also to make the trip, had arrived earlier than Lord Thomson. Anyone studying the monocled geniality of Brancker as he shook hands with the Minister would not have suspected that the two men had already disagreed violently on the airworthiness of R101. Brancker was one of those who had called for the postponement of the flight. Thomson had overruled him.

Making trip after trip, the electric lift carried passengers and their baggage up the great tower, far taller than Nelson's Column. The crew had to clamber up 170 steps to get aboard. In the engine cars the engineers were making final checks of the starting motors which would soon set off the roar of the diesels. By the time she was ready to cast-off, at 6.36 p.m., there were aboard her 42 officers and men, 5 Government officials plus Lord Thomson's valet, and 6 officials of the Royal Airship Works, making a total of 54 men.

As soon as her nose backed out of the masthead cone the airship dipped, heavily weighted as she was with fuel and passengers and crew. Her commander, Flight-Lieutenant H. C. Irwin, immediately ordered four of her nine metric tons of water ballast to be jettisoned. It would have cascaded on the throng below, had not the propellers whipped it to nothing more than a fine spray. For all the spectators knew, the long-threatened rain had started to fall at last.

Slowly, perhaps almost as though with reluctance, R101 began to move. After 127 hours 11 minutes of trial flying, Britain's biggest contribution to the airship age was off. The crowd raised a great cheer. Car headlamps flickered and horns sounded in salute. Now R101 was lifting her nose well above the masthead, slowly pulling herself clear. As she moved forward in the darkness, it seemed to those below that the searchlights were reluctant to let her go and for a long time she remained lit by their beams. On the ground, a journalistic horde was telephoning copy for the morning papers of the world. Cold but contented, the spectators watched until the red, green and white navigation lights which outlined the craft's silvery shape, and the beams of torches being flashed downward by the passengers, could be discerned no longer.

The diesel engines increased their roar. The airship circled Bedford and made for the south-east. Then the rain really came, gently at first, but with increasing strength, accompanied by wind. It was quite dark. The passengers were glad to turn their attention from the world below to the luxuries of the smoking-room as stewards circulated with drinks, cigarettes and cigars. There was dinner to be anticipated, with champagne, crates of it embossed with the crossed flags of Britain and India. Until then there was time for those who felt like it to make a leisurely tour around the airship herself.

From the white-and-gold lounge steps led to a special observation deck with big windows. Above again were the passenger cabins, each with ship's-type bunks which had sides of thin, protective net so that the sleeper could not be pitched on to the rug-covered floor. Under the bottom bunk, hot air was blown through a metal grating from a network of ventilation pipes.

The seventeen gasbags inside the frame of the airship would not have fitted into the entire length of Westminster Abbey. Any previously constructed airship could have flown through the supporting girders of the waist of R101 without a touch. The length of longitudinal steel girders within her frame would, if placed end to end, have reached the entire length of London's Oxford Street and back. It was all very awesome, even to passengers officially connected with the airship project.

Amongst the crew there was some feeling of disappointment. The height at which the airship was flying was only 1,500 feet and she was making the decidedly tortoise-like speed of 25 miles per hour. The Captain would have liked to have climbed and gone faster. But if R101 were to go higher the gas inside the gasbags would expand as the pressure of the air outside grew less, the safety release-valves would automatically open (if they did not, the bags would burst), and the more gas that escaped, the more "lift" R101 would lose. Gas could not be replenished until she reached Ismailia — and at such a speed that seemed a long, long way. The weather, too, was not promising. A radio message from Cardington warned of winds of between 40 and 50 miles per hour, a velocity previously outside the experience of airship crews. Everyone connected with R101 had hoped for winds of not more than 25 miles per hour. To turn back was out of the question. The airship must go on, and at that uncomfortably inadequate height.

The suburbs of North London were seen. R101 passed over Mill Hill in driving rain and buffeting wind. Mr Leech, the foreman engineer, was to recall later that at this point he was remembering the trouble R101 had experienced with her propellers, and noted that she was pitching and rolling more than she had done on previous flights he had taken in her. Already, the lack of height of R101 had caused comment on the ground and there were reports that her engines had sounded extremely weak.

At 8.21 p.m., Cardington was radioed: "Over London. All well. Course now set for Paris. Intend to proceed via Paris, Tours, Toulouse and Narbonne." The passengers finished their evening meal. A further radio message indicated that some of the jettisoned water ballast was now being made up — rain falling on the top of the envelope could be caught and stored. The Channel was approached over Hastings; and now the first hints of real trouble presented themselves. A weather report warned of a turbulent area over southern France. Then came an engine breakdown in the after gondola which took three hours to rectify.

Crossing the Channel, the airship was still flying very low — some of those aboard could make out the crests of the waves below. The "height coxswain", responsible for the elevator controls, was ordered to keep her somewhat higher. Yet there was no hint of concern about altitude-keeping, engine performance or weather in the R101's radioed reports. At midnight she was telling Cardington, "15 miles S.W. of Abbeville. Average speed 33 knots... Altimeter height 1,500 feet... Weather intermittent rain... After an excellent supper our distinguished passengers smoked a final cigar and having sighted the French coast have now gone to bed to rest after the excitement of their leave-taking. All essential services are functioning satisfactorily. The crew have settled down to watch-keeping routine."

At 1.51 a.m. two French wireless stations told R101 her position — one kilometre north of the landing ground at Beauvais. She made routine acknowledgment. It was her last transmission. At 2.07 Le Bourget asked R101 for her speed: there was no reply. The same thing happened at 2.13. Minutes later Le Bourget reported generally, "*G-FAAW a pris feu.*"

From the later testimony of the six survivors of R101, the airship's last minutes went something like this.

At 2 a.m. a new watch came on duty. Mr Leech, having carried out his inspection of the engines, proceeded to relax on one of the smoking-room settees. A few minutes later some glasses and a soda syphon which had not been cleared from one of the tables began to slide. Mr Leech caught and replaced them. There was nothing disturbing in this. There had clearly been a slight dive, but R101 had quickly righted herself. One minute later, the airship lurched again, this time to the accompaniment of jangling telegraph bells. Mr Leech noticed that the smoking-room door had swung open. Beyond it was a great wall of flame. A matter of seconds later, R101 struck trees above the soft, wet earth of the northern French countryside.

The control telegraphs had tinkled their warning in the split second before impact. The engines had already slowed down, preparatory to stopping. A member of the crew had been on his way to release emergency ballast, but there had been no time for the slow process. The aircraft struck and the man was thrown clear on impact. He died in hospital.

The electrician, Mr Disley, who, like most of the rest, had not been unduly perturbed by that first dive, heard the Chief Coxswain yell, "We're down, lads!" Disley at once made to cut off the live electrical circuits, but only got the chance to pull one switch. He said later: "I heard a crash and a series of explosions. There were blinding flashes all round and the next thing was that the ship was on fire. She flared up in an instant, from stem to stern, and I cannot tell how the fire started, but I think it began amidships rather than in the bows." He went on to describe R101 as a solid mass of flame, roaring like a furnace: "My one idea was to get out of the ship. I threw myself at the fabric covering and tried to break through but could not. Then I sat down and I found myself sitting on wet grass. I was under the airship, you understand, and the fabric was already torn where I sat. So I crawled on the ground following the tear, until I found myself outside. I went along to see if I could get anybody out, but nothing could be done. It was all over in a minute."

Just before the first dive, one of the engineers, Alfred Cook, had been one of those to come on watch in the port midship gondola. After the usual torchlight inspection of engine and instruments he heard the telegraph ringing "slow". At the same time the airship dived. He had obediently slowed the engine, but immediately there came the second dive. At the very instant of impact, Cook stopped the engine. As he did so, the whole gondola fell away from the ship; almost miraculously, Cook survived.

Many people in Beauvais had seen the airship or heard her pass over. Some declared later that the engines, which had wakened them, had seemed to be labouring, but this was most probably an acoustical effect caused by a storm of wind and rain at the time. Only one person saw the crash itself. Shortly before 2 a.m., Eugene Rabouille, a button-factory worker who was also an industrious poacher, was fixing rabbit snares in a field. Suddenly, he heard the drone of engines which became increasingly louder. At first he thought it was an aircraft flying very low. Then he saw the widely spaced lights of an airship. Curiosity robbed him of any fear and, poaching forgotten, he merely stood and watched. It seemed to Rabouille that his presence appeared to act as a sort of magnet to the craft. It was as if it could no longer control its movements and was drawn irresistibly towards him, filling his vision with its sheer size and dazing his senses with the heavy, deafening roar of its engines. The lights flickered and the whole craft suddenly ceased its onward movement, stopped by the tall trees on the edge of a nearby wood. It ploughed into these with a thud and a roar. Its silvery contours, which had been dimly discernible in the early dawn, now became as red as blood. The explosions flung the petrified poacher to the ground, where he lay dazed. Despite himself he could not take his eyes off the scene. He was looking at 5½ million cubic feet of hydrogen ablaze, roaring to engulf the entire envelope which had been R101. For how long he watched he never knew. Eventually, he found his feet and fled — but never from his memories of the screams of men, blinded, choking and burning.

The explosions were also heard by people in Beauvais who said that at first there had been a rumble like thunder, and then loud roars that made the houses tremble. It was Disley who was the first survivor to get to a telephone. At once he had set out across the sticky sodden field towards the town, struggling in his halting French to convince the operator of the urgency of his call.

Searchers came across wreckage that was little beyond a gaunt skeleton; a child's Meccano set half-consumed by flames. Giant girders, buckled and twisted in the murderous heat, reared hideously above the charred grass. Rudder and elevator fins stretched from the pointed tail in the form of a cross. Everything that had not been of metal had perished completely.

The bodies, most of them unidentifiable, were taken by French army lorries and carts to Beauvais town hall, whose concert room had been quickly converted into a mortuary.

Fifty-four people had set out in R101 on 4 October 1930: only six now survived.

Later, the coffins were taken to Boulogne and carried aboard two British destroyers. From Dover, the bodies went by special train to Victoria and from there to lie in Westminster Hall. Then, exactly a week after the disaster, the dead passengers and crew were brought back to Cardington to demonstrations of sorrow usually associated with the death of kings. As the coffins were removed from the trains at Bedford station, two flights of bombers flew overhead in spearhead formation. At the church in Cardington village, the bodies were buried in one massive T-shaped grave. Of the 48 coffins, only 14 bore the names of the dead on aluminium plates. On all the rest the inscription read, "To the memory of the unknown airman who died on October 5th."

A Court of Inquiry, presided over by Sir John Simon, lasted many weeks and every available witness was called. There was very little tangible evidence left to examine. The crew members Cook, Disley and Leech could really only speak with certainty about the two dives, the ringing of the telegraphs and of their own lucky escape. Those who must have known more had not survived. Assuming that R101 had first dived some 800 feet, too much to be recovered by use of the elevators, and that steps were being taken to lift her by jettisoning ballast when she had forestalled them by hitting the trees, then catching fire, the Court concluded, "the accident was not due to structural weakness and there had been no failure of the control gear".

These judgments were hotly contested by a Mr E. F. Spanner, Naval Architect Assessor to the Board of Trade, who wrote, "Undoubtedly the findings ... are contrary to the evidence. The R101 broke her back in the air owing to serious structural weaknesses." It was Mr Spanner's belief that violent application of the elevator control cable broke the airship's back before she reached the ground. But this was later contradicted by those who said that R101's hull was so strong that she could not possibly have broken in two. There was no doubt at all that full elevator had been applied, for the cable was found fully wound on the drum. If any further confirmation were needed it was supplied by Mr Cook, who described his impressions immediately after the crash: "On leaving my engine car I walked through the wood a few yards and then looked back towards the tail of the ship. The only part of the ship on which I saw any fabric left was the port elevator which was in an upward position... It was absolutely clear. There was not any smoke at that time on that side of the ship. The flames lit up the whole of the frame of the ship, and the light was shining on the fabric of the elevator."

Mr Spanner believed that the control cables had become jammed at the point of impact because of the structural breakage, thus making all attempt to gain higher altitude impossible to fulfil. Dr Eckener, the German authority, was of the opinion that there was truth in both explanations — there had been a leak in gas, and because the ship was too heavy it had nosedived. The Coxswain had not been quick enough to detect the slight dip until it was too late and all efforts with a corrective elevator had been in vain. Another popular theory was that R101 had been flying at something less than twice its own length above the ground, the recommended height for airships. An unnoticed change in barometric pressure, it was argued, may have led the crew to assume she was higher than was in fact the case. By the time she reached the Beauvais ridge, R101 was flying approximately her own length above the ground. Could her bow have been quite a bit lower than the altimeter indicated?

In his book, *Slide Rule*, the late Nevil Shute recalls a visit he made to Cardington in the year of the disaster. He encountered Squadron-Leader Booth, the captain of the private enterprise aircraft, R100, with another officer examining a small portion of tattered linen that came, as Squadron-Leader Booth was at pains to point out, not from his R100 but from R101. This fabric, which covered the frame, was treated with a dope solution in order to prevent it from rotting away in bad weather. The idea was to dope the canvas first before it was stretched over the framework. Unfortunately, the effect had been precisely the opposite to that intended; the fabric had absorbed moisture and rotted away after shrinking. Nevil Shute described it as "friable, like scorched brown paper, so that if you crumpled it in your hand it broke up into flakes". He asked if every bit had been stripped away from R101. It had: but supposing some tiny portion of the ruined fabric had remained to let in the rain during that terrible storm?

The crash of R101 had, the Court believed, been due to the deflation of a gasbag. Many authorities believe this to be unlikely. In his study, *The British Rigid Airship, 1908–1931*, Mr Robert Higham points out:

"It had been laid down that she (R101) was to be able to fly even if one of the largest gasbags collapsed — and this had been responsible for her additional size rather than the compulsory carriage of additional ballast, jettisonable in an emergency. Her Certificate of Airworthiness was granted in part because she had theoretically fulfilled that condition."

In his book, *Leaves from a Psychist's Case-Book*, the late Harry Price gives a remarkable account of a séance held on the day after the news of the crash had reached the English newspapers. The medium was the well-known Mrs Eileen Garrett. Speaking in a man's voice, she claimed to be "Flight

Lieutenant H. Carmichael Irwin" who had been the captain of R101, and stated, "The whole bulk of the dirigible was entirely and absolutely too much for her engines' capacity. Engines too heavy. Useful lift too small. Oil pipe plugged."

To the fascinated hearers, the voice went on to speak of a too-heavy load, of a bad cruising speed and of chafing fabric that was subject to severe tension: "Too short trials. No one knew the ship properly. Weather bad for long flight. Fabric all waterlogged and ship's nose is down. Impossible to rise."

The medium related how R101 had almost scraped the roofs at Achy, a small village north of Beauvais which was on its line of flight. Achy was too small to appear on ordinary maps, but it did appear on special large-scale flying maps of the sort used by R101. The voice also mentioned that the oil pressure had given cause for concern when R101 was over the Channel, a fact which was known only to the survivors. It had not been included in any radio messages sent from air to land. The testimony of survivors on this point was not released until after the inquiry. Mrs Garrett's "account" of the disaster and of the condition of the airship was full of technicalities of which she herself had no comprehension.

Price's book is now out of print, but this séance is dealt with in detail in James Leasor's *The Millionth Chance*. Mr Leasor also describes another psychic intervention which occurred three weeks later. It began as Major Oliver Villiers, who had driven his friend Sir Sefton Brancker to Cardington for the trip, was musing on the tragic death of those aboard R101. Suddenly, he claimed, he "heard" Irwin's voice implore him, "For God's sake, let me talk to you, it's all ghastly; I must speak to you." On the advice of a friend, Villiers contacted Mrs Garrett who agreed to act as medium. The first séance took place at 7 p.m. on 31 October. During it, the voice of Irwin admitted that

R101 had been too heavy by several tons and that the gas indicator had shown a leakage or escape around the valves which could not be rectified in time. Irwin had mentioned this to Lord Thomson on his arrival at Cardington and the latter had protested, "But this is negligible — and surely for this small matter you don't contemplate postponement? It's impossible. I'm pledged to be back for the Imperial Conference. We must leave according to scheduled time." Irwin admitted there was a tear in the cover and that the wind was blowing hard in the rain.

"The rush of the wind caused the first dive and then we straightened again. Another gush surging through this hole finished us." The first explosion, Irwin testified, had been caused by a diesel engine backfiring and igniting the escaping gas. It is perhaps significant that an article in *The Aeroplane* of 8 October 1930 describing the start from Cardington, stated, "The starboard forward engine was giving trouble. The main engine ... exhaust was a torrent of sparks which persisted for some minutes."

Villiers also claimed to have "got through" to Sir Sefton Brancker and the transcript of their conversation reproduced Brancker's jocular style of speech. He confirmed that Thomson had overridden everyone's objections and had insisted that the flight could not, under any circumstances, be postponed. The transcript of the séance had Brancker concluding, "We discussed the weather charts and saw that if we managed to cross the pond and could land somewhere in a foreign country, our honour would be vindicated and we could then bless the bad weather and say weather forced us to make a descent."

The medium next made contact with another victim of the disaster, Major G. H. Scott, the Assistant Director of the Royal

Airship Works. With much emotion, he admitted that he and others had been aware of the amount of gas that R101 had been losing, and that in view of the prestige involved "We *had* to go and take the 1,000th chance of making a landing in France. We started off with that idea, but being already late were taken off our course and after crossing the water we knew we had very little chance. It was hopeless to consider landing." The original idea had been to try for Le Bourget, but no request could have been made for a landing party until the Channel was crossed, or everyone would have known that R101 had been in trouble even before she started. Le Bourget proved impossible to reach anyway — there was a bad rent in the cover on the starboard side, there was heavy pressure on the gasbags and a merciless wind.

Describing the first dive, Major Scott's voice testified, "The rent had become bigger and the gusts of wind were hitting her hard, making her difficult to steer and the girders were being badly strained. Our only chance was to try a slow turn and land downwind, which would enable the damaged starboard side to get shelter from the wind... We tried to correct the bump downwards, but she would not respond. Then she practically went into a perpendicular nosedive... Since we had just commenced to try and turn, the gusts of wind blowing through the rent on her starboard put a terrific strain on her port side and she sort of got a drag on and heeled to port, thereby she finally landed on a more or less even keel. Previous to that, orders had been given to slow down the forward port and starboard rear engines. This left the forward starboard and rear port and rear after engines running which were required to carry out the turn. But by then it had been too late."

Major Villiers took these pronouncements extremely seriously. It was his view that the transcripts should have been presented at the official inquiry. They never were.

Speculation must for ever surround the exact cause of the terrible end of R101. But when one reads the report of the inquiry it is very hard to doubt that, had personal and political ambitions been laid aside in the pursuit of absolute safety, the risk of the disaster could have been minimized:

"In the construction of R101 the designers broke away almost completely from conventional methods... Originality and courage in design are not to be deprecated, but there is an obvious danger in giving too many separate hostages to fortune at one time... During the construction, and in the early flights of R101, this policy of cautious experiment at each step was admirably fulfilled; but in the later stages, when it became important to avoid further postponement and the flight to India thus became urgent, there was a tendency to rely on limited experiment instead of tests under all conditions ... and the R101 started for India before she could be regarded as having emerged successfully from all the exhaustive tests proper to an experimental stage...

"It is clear that if those responsible had been entirely free to choose the time and the weather in which the R101 should start for the first flight ever undertaken by any airship to India, and if the only considerations governing their choice were considerations of meteorology and of preparation for the voyage, the R101 would not have started when she did. She was undertaking a novel task in weather conditions worse than any to which she had ever been exposed in flight, and with the prospect of more unfavourable weather after she started. She had never gone through trials which proved by their length and conditions that she was well able to cope with a continuance of unfavourable circumstances. The programme of trials drawn up by her Captain had never been carried through, and the intended length of her last trial was avowedly cut down in order to provide a little more time for preparation before the date which was contemplated for her start for India. No adequate speed trials had been carried through, and indeed this fact was so clearly recognized that an official of the Air Ministry urged that she should conduct such speed trials on her voyage to India.

"It is impossible to avoid the conclusion that the R101 would not have started for India on the evening of 4th October if it had not been that reasons of public policy were considered as making it highly desirable for her to do so if she could..."

The R101's fate led to the cancellation of the R100 project and the end of British airship production. It has been remarked elsewhere in this book that the aircraft industry has been notable for its ability to learn from disaster and to create safety out of misfortune. Airships provide the exceptional case. Despite the convictions of their supporters, their disasters and the elements of the mysterious and the plainly insurmountable which caused them killed off airships more effectively than any contentions by their opponents.

3: FLIGHT INTO MYSTERY

As a number of the cases recounted in this book show, most mysteries involving aircraft are sooner or later solved through painstaking investigation and deduction. Those which are not are generally capable of some hypothetical solution, convincing to a majority of airmen and other experts and only lacking clinching proof. Yet in a few instances aircraft have flown off into mysteries upon whose explanation there is no unanimous agreement, and seemingly never will be.

Why, for example, did the four-engined DC-6 carrying Dag Hammarskjöld, Secretary General of the United Nations, crash in Rhodesia in September 1961, killing all on board? It had been in perfect functioning order, flown by an irreproachable crew. Nothing untoward had been revealed in either the content or the manner of its last radio communication with ground control. Examination of the wreckage disclosed no sign of sabotage, a possibility which had been anticipated and guarded against with elaborate precautions. The one man who lived briefly after the crash gave a scarcely coherent account of Hammarskjöld's having begged the pilot to turn back, as if suddenly aware of approaching danger; but what that danger was, or how, perhaps, it was transformed from threat to reality, cannot be known.

No one can say for a certainty what happened to a DC-4 of the Canadian Pacific Airline which disappeared in July 1951 over Alaska in circumstances which drew forth the official verdict: "As no trace of the aircraft or its occupants have been found the cause of the disappearance has not been determined." Once again, here had been a fully serviceable aircraft in experienced hands, carrying enough fuel but not overloaded, on a routine flight in seemingly unquestionable weather. No other aircraft had gone missing at the same time, so there can have been no collision. It is as though the DC-4 had been plucked from the sky into oblivion, leaving no trace for an intensive 10-day search to find.

There have been several other equally baffling disappearances against all likelihood. Two of them occurred just one year apart to identical aircraft, named with close similarity, flying in the same part of the world for the same airline. The years were 1948 and 1949, and the aircraft were Avro Tudors *Star Tiger* and *Star Ariel*.

The Tudor was one of many types of passenger aircraft being built in Britain when the war ended, for service either as civil airliners or as troop carriers. It was a big, all-metal monoplane, powered by four Rolls-Royce engines and well equipped with navigational and safety aids. *Star Tiger* was one of three bought by the newly founded British South-American Airways, whose pilots were nearly all former members of that elite arm of R.A.F. Bomber Command, the Pathfinder Force. Their hazardous wartime job had been to fly in advance of the big bomber formations and seek out and mark with flares the targets for attack. The chief executive of the new airline was, in fact, their former commander, Air Vice-Marshal Donald ("Pathfinder") Bennett, C.B., C.B.E., D.S.O.

With characteristic boldness the airline took on what was perhaps the toughest assignment open to post-war civil passenger operators, a Transatlantic service from London to the Caribbean by way of Lisbon, the Azores and Bermuda. It meant, on the Azores-to-Bermuda leg, a crossing of the Atlantic at its widest point. No civil airline in the world had to span an ocean reach to match this one of 2,000 miles.

The Tudor was equal to it; but the flight was a taxing one. The fully-fuelled aircraft would have an endurance of some sixteen hours against the twelve or so hours needed for the flight in ideal conditions. Winds and weather could vary both these figures quite considerably, thus reducing the safety margin to a slender one. This had been foreseen and catered for by a strict drill. Having received a weather forecast favourable enough for the flight to take place (although no forecast could guarantee conditions all along a route so extended and not serviced by weather ships), the pilot was required to compute a "point of no return", the point on his route from which it would take equal time to go on to the destination or get back to the starting place, calculated on the basis of the speed available from only three engines. Even having passed the point of no return and committed himself to fly on, the pilot had another alternative open to him. If wireless reports from Bermuda told him that conditions there were such that his approach might be badly delayed — strong headwinds and squalls often sprang up quickly and persisted — he could change course for Newfoundland, the nearest land. There was no further alternative.

The seasoned ex-Pathfinder pilots of B.S.A.A. doubly computed their point of no return, on the ground before take-off and in the air. A company regulation laid down that if they could not be certain to reach Bermuda with at least two hours' fuel reserve against the possibility of a delayed landing they must go to Newfoundland. Thus, despite the length and difficulty of the route, passengers could rest assured that they were in the best of individual hands, in one of the most modern types of aircraft being flown in accordance with stringent regulations.

This was certainly true of the flight which left Santa Maria, the most southerly island of the Azores, at shortly after 3.30 p.m. on 28 January 1948. The aircraft, *Star Tiger*, was under the command of a notable pilot even amongst Pathfinders, Captain Brian McMillan, A.F.C., D.S.O., D.F.C., a New Zealand-born former master bomber, assisted by an experienced crew which included one of the "characters" of British aviation, Radio Officer Robert Tuck, an irrepressible former Merchant Marine "Sparks" who had served with the R.A.F.'s Transatlantic Ferry Command during the war. There were 25 passengers, among them Air Marshal Sir Arthur Coningham, formerly officer commanding the Desert Air Force and later the Second Tactical Air Force during the invasion of Europe.

The mid-afternoon timing for departure on the long flight was standard B.S.A.A. practice in order to allow astronavigation (obtaining bearings from the stars) to be used.

The Tudor had a companion in the air this day. A Lancastrian, the civil version of the celebrated Lancaster heavy bomber, was making for Bermuda with a load of freight. It had taken off an hour earlier and its pilot, Captain Frank Griffin, another ex-Pathfinder, had arranged to radio back weather reports for Captain McMillan's assistance. Heavily overcast sky had been forecast for at least the first half of the route, implying limited possibilities for the navigators to obtain star-shots, but there were no more sinister expectations. *Star Tiger* carried a full fuel load: the possibility of adverse headwinds nearing Bermuda was amply provided for.

It was soon after four o'clock when Tudor and Lancastrian communicated with one another. Captain Griffin's report was not the most encouraging: he was meeting stronger headwinds than expected. This was confirmed at about six o'clock by a contact with Kindley Field, Bermuda, of the then United States

Army Air Force, but this report added that the winds were decreasing in strength near Bermuda itself. Captain McMillan had to make the first amendment to his flight plan, reckoning on something like an hour's setback to his estimated time of arrival. It still left him more than the two hours' safety margin. He reached the point of no return, and went on. Some three hours more and he was approaching the second and last point of decision, where he must settle for Bermuda or Newfoundland. A star-shot revealed nothing untoward about the course *Star Tiger* was flying. McMillan pressed on for Bermuda.

Soon after he had committed himself he received a disturbing message from the Lancastrian. Captain Griffin's navigator, having had to wait a long time to take a star-shot because of persisting cloud, had now managed to get one. It had shown that strong wind from an unexpected quarter had blown the Lancastrian 68 miles off course. When *Star Tiger*'s navigator was able to get his next shot, he too found his aircraft well off course. McMillan righted her, but it took her directly into a fierce headwind, slowing her progress still more and cutting the safety margin still further. Instead of more than three hours to spare, then two, Captain McMillan now had little more than one.

As Captain Griffin landed the Lancastrian at Bermuda, *Star Tiger* ploughed along in his invisible wake. Steadily thickening cloud was surrounding Bermuda and its approaches in cotton-wool packing. Cyril Ellison, *Star Tiger*'s navigator — yet another ex-Pathfinder — could get no glimpse of the stars to take a bearing. All would now depend on Tuck's radio. He called Bermuda radio, requesting a bearing to be taken on his signal. Bermuda answered that he was being received too weakly for the purpose. Tuck called again shortly after. His counterpart some 400 miles distant was able this time to pass the encouraging news that *Star Tiger* was virtually on course.

The pattern now would be that Tuck would call Bermuda at intervals, enabling his Captain to home *Star Tiger* on to its destination by the straightest line. Even with the safety margin now eroded to well under an hour, there should be no more difficulty. But as time passed the Bermuda operator did not hear from the aircraft. He called it up, but got no reply. More time went and there was still no sound from *Star Tiger*, either on its own initiative or in response to the Bermuda signals. An emergency alert was sounded at the waiting airport.

Captain Geoffrey Rees, the B.S.A.A. pilot waiting at Bermuda with a crew to take *Star Tiger* on to Cuba, took off in Captain Griffin's Lancastrian to fly back along the path it had recently taken, searching for the Tudor which should have followed it safely in. Griffin went with him as an anxious observer. An American Flying Fortress equipped with radar searching apparatus also went out. So, during the next few days, did many more aircraft and boats. Neither *Star Tiger* nor any part of her was seen, or ever has been.

It was unaccountable, and still is. As Captain Griffin could confirm in later years to Mr Ralph Barker, who deals with the *Star Tiger* case in his interesting book *Great Mysteries of the Air*, there had been nothing about the weather which he, too, had flown through, to cause disaster to an aircraft — no icing, fog, electrical storms or turbulence. He had been in touch with *Star Tiger* only minutes before her last signal to Bermuda and had been told nothing of any difficulty or sensed anxiety. Ex-Pathfinders or no, pilots do not allow themselves false pride. If they are in trouble, they tell someone quickly. If they need help, they ask for it.

Perhaps this was the explanation: that Tuck's radio somehow failed immediately after that last signal, leaving *Star Tiger* without means of communicating distress or asking for the vital bearings which would keep her on course. If the radio did not fail, and some other form of disaster occurred, there should have been time for the briefest signal from the plane, even if broken short; even the merest "blip" from Tuck's morse key.

Either something happened so suddenly, so violently, that Tuck was killed outright; or the radio failed, leaving *Star Tiger* to fly on helplessly, unable to make a landfall, until she finally ran out of fuel and crashed into the sea. Yet even here is mystery. Aircraft which crash into the sea, whole or in broken pieces, do not disappear without trace. Something floats — light metal fragments, cushions, papers, oil, automatically inflating life rafts, the bodies of those aboard and items of their baggage. Some of the parts which do sink do so quite slowly, remaining visible from the air for even days after the crash. An intensive search of a wide area was made in this instance without finding so much as a fleck of oil. Nothing was ever washed ashore. There came the usual reports of an unidentified aircraft having been seen at many points quite distant from Bermuda — too distant for *Star Tiger* to have reached when she had had little more than enough fuel even to get her to her destination. It remains just one of those mysteries.

Star Tiger disappeared in January 1948 between the Azores and Bermuda. *Star Ariel* vanished, equally without trace or explanation, between Bermuda and Jamaica in January 1949. The flight she was on was far shorter than the tough 2,000 miles which *Star Tiger* had had to cover. She took off at 12.42 p.m. on 17 January with a crew of 7 and 13 passengers. Again a British South-American Airways machine, she had an ex-

Pathfinder pilot of great experience and, also like *Star Tiger*, a notable radio operator, formerly of Transatlantic Ferry Command.

The flight was scheduled to take five and a half hours. The aircraft took off with fuel enough for nearly twice that time, yet with a considerable under-load, and into perfect weather with clear visibility, almost no wind and a calm sea below. She was in perfect flying order and, in addition to the navigational and communications equipment *Star Tiger* had carried, she had radar and radio direction-finding aids.

She signalled her position twice, just under an hour from take-off — and was never heard of again. A big air-sea rescue operation involved some 80 aircraft and many surface craft for nearly a week.

Never a trace was found. The same questions can be asked about *Star Ariel*'s fate as about *Star Tiger*'s. The same negative answers are all that can be returned.

4: TWO STARS FALL

What makes a spy? To avid fans of espionage novels, films and television series the question is almost contemptuously elementary: the modern spy is a ruthless professional with an enormous sexual appetite who devotes his short but spectacular life to planting spokes in other nations' wheels, aided by all the highly sophisticated gadgets which modern science can devise for him. Or else he is the reverse of glamorous: a seedy, frayed little insignificant, with bad breath and the scruples of a stoat, trapped by suave professionals into a trade he hates and fears but cannot escape.

Once, though, there was the cult of the gentleman amateur. John Buchan's Richard Hannay was one, an officer who became involved in espionage more or less by accident and who stuck to it out of patriotism. Somerset Maugham's Ashenden was a writer who was asked casually at a cocktail party whether he would like to try a spot of espionage. Both Hannay and Ashenden would seem to have had their day, in fiction as well as in real life. The technocrat spy is more in keeping with our times; yet both Hannay and Ashenden would quite probably have got jobs as recently as the Second World War. The most improbable-seeming people did. So it is far from absurd to accept the story that the British secret service approached a certain internationally famous film star with the suggestion that, using his work as a handy cover, he could usefully pass on any appropriate information he could pick up while touring a neutral country. All of which adds up to the questions which still perplex after nearly thirty years: was the gentle, unassuming Leslie Howard — the charming Ashley

Wilkes of *Gone With the Wind* — in fact a sort of mild prototype of James Bond? And did he die because the twin-engined DC-3 civilian aircraft in which he was flying from Portugal to England in June 1943 was shot down by Germans who did not wish him to get home with information he had gathered during a seemingly innocent British Council lecture tour? Neither question has been answered definitively, and almost certainly never will. We know exactly what happened to Flight 777 of KLM, the Royal Dutch Airline, by which Leslie Howard was travelling. What we do not know is *why*.

As an actor, Leslie Howard represented in the 1930s and early 1940s the idealization of the then "typical Englishman". America in particular idolized him, even if her views about British films were quite the reverse of idolatry. He was the nonchalant Briton of lazy charm and concealed strength and courage. Off the screen as on he was shy, somewhat vague in manner, slight in build. Once destined for a bank career, this son of an obscure London businessman had started as a poorly paid actor in repertory after the First World War. In his early days he was cast very much as a drawing-room comedy lightweight. He arrived on Broadway from the London stage in the early 1920s in plays of that kind.

He was refreshing and unusual; he became instantly popular. Inevitably, Hollywood beckoned. Then the studios of Pinewood and Denham called him home. He played a romantic role in *Escape to Happiness* with Ingrid Bergman. He was an equally romantic dreamer in *Berkeley Square*, with Heather Angel. He was Sir Percy Blakeney in *The Scarlet Pimpernel* and had a similar role in a setting of the Second World War, in *Pimpernel Smith*. It may not be fanciful to suggest that these two parts, each a deceptively casual Englishman, were the most accurate reflection of Howard's own character.

At the outbreak of war in 1939, Leslie Howard, who at that time was enjoying a secure and comfortable career in Hollywood, announced immediately that he would return to Britain. His intention, he said, was to make films that would help to boost morale and expose the evils of Nazism. He said quite simply, "I'll do anything that I'm asked to do." The amount of money available for film-making was limited in wartime, but the British Council, a shrewd organization with the job of making the country's way of fife as well known as possible abroad, soon found a role for Leslie Howard. He would travel in a number of countries, lecturing on his art and, at the same time, introducing showings of existing propaganda films, together with his own pictures whose spirit was such as to counter Nazi influence. Obvious choices were *The Scarlet Pimpernel, Pimpernel Smith*, and *The First of the Few* about R. J. Mitchell, the £6-a-week draughtsman who had designed the Spitfire.

Howard's first mission was in neutral Portugal and Spain. In 1943 these countries seethed with spies who would have sold anyone and anything for the price of a bottle of champagne. Some worked for Vichy France, others for Gaullist France. Many were agents of Nazi foreign intelligence or of the Allies. Many cheerfully took money from all of them. The riff-raff of Europe chanced their luck. Into this vortex of dubious loyalties came the sometimes bewildered, but always good-humoured, figure of Leslie Howard. He gave the impression, probably genuinely, of being the classic innocent abroad, touchingly willing to help and easy to take in. In pure propaganda value the tour was an immense success. A highlight was a lecture on *An Actor's Approach to Hamlet* which drew a packed audience at Madrid's British Institute. A more spectacular achievement was that, at the time of Howard's trip, cinemas in Spain and

Portugal were showing no less than nine hundred British films. It was the actor himself who insisted on having *The First of the Few* flown out for showing on the Iberian peninsula. The innocent abroad was not so innocent after all.

We do not know whether Leslie Howard was engaged in espionage; but we *do* know that German agents in Spain and Portugal thought he was. He and his manager, a bluff Churchillian figure named Alfred Chenhalls, were kept under surveillance night and day by undercover Nazis.

Real-life stories of espionage frequently read like storylines for second feature movies. It is nevertheless true that while he was in Estoril Leslie Howard was vamped quite openly by a beautiful *femme fatale* whom we will refer to here as Madame X. She was a known Nazi agent. This lady was straight out of the most purple penny-dreadful, the type of international adventuress belonging to the 1890s rather than to the Third Reich. She was said to be of Hungarian-Argentinian origins, the wife of a German count whom she had married in order to secure European nationality. In the 1930s she hobnobbed with leading Nazis and was soon having an affair with an influential diplomat who was a useful source of information of marketable value. When Howard met her she soon began to whisper sweetly into his ear.

If the actor had in fact been instructed to report on what was happening among the Nazi colony, he would probably have been made aware of Madame X's game and been especially cautious. He could still have been flattered by the interest this undeniably attractive Mata Hari was showing in him, and responded to some extent. This seemed to be happening. It worried Alfred Chenhalls and a Mr Neville Kearney, a British Council official, who made it his business to find out all about Madame X. We can never be sure if Leslie Howard was completely unaware of her real role, but he made one bad slip which even the rankest amateur in the spy game would have avoided. In the lady's hearing he referred to his departure for England from Lisbon Airport on 1 June. For this he received a well-merited rebuke from Chenhalls. It was too late. There is not the slightest doubt that the information was passed on to interested ears.

The scene now switches to the airport at Lisbon's Portela, where a twin-engined 210mph DC-3 (Dakota) aircraft, Flight 777, stands ready for departure to the United Kingdom. This plane — codename G-AGBB — was one of those on the wartime service from Lisbon flown by pilots of KLM, Royal Dutch Airline. War or no war, a certain amount of civil flying had to continue to neutral countries. It was essential to keep some links, however small, open with Europe. British pilots had their military role to fulfil elsewhere, so an agreement had been worked out between the Air Ministry and the Dutch Government in exile to keep open the Britain–Lisbon route. The Dutch operated from Heston Airport near London until Goering launched his fierce blitz against the capital and the flying of civil passengers on the original route became impossible. The Dutch crews moved to "somewhere in England" — in fact, to a civil airfield at Whitchurch. The exact location was, as far as possible, kept secret, with elaborate precautions to ensure that passengers did not know exactly where they were on take-off or landing.

But Portugal was neutral. Anyone could operate an airline from Portela, and all the big airlines including KLM, BOAC and Swissair did. So, incidentally, did the German line, Lufthansa. It was clearly impossible to keep the departure of an aircraft bound for England a secret when all someone on the Lufthansa departure desk had to do was lift a telephone.

German mechanics had, of course, access to the tarmac which meant a risk of sabotage. All the security in the world could not make the Dutch pilots and their passengers absolutely safe.

Naturally, other passengers were aboard the plane carrying Leslie Howard and Alfred Chenhalls. There was an oil executive, Tyrrell Shervington, whom the Germans suspected of being a spy; Berthold Israel, who had been in Lisbon on behalf of the Jewish agency in Palestine; and Foreign Office diplomat Gordon Maclean. These — and particularly Israel — were doubtless of more than passing interest to the Nazis.

There is one passenger upon whom it might be instructive to linger a moment — Alfred Chenhalls himself, a large, pink-cheeked devotee of the good things of life. He had been in lucrative practice as a solicitor in the City before becoming business manager of Leslie Howard Productions, Ltd. Like many ample individuals whose feet have to support a generous body, he walked with a shambling gait. His head would pitch forward to give him a probably unmerited air of pugnacity. He smoked enormous cigars. In short, he bore something of a resemblance to an infinitely more celebrated figure, also large, also given to shambling and addicted to cigars. Chenhalls knew perfectly well that he looked like Winston Churchill: it would appear that he took great delight in trading on it. He had a taste for black Homburgs, and went for them to the same hatter as the British Prime Minister. He got his suits from the same tailor as the great man. The resemblance — part coincidental, part contrived — is important in the light of what happened later.

The passengers of the Dakota climbed aboard, Leslie Howard much concerned about the safety of gifts for his family and for film friends. Captain Quirinus Tepas taxied across the runway and, at 9.35 a.m., took off towards the Bay of Biscay in weather which promised rain and poor visibility. Behind the passengers lay prosperous Lisbon whose tawdry glitter and obvious complacency contrasted sharply with the dour London of blackout and ration cards. The route lay across the Portuguese and Spanish coasts to Cape Finisterre and then out across the Bay of Biscay. The danger point of Brest was given a wide berth. The aircraft would turn east-north-east for Whitchurch. Sinister sentinels were prowling under the waters of the Bay and they merited the protective patrolling of the Luftwaffe at a time when it was vital to the Germans that the U-boat lanes should remain unmolested. The civil aircraft on the Lisbon–United Kingdom route had twice been attacked. No serious damage had been done on either occasion. So far the route had led a charmed existence; yet the crews were not underestimating the dangers.

One may well wonder why the Germans did not make greater efforts to blast the Lisbon routes out of the sky. After all, Hitler was not noted for respecting neutrality. The answer is probably that such sabotage would have killed quite a few geese capable of laying golden eggs. Not a few undercover Nazis tried to smuggle themselves in and out of Britain; some doubtless succeeded. A civil air-route could be a handy aid. In addition, aircraft like this Dakota frequently carried diplomatic documents, mail and newspapers. All of them might afford useful clues to what the British were up to. German spies in Britain and Portugal had generous budgets, and money had a habit of talking to men who might be able to get their hands on these transit documents. So long as it served them a purpose the Germans were prepared to leave the route more or less alone, though of course some Luftwaffe crews did suffer from an excess of zeal. There is no doubt that the route would have been forced out of business if it had suited Germany's plans.

Until the Dakota reached the edge of the Bay, passengers relaxed in something approaching pre-war comfort. A steward circulated with drinks. There were books and magazines. A traveller might well rub his eyes and wonder whether or not he had dreamed the war. Then he would remember the injunction he had received on embarking: "Passengers are asked to look out of their window during the flight and to announce the approach of *any* aircraft."

Although visibility over the Bay was bad there was a patch of clear weather some 500 miles west-north-west of Bordeaux, near where the Luftwaffe had an airfield. It was on the cards that the Dakota must fly somewhere near the bright patch: so, unfortunately, it proved. Eight Junkers 88s of KG Bomber Group, from Kerlin-Bastard near Bordeaux, were waiting. The attack began at 12.54 when Captain Tepas, doubtless peering into the mists of the Bay, saw a single aircraft on his port side. Radio operator Cornelius van Brugge flashed, "GKH from G-AGBB. An unidentified aircraft is following." Whitchurch did not pick up this message, but Lisbon did. Then came another desperate signal: "I am being attacked by enemy aircraft."

The Junkers each mounted three 2-centimetre cannon firing ahead and three 0.79-centimetre machineguns in the armoured nose, as well as two turret-mounted cannon. The Dakota was unarmed, except for a pistol carried in the pocket of one of the crew in case of trouble from the German mechanics in Lisbon. It was, even by Nazi standards, a cowardly attack. By now Whitchurch was receiving the signals... "From G-AGBB to GKH, am attacked by enemy aircraft." Whitchurch attempted to reply, but there was silence. The Junkers had held off for a few minutes. Then, like unleashed bloodhounds, they swept in to an obviously premeditated kill, their cannon blazing. The airliner had no chance. Her engines streaked smoke and flame, and the bullets peppered the fuselage.

Whether Tepas was still alive we do not know. It made no difference. The Dakota nosedived and streaked towards the sea. What happened next was horrible. The fuel tanks exploded, the after-door flew open, and four bodies — whose, was never discovered — were catapulted out of the plane. Eyewitnesses among the German pilots said that one parachute opened half-heartedly, then caught fire. For a moment, the bodies seemed to dangle in space, then they fell like stones, the blazing hulk of the aircraft following. For the whole of this account of the end of the aircraft we depend on the testimonies of Luftwaffe officers and crew questioned after the war. There is no reason to doubt their story.

The Nazis lost no time in disclaiming allegations of a cowardly attack on a civil aircraft. Goebbels declared that the Dakota had been camouflaged and, as such, deserved to be treated as a military plane. The Bay of Biscay, the Germans claimed, was war territory, with the Dakota a threat to U-boats: thus the attack had been fully justified. Furthermore, it was hinted darkly, all on board had been of military importance and had been, in effect, executed as spies, in accordance with the rules of war. Dr Goebbels was far too shrewd a propagandist not to mix a speck of truth with his poison. Was that last allegation partly true? The Nazis named specifically Leslie Howard and the oil man, Tyrrell Shervington, as British agents.

British official sources have rejected utterly the assertion against Leslie Howard. He had simply been a patriotic British actor doing his bit for the war effort. As for Shervington, we know even less about his activities. But the Luftwaffe would have been kept far busier than was healthy for them if they had planned to kill every business executive of anti-Nazi sympathies who flew out of Portugal. Neither was the Foreign Office man, Gordon Maclean, of any outstanding importance. This brings us to Berthold Israel. He is, on the surface, a likelier prospect than Howard or Shervington. He was a Jew. His known dream of re-establishing his people, after the defeat of Germany, was a raging heresy in Nazi eyes. Did this make him worth the attention of eight Junkers? The Germans had enough problems implementing their "final solution" in Europe without pursuing a single vendetta of this kind.

We have deliberately left the Churchillian Alfred Chenhalls to the last. Photographs suggest that his strong superficial resemblance to Winston Churchill could have deceived almost anyone, across room, airport lounge or tarmac. At the time of the departure of the Dakota, Churchill was in conference at Algiers. But even if he had been in Lisbon, he would neither have taken — nor been allowed to take — the risk of travelling in an unescorted aircraft, when he had the pick of everything Britain had to offer. Even for someone as unpredictable as Churchill the idea is ridiculous. Yet the Nazis frequently could be stupid in matters of simple logic, usually when Foreign Minister Ribbentrop interfered, as he had done with a preposterous plot to kidnap the Duke of Windsor. What we now know of the failings of the Nazi mind, and of Ribbentrop's monumental denseness, place the mistake within the bounds of possibility. The Chenhalls-Churchill confusion — even the names have a ring of similarity — cannot be totally disregarded when we look for the real motive for the Dakota massacre.

Leslie Howard's actor son, Ronald, was 22 at the time and, over the years, he has studied the affair probably more closely than any man alive. He inclines to the Chenhalls-Churchill theory. Of one thing he is absolutely certain: his father was *not* a secret agent. Ronald Howard insists, "My father had a lot of plans for war propaganda through lecture tours, film shows and the arts. His trip to Lisbon was to further these. He had, I am convinced, no other motive." Ronald Howard believes that "Churchill" was the intended victim all along. Someone saw Chenhalls board the aircraft and, seeking a moment of glory, put a telephone call through to the right quarters saying that the Prime Minister was on the way to London. It is a persuasive theory which fits all the facts as we know them. There is no evidence whatever that anyone in the Dakota was of sufficient importance to be eliminated. Therefore, it may be reasonable to assume that someone simply made a bad mistake and set the Junkers rolling for the attack.

There is, however, another possibility. Although the Lisbon line was of considerable use to the Germans it was also doing considerable damage to their cause in Spain and Portugal. All sorts of influential people were travelling back and forth, despite the supposed siege-state of the British Isles. The flights could have increased in nuisance value, and quick action was decided upon to prevent them doing so. As it happened, after the Dakota disaster the aircraft on the route switched to night-flying with considerable inconvenience to everyone. Only after the Allied invasion of Europe, when the Luftwaffe was near total collapse, was the old routine resumed.

It is certainly tempting to cast Leslie Howard in the role of the spy. If one believes that he was, the story has everything — a handsome actor donning cloak and dagger, a beautiful vamp who may have betrayed him, and, above all, a final martyrdom. There are no facts to warrant this interpretation.

When it was clear that Flight 777 had crashed in the Bay of Biscay there was a widespread search. No bodies were ever found. Leslie Howard died serving his country, one way or another. He knew perfectly well the risks along the Lisbon route. While many British actors sat out the war in comfort in Hollywood, Howard chose to come home and do what he could for England at war. *The Scarlet Pimpernel* and *Pimpernel Smith* were ideally cast.

Another leading member of the entertainment profession died — or is taken to have died — in mysterious fashion during the war. He was Glenn Miller, the American bandleader whose brilliant gift for instrumental arrangement gave his band a "new sound" — crisp, sweet-sour, equally satisfying both to American and British tastes. Some say that when he disappeared on a flight from England to France in 1944 he did so deliberately, as a defector, and is alive to this day (at the time of writing), living on the interest from ill-gotten gains as a wartime black-marketeer. Kinder souls have put it about that he suddenly went insane and was shut away; or that he was in a genuine air accident and suffered such terrible injuries that he could never again be seen by any but those who tend him.

More than likely none of this is true; but the Glenn Miller mystery remains, just as there lingers, for all who ever heard it, the unforgettably distinctive sound of his band playing "In the Mood", "Tuxedo Junction", or any of the other tunes of the 1940s which are associated first and foremost with him.

In 1944 he was 39 and at the peak of a success for which he had worked since boyhood. Thankfully, not many schoolboys gravitate to the trombone, but young Glenn Miller did, buying the instrument with the proceeds from milking cows in his native Iowa. Music was in the forefront of his mind throughout his college and university years and he had already made arrangements for a number of bands when Ray Noble enlisted him, in his late twenties, to help him organize a new one. He served Noble as arranger for several years, until the realization came that he would never obtain the blend of sound that he could hear in his mind, but had never yet achieved, until he could have a band of his own to experiment with.

He formed his band in 1937 but found even then that what he could conceive and what achieve were still frustratingly different things. The sound would not come right. He broke up the band, went back to arranging for a while, then formed another. Like an artist chasing an inspiration, or a writer an elusive idea, he found success almost accidentally. A trumpeter was unable to play. Glenn Miller did a last-minute reshuffle of parts, scribbled an arrangement for a clarinet to take the trumpet's place — and the Glenn Miller sound was born. Success came immediately and hugely. By the time America entered the war, Glenn Miller and his band had been top of almost everyone's list of favourites for years.

Tall, rangy and almost ascetic in appearance — in fact, rather like the film actor James Stewart who would one day depict him in the film of his life-story — Glenn Miller could have stayed well away from the war. He was too old to serve; in any case, his eyesight was poor — the rimless glasses are an essential feature of his image. He chose to do his share by taking his band to England to broadcast and play at concerts for the American and Allied forces concentrating for the invasion of Europe. For one reason and another this was not permitted, but he was invited at length, by General Eisenhower's order, to come to England and direct the American Band of the Allied Expeditionary Force, a new combination of grandiose proportions — sixty instrumentalists, one-third of them violinists from the great American symphony orchestras. It was a strange mixture and an exciting challenge to which Miller rose as perhaps no one else could have done. He created yet another "new sound" and ensured, by personal dynamism and the incisive discipline of which he was capable, that the essence, once bottled, never escaped.

The invasion took place and the Miller sound accompanied the advancing forces by way of radio. To his regret, Miller was instructed to remain in England from where he could entertain more people, soldiers and civilians by his broadcasts than he could ever have done by chasing all over France. Besides, the Allies' job on the continent was to move forward fast, not pause for music.

It did not stop Miller wishing to go, and when Paris fell in 1944 he saw his chance, arguing that he wished to broadcast a live Christmas show from there: "You boys bust through to Paris. When you've kicked the Germans out I'll come and play for you," he had often told his audiences. The show, he knew, would not reach more than a fraction of the audience his BBC broadcasts were enjoying; he seems to have seen it rather as a gesture to the troops fighting on through Europe that he should keep that promise. His persistence paid off. It was at last agreed that he might take the band to Paris in December for six weeks, having first completed the stiff task of recording enough programmes — more than a hundred of them — for the BBC to transmit in the regular spots when millions of listeners would tune in for the pleasure of listening to Glenn Miller "live", announcing, in those characteristic tones, such numbers as "Pennsylvania 6-5000", "Moonlight Serenade" and "Chattanooga Choo-Choo", which no one could put across like he.

The not inconsiderable airlift of the large band and its instruments was arranged for 14 December, a Saturday. The weather proved too bad for take-off. Miller, reflecting the impatience of "In the Mood", was raring to go and took the delay badly. There were countless things waiting to be done in Paris, from supervising their accommodation arrangements to conferring with radio officials and concert managers. He determined to get across the Channel himself, even if his band would have to wait a few days before joining him. A "lift" in an operational aircraft seemed the best possibility, and this was soon offered by an American colonel named Basselle who undertook not only to get him aboard an aircraft the following afternoon, but to go to France with him.

December fog hung depressingly that Sunday morning outside Glenn Miller's room in a block of officers' apartments in Bedford, the wartime centre for BBC music broadcasts. The R.A.F. had already decided not to operate training flights from the nearby aerodromes that day; yet Miller was relieved, after lunch, to find Colonel Basselle still game to get him to France. Although the fog was, if anything, thicker, and R.A.F. meteorological advice was against the flight, when the two men reached their airfield they found their pilot, an experienced American, awaiting them and the small, single-engined Norseman monoplane standing ready. Minutes later they had taken off and been swallowed up by the fog.

The band managed to fly to Paris at last on the Tuesday. As their big aircraft landed at Orly they peered from its windows, trying to catch sight of the scholarly figure in Major's uniform waiting to meet them. He was not there. No doubt he was tied up with meetings — but there was no message for them, either. Odder still was that no one who was asked could say where he was or might be. It seemed clear to the band, boarding transport awaiting them outside the airport, that Glenn Miller had not passed that way.

So unofficial had his flight been, it transpired, that no one knew where the Norseman had landed. Inquiries began to be put about for news of it. It was not long before inquiries were giving way to orders for an immediate air search along the cross-Channel route the Norseman would have flown; for no airfield could report its landing. Even if it had been forced to put down at a place quite some distance from Paris, Miller and his companion had had two days in which to reach the capital by other means, or at least communicate with someone. They had done neither.

Unless any of the possibilities mentioned at the beginning of this account is true, Glenn Miller has never been seen since that Sunday afternoon in December 1944. The news that he was posted missing was released on Christmas Eve, the last possible moment before the Christmas show which he was to have presented. Those who heard it were stunned; for while all entertainers subscribe to the wish that "the show must go on" in the event of their sudden incapacity or death, bizarre circumstances had attended Glenn Miller's case. Hoping fervently for firm news about him, good or bad, the authorities had decided to keep his pre-recorded broadcasts going on the BBC. While the search for him was in progress, listeners were still hearing his voice introducing the "Glenn Miller sound", unaware that he was not speaking to them by live microphone at that very moment.

Perhaps this well-meant deception helped to create the rumours that arose and to nourish the exaggerated reports which inquiry into them produced. Glenn Miller was variously said to have been kidnapped at the orders of the Nazi propaganda chief, Goebbels, in envy of his morale-raising appeal; to have hijacked his own aircraft in order to get to South America and "away from it all" (South America in a single-engined aircraft!); to have been shot down by a British or American fighter, in mistake for a German plane. The latter explanation is the least ludicrous, but can be discounted: no R.A.F. aircraft reported contact with Germans in that area on that day, and the only American combat involved the elite Black Widows squadron, far too skilled and experienced to have mistaken the small passenger plane for — as was rumoured — a JU-88.

Not many hours before his death, Glenn Miller had had drinks with the British bandleader and impresario Jack Hylton at the latter's London apartment. Looking back to that time, the late Jack Hylton used to recall the American's farewell remark to him before he stepped out into Piccadilly to return to Bedford: "I've never seen a shot fired in this war, Jack. I feel kind of ashamed about that. I'm going to do my darnedest to get a look at some fighting. I'll tell you about it when I get back."

Indeed, yet another of the rumours is that Glenn Miller persuaded his pilot to take the little Norseman monoplane towards enemy territory in France — a detour which would have meant a considerably longer flight than the 160 miles from Bedford to Paris, for the nearest centres of fighting then were in Belgium and Holland, and to reach them would have meant a long loop from the Channel. Jack Hylton believed that something of this sort was attempted, but that the aircraft had iced up and fallen into the sea, or possibly had reached or neared enemy territory and been shot down. The whole notion is, surely, a most unlikely one. The little party may have been flying unofficially — and just how unofficially is not known — but the experienced pilot would scarcely have added sightseeing to a hazardous flight in fog.

The prosaic, but sorry, truth is, no doubt, that Glenn Miller's eagerness to get to Paris was so great that the flight was undertaken rashly, leading to a crash into the Channel. No one in authority appears to have missed him during the two days between his departure and his band's arrival in Paris, suggesting that no one expected him to arrive ahead. There has been no official verdict on the case, leaving rumour to flourish where it can.

The Glenn Miller Band, as it now called itself, remained in being for some time. But although its members were the same, with its combination of instruments, its arrangements and its repertoire, the catalyst was gone and with him the magic. Even now, from many parts of the world, members of the thriving Glenn Miller Appreciation Society make periodic pilgrimages to what was the wartime airfield from where he took off on his last flight. No doubt, blended with that Glenn Miller sound which is their *raison d'être*, they hear on those occasions the receding drone of a little aircraft in a December fog.

5: A 27-YEAR MYSTERY SOLVED

At seven o'clock on a blustery autumn morning — Saturday, 21 March 1931 — a ground crew huddled on to the tarmac of Mascot Aerodrome, Sydney, Australia. Its task was to prepare the blue-and-silver tri-motor Avro–Fokker airliner *Southern Cloud* for its scheduled passenger flight to Melbourne at 8.15, a 450-mile journey on which it would be piloted by 33-year-old Travis William ("Shorty") Shortridge, former British Army officer, Sandhurst-trained and born in India, now senior pilot of the 3-year-old Australian National Airways.

For all its youth, the company was meticulously professional. Its highly-trained engineers, under a chief — F. Wyndham Hewitt — who had studied at first-hand the factory and workshop practices of such thorough-going European firms as KLM in Holland and Lufthansa in Germany, observed a rigorous pre-flight checking routine on *Southern Cloud* this morning as on every occasion when one of their aircraft was about to fly. When *Southern Cloud* took off five minutes ahead of schedule she was in perfect order.

Like all ANA pilots, Shortridge, who had learnt his flying in the R.A.F., knew every detail of his route visually, but was also a skilled blind-flier. Pilots at that time were not restricted to precise flight paths; their slow machines were too much at the mercy of the winds to maintain undeviating lines. Only one thing was thus certain about the course *Southern Cloud* would follow on this as on other trips; this was that, because of bad weather and very strong headwinds, it would be forced to land for refuelling at the emergency strip at Bowser, some 4 miles from Wangaratta on the main Sydney–Melbourne highway, or farther south at Benalla, another of ANA's emergency fuelling points.

In the event, it did neither. After leaving Sydney it vanished — for 27 years.

The story really begins on the day, in 1927, when Charles Edward Kingsford Smith met Charles Thomas Phillippe Ulm. During the First World War, Kingsford Smith had served with the Australian Imperial Force and won the Military Cross for operations over the German lines. His dream was to make an England–Australia flight, but since he was only in his teens during the war the idea was not treated seriously. Eventually, he found a job with West Australian Airways, but could not lose the obsession of making history in aviation. He set his sights on amassing enough money to enable him to fly the Pacific from America to Australia.

Charles Ulm had the same idea and an equal ambition. Already, in 1919, he had tried to float a company to run a passenger air-service from Sydney to Melbourne and from Sydney to various inland centres. He never secured the backing, but decided to pool his considerable business talent with the greater flying know-how of the more mercurial Kingsford Smith. The two men went into business together. The story of the thrilling and hazardous America–Australia flight made in *Southern Cross*, first of the Avro–Fokkers which were to make them famous, has been described exhaustively. Our concern is with later events.

Australian National Airways, Ltd (ANA) was the biggest project of the redoubtable pair. Its aim was to cover all major Australian locations with scheduled flights. ANA was formed on 12 December 1928 with a nominal capital of £200,000. Those were still pioneering times. Scheduled flights were as novel as regular railway journeys must have been to the more elderly subjects of the young Victoria. ANA was very far from being a whim, something to be run on a shoestring with a scratch fleet of stunt aircraft. Kingsford Smith and Ulm went for the best, earmarking £37,000 for the latest Avro–Fokker aircraft. An elaborate and expensive hangar was built at Mascot. Offices were opened in Sydney and Melbourne. Amateurs, no matter how enthusiastic, were not employed. ANA combed Australia for its staff which eventually numbered around seventy, many of whom had learnt their trade in British workshops. Kingsford Smith's job was to put the newly-acquired aircraft through their paces. Pilots were taught, amongst other things, to rely completely on their instruments to tell them their position. Kingsford Smith accompanied candidates for jobs over the Sydney–Melbourne route more times than he ever counted, a taxing flight and a splendid test of a pilot's suitability to join ANA.

One fundamental shortcoming was the absence of radio on the Avros. For technical reasons, an Avro was not suitable for receiving radio messages even over a few miles, although transmission presented few problems. Added to this shortcoming, the Australian authorities felt that they should own and operate all ground radio stations. This might have been all very well if they had proceeded to set up an efficient and comprehensive service, but there was no sign of their doing so. ANA protested vehemently, arguing that it could do the job itself if permitted, whereupon the government moved in the classic way of governments — it formed a committee. This was in 1931. When war broke out eight years later there was still no suitable ground wireless network for the aid of Australian aircraft. The committee had met conscientiously, and that was all.

Even before the *Southern Cloud* affair it seemed as if Kingsford Smith and Ulm were under a cruel curse. In April 1929 both men planned a business trip to England from Richmond, New South Wales, and set off in their Avro *Southern Cross*. They flew into a blinding storm and were forced down in the Kimberley area of Western Australia. They were not sighted for twelve days and the search for them brought the death of two colleagues whose aircraft had to make a landing in desert. The whole expedition was sharply criticized, although Kingsford Smith and Ulm were acquitted of personal responsibility. ANA was lucky to survive the unfavourable publicity, but the fates were frowning and there was worse to come.

During March 1931 it seemed as if hell had come to Melbourne, destination of *Southern Cloud*. The place was lashed by heavy seas whose spray deluged the roads. Streets had become fast-moving, debris-choked lakes. Battering rain, stinging like glancing needle-pricks, lashed down on the city. The weather forecasts continued grim. On the day of *Southern Cloud*'s flight Melbourne was threatened with 48 hours of thunderstorm and hail. Although these conditions were exceptional, the weather along the Sydney–Melbourne route was never exactly mild, particularly over the Australian Alps which covered about a third of the way. Conditions were always variable and could change from frowning cloud and driving rain to air too turbulent for flying.

Sydney, that March, had blustery weather that was for ever threatening something worse, although conditions were nothing like those in Melbourne. When "Shorty" Shortridge took off it was in weather no worse than he was used to. At mid-morning, however, the Sydney Weather Bureau released a forecast which struck a chill even into the hearts of Kingsford

Smith and Ulm. Gale-force winds, thunderstorms, hailstorms and, above all, murderous rain were all awaiting *Southern Cloud*. Shortridge was to know none of this. He was in the air, beginning his scheduled 450-mile run, accompanied by his co-pilot Charlie Dunnell and six passengers.

At the refuelling points along his route men waited in vain for the drone of the approaching airliner. There came no sound. By evening, Melbourne was telephoning to a seriously alarmed Charles Ulm who had to break the news to his partner: the aircraft was missing. For a few more hours both men consoled themselves with the hope that it had been forced to ride out the storm at one of the refuelling centres. As time passed this slender hope died, the news leaked out, and ANA offices in Sydney and Melbourne became crowded with friends and relatives anxious for news. It was calculated that Shortridge's fuel would have lasted him until the early evening. When there was no news of him by the following day there seemed no doubt of tragedy.

A search for a missing aircraft in the 1930s was by no means the highly organized affair it is today. There were few technical specialists. Everyone lent a hand, so that while there was any amount of willingness, there existed no overall command and precious little planning. After the reported disappearance ANA's scheduled services were reduced so as to enable every Avro to join the search, concentrated on the densely timbered and inhospitably rugged territory lying to the north-east of Victoria and straddling the continent's east coast. It began with rising foothills some 40 miles outside Melbourne which covered mile upon mile until interrupted by the mountain peaks. Here an aircraft could have fallen without a soul having seen it: it could be lying hidden and its occupants marooned.

The pilots of ANA were reinforced by volunteer help from the Royal Australian Air Force and numerous private individuals. Aircraft were offered in profusion, but the call still went out for more and more searchers. In country like eastern Australia, looking for a missing aircraft is not just a question of flying low and keeping your eyes peeled. To search anywhere near the Australian Alps means getting as near to the ground or mountainside as possible, a hazardous business even in good weather. But for a good part of the year weather in that region is anything but favourable. Mists that resemble nothing so much as a thick plate of substantial Celtic porridge impede the progress of any aircraft unwise enough to fly too low. A clear ridge may stand out in seeming clarity, but at the side of it, screened by the soggy grey, swirling mist, can be razor-backed ridges and jagged escarpments that will slice a speeding aircraft to ribbons in a second. It was in these sort of conditions that search parties operated, Kingsford Smith among them flying *Southern Sun*, one of the Avro fleet. He elected to tackle an area called the Strathbogie Ranges. His aircraft's manoeuvres resembled those of a nimble fighter in the thick of a dog-fight, rather than a sedate passenger machine. One moment Kingsford Smith was zigzagging across countryside that was alternately steep and flat without warning; then he was gritting his teeth as tall trees threatened to shave the underbelly of the aircraft or seize him prisoner in their branches. As well as the preoccupations of flying, a sharp lookout had to be kept for even a hint of wreckage. It was a toss-up whether any aircraft landing in such country would ever be discovered. *Southern Cloud* had probably come down in mountain country amongst trees towering 100 feet, their branches concealing ground fractured by gorges and ravines.

Other promising leads all petered out when investigated. The usual quota of cranks who inevitably seek the limelight when there is a disaster swamped Sydney and Melbourne with statements that they had seen *Southern Cloud*. Most of these claims were patently ridiculous and contradicted each other hopelessly. One, however, seemed less so. Two days after the disappearance, Kingsford Smith received an excited telephone call from Squadron-Leader A. H. Cobby, Commanding Officer of No. 3 R.A.A.F. Squadron, Richmond. Cobby, whose word was obviously worth respecting, explained that on the day of the flight he had been in Melbourne on family business. At about 3.30 p.m. he had heard a three-engined aircraft overhead; as an experienced airman he had had no difficulty in identifying the sound.

The presence of an aircraft at that time was confirmed by other witnesses, but what precisely did this amount to? How could *Southern Cloud* have managed, in the storm, to get to Melbourne without stopping at the refuelling points? If Cobby's evidence was accurate, it would have meant that *Southern Cloud* must then have overshot the airfield, in which case it would have turned back. No one had noticed it. If it had come down on the sea it was likely that someone would at length have spotted it.

Could Cobby have heard some other aircraft? It had certainly not been one of the ANA fleet. There had been no other Avro over Melbourne that day save for *Southern Star* and *Southern Moon*, which had many hours earlier left there for their destinations. It looked very much as if Cobby had been mistaken. Nevertheless, a R.A.A.F. Seagull amphibian was sent to comb the area south of Melbourne, but nothing was found.

The tragedy of *Southern Cloud* was both a mental and physical agony for Kingsford Smith and Ulm. Both men worked around the clock, sometimes flying for eight or nine hours at a stretch. Even for men well used to doing without sleep, a schedule as rigorous as this began to take its toll. Both began to lose most of their spirit as the days passed and they had no word of comfort for the anxious crowds who haunted the airfields.

The search went on for six days and nights without a break. The most spectacular foray occurred after there had been reports of flashing lights near Tintaldra, 40 miles from the 7,328-foot Mount Kosciuszko, lying roughly on the last three-quarters of the Sydney–Melbourne route. Could these have been signals? Kingsford Smith flew *Southern Sun* a mere 50 feet over Kosciuszko and circled the mountain area until sunset. As the shadows lengthened the *Sun* banked away and in the encroaching darkness returned to Melbourne, its tanks almost dry.

Friends, relatives and well-wishers joined in equally fruitless expeditions. They meant well, but with limited flying experience and in some cases only the haziest knowledge of the terrain between Sydney and Melbourne they could scarcely hope to succeed where seasoned pilots had so conspicuously failed. The ANA Avros pressed on, working in pairs, so that if one should have to force-land the other would know its position. As far as was possible every square mile of territory had been combed, something like 100,000 in all. A search party on foot, had it been possible to organize one, would have taken years to cover such an area; besides, there were regions no human being had ever penetrated.

On 29 March, at a series of Press conferences throughout the flight area, reporters were told that the search had been called off. Two days later, and ten days after the disappearance of *Southern Cloud*, a government announcement stated that the death of all aboard must now be assumed. A public inquiry would be held.

The inquiry was, inevitably, an anti-climactic formality. In essence, its findings were that everything possible had been done to find *Southern Cloud* and that no definite reason for her disappearance could be established. Then came a belated recommendation that two-way radio should be made compulsory, that accurate weather reports should be more speedily available to pilots and crew, and that aircraft should be equipped with Very lights. The suggestion regarding radio, coming as it did from a government source, must have provoked a few grim smiles between those in ANA who had pressed so long for just such a facility.

A few undaunted souls continued with the search, but soon the Australian Alps were gripped in the iron vice of winter and everyone knew that Travis Shortridge, Charlie Dunnell and their six passengers, even in the unlikely event of having survived the crash, must now be dead.

What had happened to *Southern Cloud*? Kingsford Smith and Ulm were never to know the answer. Nor might Australia or the world, if it had not been for a lucky chance.

As the 1930s wore on, Australia found herself involved first in the universal economic depression and then in a Second World War. The Australia of the mid-forties and fifties was, in the exhilaration of victory, in no mood to look back over a decade. Still a young country, she plunged with gusto into expansion, making habitable for the first time in history vast sections of land that could not previously have sustained human life. It was, in a sense, this expansionist policy which led to the solution of the 27-year-old mystery.

One of the great problems Australia faced was how to harness new water supplies needed for irrigation and hydroelectricity. She had water in plenty, but a good deal of it was being allowed to go to waste, notably that of the most famous river of all, the Snowy, which ran from a ridge on the Australian Alps to cascade and spill into Bass Strait. This was doubtless picturesque, but useless. Far-seeing geologists and scientists viewed it as a criminal waste, and planned to divert the waters of the Snowy to link up with two other rivers, the Murrumbidgee and the Murray, through a series of tunnels beneath the Great Dividing Range. The result would be a vast source of desperately-needed water which could supply the multiplying post-war communities.

As the ambitious project got under way, this part of Australia began to reflect the Gold Rush era of the previous century. Labour, recruited from all over the world, swarmed into the villages and settlements, bringing bustle and colour. Many firms had contracts to work the Snowy. One of these, a subcontractor to a major company, had working for them a bright young carpenter named Thomas Reginald Sonter.

On Sunday, 26 October 1958, Sonter had a day off and decided to spend it taking photographs of the country around. The Australian Alps are nothing if not photogenic and Sonter, oblivious of time, wandered about casually, marvelling at the beauties awaiting his camera amongst the towering trees. He found himself in a world of perpetual twilight, where there was a solitude which reminded him of the interior of a vast cathedral. Not even a bird sang. In the distance could be heard the faint rush of the river far below. It was here that Sonter found *Southern Cloud*; or at least, parts of it.

His curiosity was aroused by some tangled and rusted metal which was entwining a bunch of saplings. As he pulled it free, Sonter felt heavy objects beneath his feet. He began to scrabble in the undergrowth, finding movement difficult amongst the close-set saplings. As evening approached, he found the whole place oddly depressing and, with as many pieces as he could carry, he left.

In no time at all a party from the Department of Civil Aviation was on its way up the mountain slopes to a point at the south-west side of a ridge in the Toolong Mountains, of the Great Dividing Range overlooking the Toolong River. It was within five miles of a gorge on the Eucumbene River which Kingsford Smith had explored on one of his fruitless flights. There was no doubt that *Southern Cloud* had now been found. A brass plate was unearthed from the mud and mouldering leaves, inscribed "Avro type X DWG. No. P1131".

The surroundings were depressingly apt for an exhumation. Twenty-seven years in the open is certainly enough to annihilate human remains and reduce them to a few softening bones. Objects have greater resilience. In this lonely graveyard they had survived as mildewed relics of three decades before: a string of chunky, 1930-ish red beads; a pair of binoculars; some sovereigns; a razor; a scent bottle. These were poignant enough, but there were grisly finds as well. One of the investigating team picked up a pair of shoes and bones fell out of them. The searchers turned with relief to items of less evocative kind: an aircraft clock, a rev counter, an altimeter. The years had not been kind to anything perishable in *Southern Cloud*, but it was perfectly possible to identify most of the components. A rusted cylinder head of the centre engine stuck out of the ground like a tombstone. The remains of another engine had sunk in the hillside. Carburettors and magnetos were blackened and charred, but many parts of the three Lynx engines were as good as new. Some of the nuts and bolts seemed freshly greased and oiled and would have been as usable as on the day of the disaster.

Southern Cloud lay on her right side on top of the starboard landing wheel which had been pushed 6 feet to the rear of where it would normally be. The starboard and centre engines were still in their correct positions, but the port engine was 4 feet in front and 2 feet to the left of the centre engine.

It seemed likely that the pilot had been on a level turn, but had banked to starboard at the moment of impact. The centre section was more or less intact. The flight controls had not been smashed out of all recognition; many were in reasonable condition. Plainly, *Southern Cloud* had not sustained any damage before it struck the ridge; neither, since the engines were embedded so deeply, could it be presumed that Shortridge had cruised gingerly and slowly in search of a suitable crashlanding spot. The ridge had therefore caught him by surprise. One puzzling fact was that the nose of the aircraft was found pointing *towards* Sydney.

Here was a fresh mystery. It was only too easy to picture Shortridge, battling on in that dreadful storm, praying every second that his passage would remain clear. Then he would spot, too late, that dreadful ridge. He would make a last minute starboard turn to dodge it. The noise of the impact would have been snatched away in the fury of the storm and the resulting blaze would soon have been quenched by the cascade of rain. The site of the remains of *Southern Cloud* was 219 miles from Sydney in a direct line, and a mere 16 miles east of the aircraft route. The search parties had flown time and again overhead, but had missed the ridge.

What had happened on 21 March 1931? There are plenty of theories and obviously the truth can never be known. But there have been some educated guesses. In his book *Southern Cloud*, Mr I. R. Carter has two theories to put forward. One theory assumes that for the early part of the flight Shortridge kept to the accepted route. That would have brought him to a place called Goulburn at 9.40 a.m. The weather reports suggest that, instead of a northerly wind which he was expecting, Shortridge was buffeted by a violent west-south-westerly. At this point it is sensible to assume that the normal route was abandoned. The logical place for Shortridge to make for next was Yass, which lay north of Canberra. But winds were such that at times they held *Southern Cloud* virtually motionless in the air, any movement merely a drift towards mountains over 7,000 feet high. How many of these *Southern Cloud* missed will never be known, but eventually it struck the Toolong Range.

The second theory supposes that at 3 p.m. Shortridge was within reasonable distance of Bowser, one of the emergency landing fields. This time is arrived at by assuming that *Southern Cloud*'s average speed was 45 miles per hour in the weather he encountered. With only an hour's fuel left he would have known that making it to Melbourne was out of the question. Seeking to get clear of the merciless rain and the mountains, he turned round for Bowser. What he found eventually was not reassuring flat land, but the Toolong Range.

Whatever the truth, Shortridge could not have been expected to deal with 100-mile-an-hour winds when he had expected 20–30-mile ones at the very worst. The fate of *Southern Cloud* was probably inevitable; it is only remarkable that the aircraft was not ripped to pieces in the air.

The missing *Southern Cloud* formed but one tragedy in the fated history of Australian National Airways. Both Ulm and Kingsford Smith were long dead by the time the aircraft was found. On 4 December 1934 Charles Ulm vanished while flying *Stella Australis*, an Airspeed Envoy monoplane, from California to Hawaii. Kingsford Smith was to disappear in October of the following year over the Bay of Bengal on a flight to Australia from Croydon in England. As for ANA itself, the Australian Government of the depression years had little money with which to subsidize domestic air services. Australian National Airways was forced to curtail its services. On 26 June 1931, only three months after the disappearance of *Southern Cloud*, the company was wound up.

ANA has an honourable place in aviation history, but ill-luck, of which the loss of *Southern Cloud* was only one piece, dogged it from the outset. Both Kingsford Smith and Ulm deserve the gratitude of modern Australia which, thanks to the efforts of such pioneers, enjoys one of the best civil air services in the world.

6: THE DEATHS OF ULM AND KINGSFORD SMITH

A quality common to pioneers — essential to them, perhaps — is self-confidence, with its attendant irrepressibility. The pioneers of flying had it in large measure, and none more than Charles Ulm. Standing amid the ruins of his and Charles Kingsford Smith's Australian National Airways in 1932, he was already looking forward to new achievements. He had done his best to keep the airline going, to hold fast to the first-rate team of pilots and engineers in readiness for the mail-carrying concession that could so suddenly be granted and would put the concern back into thriving business. Tenders for carrying overseas airmail between England and Australia were open until January 1934: there was always hope, although ANA's bankruptcy, the unsolved loss of *Southern Cloud* and the crash and writing-off in Malaya of one of her sisters, *Southern Sun*, weighed heavily in the debit balance.

What might have been a fillip to the company's reputation came in June 1932 when the overthrow of Australia's Labour Government cleared the way for Kingsford Smith to be granted the knighthood which his many admirers there and in Great Britain felt was long overdue. But the new knight had to continue earning his living by giving joyrides in his ageing *Southern Cross* to anyone wishing to take an aerial view of Sydney's spectacular harbour bridge, opened that March. Ulm stayed on the ground and occupied himself with negotiations.

The latter stage of the England–Australia airmail tender comprised three parts: Singapore–Darwin, Darwin–Brisbane, Katherine–Perth. Ulm and some of his compatriots maintained that it would be only fit and proper for an all-Australian airline to operate the "home" end of the service and for more than a year he engaged in talks with his country's major airline, QANTAS, in the hope that a new company might be created. But Great Britain's powerful Imperial Airways did not propose to stand aloof while a lucrative contract went elsewhere and began negotiations for a link-up with one of the Australian companies. Although Australian National Airways was amongst those considered, its unhappy record was too much to be offset even by the personal achievements and acknowledged qualities of Ulm, Kingsford Smith and their staff. Imperial Airways and QANTAS duly joined to form QANTAS Empire Airways.

Ulm fought on, hoping that ANA's experience and its readiness to begin a service at once with its remaining aircraft and team-tested organization would win it a contract. The odds were long against him, as even the ever-optimistic Ulm must have seen. He decided to shorten them by what would be a spectacular achievement: he would fly round the world in one of ANA's planes, thus attracting enormous publicity and proving the company's capability to handle the mere trifle of an Australia–Singapore run. To cap the feat, he proposed to break the existing round-the-world record, set up in 1931 by the American Wiley Post and his Tasmanian navigator Harold Gatty, the first fliers to circumnavigate the globe in continuous planned flight. They had completed the northern hemisphere route, 15,500 miles in distance, in 8 days and 16 hours. Ulm, determined to outdo his predecessors in every particular, chose the longer "Empire" route which meant crossing the equator twice. "I intend to rewrite the history books and substitute the name of Ulm for that of Wiley Post," he modestly announced.

The tough, one-eyed Wiley Post had set up his record in a trim Lockheed Vega monoplane, named *Winnie Mae*. Ulm, to the dismay of his more level-headed well-wishers, proposed to use one of Australian National Airways' obsolete Avros. They had given trusty service between cities on the Australian continent: a flight round the globe was a different undertaking indeed.

With all the money he could raise, Ulm bought *Southern Moon*. She had been standing disused for nearly two years in a hangar at Mascot Aerodrome, Sydney, awaiting a reconditioning which had been scheduled for her in 1931 but which it had seemed certain she would never enjoy. Ulm proceeded to recondition her to an extent far beyond that originally planned, to give her the extra durability, speed and fuel-carrying capacity vital to his enterprise. She was redesigned by an expert leading a team of former ANA men who knew too well that Ulm's success or failure in the aircraft they were about to rebuild for him could dictate the pattern of their own future. Accordingly, they worked day and night, substituting three new 240hp engines for the old ones; filling the fuselage with extra fuel tanks, supported in steel cradles, to quadruple the former tanks' capacity; strengthening the shock absorbers to meet the increase in laden weight from 10,255lb to 16,000lb; and almost remaking the single plywood wing, painting its top a bright orange as Ulm's one concession to the possibility that he might have to make a forced-landing, or even crash, and need to be spotted by an air search.

In June 1933 she was ready. With another of his aggressive gestures Ulm gave her the symbolic new name *Faith in Australia*. It could never be said of him that he failed to appreciate the value of publicity and the Press. But brave intentions and a flair for the dramatic do not guarantee success.

Faith in Australia took off in June on the first leg of her flight, with Ulm at the controls and P. G. Taylor and G. U. ("Scotty") Allan as crew — and was in trouble within hours. While still over Australia the petrol-feed system failed. The three men took turns at pumping by hand to keep the three thirsty engines supplied, until Ulm collapsed from the fumes. Allan had to take over the controls and Taylor worked to revive Ulm while keeping up the pumping. They landed and had new pumps installed, then made for northern India where a broken piston had to be repaired. Over Persia they had to jettison 400 gallons of fuel in order to make an emergency landing with engines smoking and threatening to burst into flame; and they were forced down yet again in France. The flight to England, when they got there, had taken 17 days, against Post's 8 to get round the world.

Ulm and his crew determined to go on: they would break no record now, but they would get round the world. They never did. Standing on the sands of Portmarnock, Ireland, taking in the excessive 6,000lb burden of fuel which Ulm had decided to carry in order to demonstrate her capacity for undertaking long flights, their aircraft began to sink. Her weight was too great for the surface on which she stood. One wheel went deep. A wing carved its way into the sand. Then the undercarriage collapsed, imprisoning the old machine for the disrespectful tide to come in and wash round *Faith in Australia*. The mishap cost them three more months' hold-up which might have become an indefinite one if a nobleman in the oil business had not given orders for the salvage and repairs to be charged to him.

There was one achievement, however. Seeing the futility of trying to get round the world, Ulm and his disappointed colleagues flew *Faith in Australia* back to her homeland, breaking the England-to-Australia record in doing so. But the object of the whole disastrous exercise was not gained; the Australia–Singapore mail-carrying contract, ANA's last hope of resuscitation, went to QANTAS. Ironically, if the Australian Government had had as much personal faith in Ulm as he had in Australia, and had given him the contract in spite of everything, he would have received enough funds to buy modern aircraft and perhaps set up a great airline. He had had to make his gesture with an obsolete aircraft; personal qualities had not proved enough to overcome the handicap.

Ulm may have been disappointed, but he was not dismayed into giving up. He still had his aircraft, now reconditioned again, and he proceeded to use her for several pioneering mail-carrying flights from Australia to New Zealand and New Guinea. His ambitions rekindled, and during the long hours flying to and fro over the Pacific he made his plans for the first passenger and airmail service between Australia and America. It was a breathtaking concept which, in terms of the aircraft, equipment and knowledge available, was several years ahead of its time. Even Ulm could not persuade himself that the service could be flown non-stop for 7,000-odd miles across the world's greatest ocean. He resolved to adopt a patient, painstaking approach: he would break the journey into a number of comfortable stages by providing his own stepping-stones across the water.

Again managing to scrape up funds he quietly, and telling no one, went about having an airstrip made on Fanning Island, 1,000 miles south of Hawaii. Native labour did the work, using crushed coral for material. Ulm's intention was to test out this prototype runway with an aircraft and then, if it proved successful, quickly to have others built on a series of Pacific islands, so creating a causeway of staging posts for aircraft to use between Australia, New Zealand and America.

The airstrip ready, Ulm took his plans to official quarters, proposing an all-British survey flight across the Pacific, by way of Fanning Island. No doubt to his relief, and perhaps some surprise, he was listened to with interest. Although it was not made public at the time, the Australian Government guaranteed him the costs of the experimental flight, to the tune of some £8,000. He was able to establish a new company, Great Pacific Airways Ltd, with himself as managing director and a well-known businessman, Sir Ernest Fisk, as chairman. At last, at the age of 37, Charles Ulm had the official demonstration of confidence he had been seeking. There were whispers of a knighthood for him if his venture proved successful. The scheme itself was visionary, yet, to all intents and purposes, soundly practical, and he would use his own acknowledged skill and courage to prove it. Australia would have been letting slip a great chance to enhance her prestige if she had failed at that moment to give him the backing he needed.

Buoyantly confident, Ulm pressed ahead with his plans. One thing was certain: there was to be no question this time of placing misguided trust in an outdated aircraft. The old *Faith in Australia* was abandoned in favour of a brand-new Airspeed Envoy monoplane, a sleek, low-winged, twin-engined British machine which he proceeded to test exhaustively in England, Canada and America before flying it at last to Oakland, California, the starting point of his and Kingsford Smith's historic first flight across the Pacific in 1928. At Oakland he received the Press, telling them: "I expect Great Pacific Airways Limited to establish a service in the next two years. Planes, one a week each way between Sydney and Honolulu to connect with the steamer service between the United States and Honolulu, would reduce the transportation time of twenty-one days from San Francisco to Sydney to seven-and-a-half days." But at first the service would only operate on a Sydney–Honolulu basis, since there were no aeroplanes yet existing capable of operating economically over the 2,400-mile nonstop stretch between California and Honolulu.

Ulm introduced his crew: his co-pilot, G. M. Littlejohn, a well-known New South Wales flying instructor, and his navigator and radio operator, J. Leon Skilling, who had come to flying from the Mercantile Marine. Never a man to let a chance of publicity pass by, he had already made the name of his new aircraft, *Stella Australis*, familiar throughout the Press of America and the British Empire.

On 30 November he made a final test flight from Oakland. Heavily laden with 600 gallons of fuel, the aircraft responded perfectly. "We can make the hop with no trouble at all," Ulm declared, and set the last preparations in motion. Four days later, on the morning of 4 December, *Stella Australis* again had her tanks filled to capacity, the three men climbed aboard, last-minute checks were carried out, and then they were off.

An amateur radio "ham" picked up a message from them at 10.30 a.m. Everything was going swimmingly; the weather was perfect, the engines performing beautifully. Another message, picked up at noon, confirmed excellent progress, aided now by a little tail wind. Two more hours, and the S.S. *Lurline* saw them pass over her: at the same time they reported, "The engine is fine, the weather perfect. Starting lunch. We do not expect to get our feet wet." After all his tribulations and frustrations any rashness on Ulm's part in making such confident predictions when he was still two or three hundred miles short of the halfway point in the flight can be sympathized with; but rashness there was, as would transpire. For the present all continued to go well. They reached and passed the halfway point. Now, in the event of trouble, there was less flying before them to reach Honolulu than behind them from Oakland. At 6.30 a.m. on 5 December *Stella Australis* was calling the U.S. Army Air Service for forecasts of weather conditions at the two Army aerodromes on Honolulu, Luke and Wheeler Fields, and estimating time of arrival at one or other of them as 8 a.m.

But now there was trouble. As well as the darkness before dawn, there was cloud. They were having to rely on dead reckoning for their course. This should not have been necessary. There was a radio beacon at Honolulu, and it had been in constant operation since midnight. They had only to follow its signals to be guided in.

It first became obvious that something was amiss when a message received at 7.30 a.m. reported that the airmen were lost and running short of fuel. It was known that they had aboard more than enough to get them to their destination; if they could get back on course soon they would easily reach land safely. What gave rise to real anxiety was a series of requests from them for the Honolulu beacon to be switched on. It *was* switched on and working perfectly. The obvious implication was that its signals were not reaching *Stella Australis*.

The messages began to be appeals:

"Must get beacon soon."

"Trying to pick up land."

"I don't know if I am south or north of the islands."

"We are south of Honolulu but are heading back towards our plotted course."

Then came the staccato symbols "SOS", repeated several times; and finally, at 9.23 a.m., "Going down into sea. Plane will float. Come and get us."

U.S. Navy aircraft were already up, circling the island of Oahu where Ulm had been expected to make his landfall, hoping to spot him and guide him in. They were instructed to begin an immediate search of the sea; but where, within the likeliest area of some 20,000 square miles, were they to concentrate their search? No one knew just when *Stella Australis* had started to go off course, or in what direction the error had taken her. Calculating from the rate of progress the aircraft had been making, and the prevailing winds, the U.S. Navy's meteorologist put the likely scene of the forced landing to the north-east of Oahu, anything up to 300 miles offshore. Some American officers argued that the plane could not have got as far as Oahu; others, that it had overshot.

Fortunately, it was early morning. There would be a whole day, if necessary, in which to search. The chances were that if the crashed aircraft could be spotted its crew would be found alive. Ulm's survival plans in the event of being forced down into the sea were well known. He had said they would climb on to the wooden wing and chop away the two engines. Relieved of the weight and buoyed up by the fuel tanks, the aircraft would stay afloat. Its crash having occurred at the end of the flight, the fuel tanks would be empty and capable of their greatest buoyancy; enough, perhaps, to keep aircraft and survivors on the surface for up to three days in so calm a sea.

With typically unsparing resource the American Services at Honolulu at once mounted a colossal search, involving dozens of aircraft and a small navy of ships, including destroyers, 18 submarines and many minelaying, Coast Guard and other small craft. The Australian Government did what it could at the distance, offering a reward of 5,000 American dollars to anyone finding the three airmen, or any one of them alive, and 1,000 dollars for the discovery of aircraft wreckage or a body. Plenty of civilian craft put out in hopes of gaining one of these prizes, while the large Hawaii-based Japanese fishing fleet mounted keen watch. But the three hopeful days passed; then more. The warships and aircraft were summoned back to base. The civilians withdrew to the seafront bars to argue with lessening urgency as to where, in all that sea, the relatively tiny aircraft had come down.

Desperate to believe that her husband might yet be alive, and hoping that he might prove to have got ashore on some small island, Ulm's wife, assisted by official Australian agencies, promoted a private search. It came to nothing. Wife became widow. In recognition of Ulm's services to his country, the Australian Government granted her £5,000. The tragic incident was ended. But the mystery of what happened to Ulm, Littlejohn, Skilling and *Stella Australis* remains.

Twenty years after their loss, an interesting and authoritative addition to the available evidence was made by the novelist Nevil Shute in his autobiography, *Slide Rule*. A distinguished aeronautical engineer, Nevil Shute Norway, to give him his full name, had in 1931 founded the firm of Airspeed Limited which had built the Envoy type of aircraft to which *Stella Australis* had belonged. He revealed that when Ulm was negotiating his order for her he specified an extra large fuel-carrying capacity. Airspeed had accordingly installed a tank which took up so much of the fuselage space that pilot, co-pilot and radio operator had to cram together in the cockpit. Recognizing the discomfort and even danger this would entail during a long flight, Ulm had things so rearranged that the navigator-radio operator, Skilling, sat in the rear of the fuselage behind the great tank. He was thus invisible from his colleagues and could only communicate with them by means of a specially installed speaking tube. In Nevil Shute's opinion the aircraft had over-flown Honolulu in cloud and had gone on to the west, well off its course, perhaps due to a navigational error made by Skilling who had had no one beside him to check it.

If this is the truth of it it is singularly ironic; for it was Skilling who, it was reported later, had remarked some time before the flight: "The chance we are taking in flying across the Pacific is no greater than walking across a busy street or sleeping in bed. In one instance you may be killed by a motorcar, while in the other you may die if an earthquake wrecks your house. You take these chances every day. We are familiar with the perils of the journey but, with the aid of science, our chances of meeting with disaster are no greater than with you who stay at home." Yet science, perhaps, let him down.

The death of Ulm robbed Australia of one of the two most distinguished of her many pioneers of aviation. It would not be long before she would lose the other; and he, also, would leave an ineradicable question mark appended to the circumstances of his fate.

Like Ulm's, Kingsford Smith's disappearance is a mystery out of a mystery; for it is tolerably certain that if their Australian National Airways had not gone out of business, largely due to loss of confidence in it in official quarters following the unexplained disappearance of its aircraft *Southern Cloud* in 1931, neither man would have been driven to the rash venture which ended in death. Irrepressible and ever-optimistic those pioneers may have been; they were not irresponsible. They were professionals who knew that every flying venture had precise limits, prescribed by what a given type of aircraft could and could not do, and that no exercise of determination by the machine's human controller could override this.

In the event, frustration and insecurity had given rise to desperation, and that in turn to fatal recklessness. But for this train of circumstances, they would probably have lived, a pair of knights, or even noblemen, in affluent retirement after a quarter of a century of steady executive work in joint-managerial offices of an airline with world-wide ramifications.

Kingsford Smith's state of mind in 1935 can easily be appreciated and sympathized with. One of the most renowned figures in civil aviation's short but spectacular history, he had been reduced from governing an airline to running a flying school and giving sightseeing flights to anyone who would pay a few shillings' fee. Far from being able to find consolation in the Australian Government's recognition of his past achievements, or in any degree of hero-worship on the part of the public, he was criticized and reviled at the least excuse as self-seeking, ruthless in his ambitions and over-conscious of the value of personal publicity, accusations which owed much to the jealousy of rivals and the ignorance of politicians and Pressmen. Yet, despite physical and financial strain, chronic disappointment and an almost paranoic belief that "They" were ganging up against him, Kingsford Smith still cherished the idea of restoring Australian National Airways to eminence amongst the airlines of the world.

The contract to carry the airmail between Australia and New Zealand now seemed his best hope, and in 1935 came the chance to carry a special consignment of mail over the route as part of the celebrations for the Silver Jubilee of King George V and Queen Mary. Kingsford Smith accepted eagerly; it might well set the seal on his bid for the contract. Thoroughly familiar with conditions over the 1,300-mile stretch of the Tasman, one of the most treacherous seas in the world, he decided to make the occasion a doubly sentimental one: it should be the last flight of the gallant "Old Bus", the *Southern Cross*.

It nearly was just that — and nearly, into the bargain, the last flight of Charles Kingsford Smith, his co-pilot and navigator Patrick Gordon Taylor — later Sir Patrick Taylor, G.C. — and radio operator John Stannage. Six hundred miles out over the Tasman, in bad weather, one of the exhausts disintegrated, showering the starboard-engine propellor with metal fragments and shattering it. Until Kingsford Smith could cut off the power the vibrations set up by the whirling propellor stump threatened to shake the plane to pieces. Tools, freight, personal belongings and many gallons of fuel were urgently jettisoned into the sea to give the old aircraft a chance of staying aloft on two engines. She managed to maintain enough height and stability, but it was clear that they could not go on. With one more major disappointment to add to his store, Kingsford Smith turned her back towards Australia. She limped homeward; then, within 200 miles of the coast, the level of the oil-pressure gauge for the overworked port engine suddenly plummeted. The engine was down to its last spoonful of oil. If it failed, the sole remaining engine would not be able to keep the heavy aircraft from falling into the storm-ravaged sea which was already only feet below them.

Balancing his own life against those of them all, P. G. Taylor found a thermos flask and, telling his companions to empty one of the remaining suitcases, took off his boots and climbed out on to the starboard wing struts. The wind and the slipstream from the still-functioning nose engine tried at once to jerk him into space; but he hung on, and, inching his way to the silent starboard engine, he held on with one hand while using the other to dip the thermos into the engine's un-needed oil supply. Then Taylor returned the way he had come, passed the thermos of oil in for Stannage to pour into the suitcase, then returned to the engine for more. Then he repeated the process in reverse, climbing out on to the port side struts to supply the engine with oil. The first thermos-full was only just in time. In all, Taylor had to make six trips, at half-hourly intervals, to keep the engine supplied. He saved the *Southern Cross* and her crew and earned himself the George Cross for his heroism. (The George Cross was instituted in 1940 and awarded to Taylor in 1942, seven years after his deed.)

As a final humiliation, Kingsford Smith had had to jettison the bags of airmail which had given the flight its whole purpose. Back safely in Australia, his situation was now approaching the desperate. Like Ulm, he knew that he could never hope to gain the mail-carrying contract without modern aircraft and an efficient organization; and he had no money for either. He wasted some of what he had by having dozens of copies made of a fifty-page report he had compiled, detailing his plans for a regular Australia–New Zealand service. Every member of the Federal Parliament received one, but the report made no impression. It seemed more likely than ever that the company Kingsford Smith had set up with the proceeds from the sale of his flying school and sightseeing-flight organization would never operate the trans-Tasman service for which it was designed. Yet he would not give in while enough funds to continue were available. The immediate question was, how to get those funds?

Once more, luck turned him a cold shoulder. The obvious source of money would be to sell *Lady Southern Cross*, the fast, single-engined Lockheed Altair plane he had bought in order to compete in the England–Melbourne air race that had helped to mark the centenary of the State of Victoria in 1934. Even this was a relic of disappointment and show of public hostility where there might have been triumph. Unable to buy one of the new twin-engined De Havilland Comets — forerunners of the wartime Mosquito — which he had felt certain must win the race, Kingsford Smith had bought the Lockheed, the best aircraft in his view to show them real competition.

The news of the purchase had enraged the Australian Press which flung at him accusations of being unpatriotic to his own and its mother country by buying American. He had retorted angrily that after his and Ulm's epic first flight across the Pacific in 1928 he could have accepted an appointment in America which would have made him rich; he had declined, because it would have necessitated his taking American citizenship. He could have sold *Southern Cross* at that time to overseas bidders for far more than she was worth; he had preferred to keep her in the service of Australian aviation. To argue with newspaper critics at any time is to court danger without hope of victory, and, despite their truth, Kingsford Smith's retorts brought down upon him only more vilification.

Then he had run into troubles of an official nature. He had christened the Lockheed *Anzac* and she had reached New Zealand aboard a cargo ship bearing that name. By the time she had been hoisted on to the quay the name had vanished — obliterated at official insistence that the abbreviated name sacred to the Australian and New Zealand Army Corps of Gallipoli fame would not be tolerated in "commercial" usage. Kingsford Smith substituted the name *Lady Southern Cross*. This was allowed to stand; but now it was the aircraft's American certificate of airworthiness that was the focus of attention. It was not valid outside the United States. That, too, had been overcome and Kingsford Smith, with P. G. Taylor as his fellow-flier, had set off for England and the starting-point of the race. They had got no farther than Queensland before the engine cowling had split too badly to be repaired in time for them to go on and reach England before the race began. Kingsford Smith had had to withdraw; it was just his luck.

In October 1934 Kingsford Smith and P. G. Taylor had flown *Lady Southern Cross* on the first west–east crossing of the Pacific. With the exhilaration of yet another pioneering achievement ended, "Smithy" put up his aircraft for sale in California and went home by sea. And now, in July 1935, with his new failure in *Southern Cross* — and the narrowest escape from death — behind him, he had still not found a buyer for her more modern supplanter. His detailed plans for an Australia–New Zealand service ignored, he took the step of trying to sell his old *Southern Cross* to the Australian Government for preservation as a memorial to the country's pioneer airmen. He asked £5,000. They offered £1,500. He had to accept, and, wearing the uniform to which he was entitled as an Air Commodore of the Royal Australian Air Force, he took *Southern Cross* up for the last time for the short flight from Mascot, Sydney, to a hangar at Richmond R.A.A.F. base where the "Old Bus" would spend the rest of her days. It was a sad occasion for the unhappy, far-from-well man, whose face bore plain evidence of the stress he had had to undergo. It was made sadder by the presence beside him in the cockpit of his lost colleague's son, John Ulm, as passenger; but it would have been immeasurably worse if "Smithy" could have had the foreknowledge that *Southern Cross* would not be displayed as the permanent memorial he had consoled himself by thinking she was to be until 1957 when the people of Brisbane, his birthplace, would raise money to have her wheeled out of an unvisited hiding place and placed behind a great glass window in a hangar at their city's airport.

Having disposed of the "Old Bus", Kingsford Smith took ship to New Zealand. If he could not persuade his own country to let him organize a trans-Tasman airmail service, perhaps the New Zealanders would listen and take the initiative. He left New Zealand again with nothing agreed, this time sailing to America, buoyed up by a new plan to use some of the proceeds from *Southern Cross* for shipping *Lady Southern Cross* back to Australia and then to use her, converted to carry three passengers, for a special fast service between Sydney and Adelaide. More disappointment almost inevitably attended this notion. His Government had not yet paid any of the money he was due. It would cost too much to convert the Lockheed in the way he wished, and Australia, in any case, would allow only British-made aircraft to be brought in for use there.

Kingsford Smith had *Lady Southern Cross* hoisted aboard yet another ship and carried to England. Only a bold stroke could change his fortunes now, he had decided. The boldest and most effective stroke he could make would be to fly from England to Australia, as he should have done in the air race of the year before, and in doing so to smash the record set up by the D. H. Comet flown by C. W. A. Scott and T. Campbell-Black in winning that race in the sensational time of only 2 days and 23 hours from Mildenhall to Melbourne.

In England Kingsford Smith fell ill with a bad attack of influenza. But there was more than illness to drag down his constitution further. *Lady Southern Cross* still had only her American certificate of airworthiness. Kingsford Smith hoped the Air Ministry in London would grant her a British one. It would not do so immediately, and informed him that any flight he made from England meanwhile would have to be governed by British regulations, one of which would have the effect of limiting the amount of fuel he could carry in his aircraft at take-off to 138 gallons, a restriction that would enable him to cover little more than one thousand miles on the first leg of his flight at the rate his 550hp Pratt and Whitney Wasp engine would drink. He argued in vain. If he could have sold *Lady Southern Cross* and thrown in his hand he would have done so. No one offered to buy; and back in Australia Lady Kingsford Smith was dismayed to receive the news in October that her husband had at last decided to make the record-breaking attempt after all. Assured by friends that an attempt to fly such a distance, so fast, in a single-engined plane would be courting disaster, she appealed to him to abandon the idea. He refused, promising that this flight should mark the end of his flying outside Australia.

For all the pioneering risks he had taken, "Smithy" had always enjoyed a reputation for level-headedness. He had many times been heard to declare that to undertake long sea crossings in an aeroplane powered by only a single engine would be inexcusable folly. Now he was about to commit this very form of imprudence. It was the resolution of a man of only 38, driven by mental and physical stress, frustration, ill-luck, and, no doubt, post-influenza depression, into staking his life on a last gamble.

Characteristically, even this rash enterprise suffered a false start. On 23 October 1935 Kingsford Smith took off from Lympne, Kent, in *Lady Southern Cross* with 28-year-old Tommy Pethybridge, one of Australia's finest aero-mechanics and formerly chief of technical training at Kingsford Smith's flying school, as his companion. In a last minute declaration "Smithy" had let it be known that he would not necessarily try to break the record held by C. W. A. Scott — who was in the large crowd assembled to see him off — but would concentrate on proving that special mail services using fast planes would be a practicable possibility. So he flew off; but two days later, instead of having reached the threshold of Australia, he was at Croydon Airport, a point behind that from which he had started.

Lady Southern Cross had reached the Greek mountains without mishap when she had suddenly plunged into tearing sheets of hail and snow of such violence that the fabric of her wings and fuselage was ripped in countless places. Unable to see in any direction and feeling the controls under great stress as ice formed on the wings and ailerons, Kingsford Smith banked sharply off course and ran. The ice cleared at length, but he was flying blind in darkness and had no idea where he was. The beam of a lighthouse, there to guide ships but equally valuable to an airman not knowing whether he was over land or sea, told him that he was, as he had hoped, making for Brindisi in Italy. He had alerted the aerodrome there by radio and eventually found himself over it; but Brindisi boasted no facilities for night landings, so *Lady Southern Cross* was forced to circle again and again while her occupants watched the growing glimmer of car headlights as the Italians mustered every motor owner in the vicinity to help illuminate the runway. Kingsford Smith and Pethybridge were glad to get down in one piece, and when they saw their battered machine from the outside they gave thanks that they had managed to do so.

Yet by early November they were ready to start again, despite further attempts by well-wishers to dissuade them. They had plans this time to beat the handicap of the petrol restriction still insisted on by the British Air Ministry by landing at Marseilles — about the limit of their 138 permitted gallons — and taking on their maximum capacity of 400 gallons.

Although "Smithy" still insisted that he was not out to break the record, he left the possibility open when he stated, "I intend to make the fastest possible trip because I believe that no flight is valuable unless it demonstrates that it is a more rapid means of transit than the existing forms. If I am fortunate enough to arrive in Melbourne in less than the air-race time it will be purely accidental."

So on 6 November Kingsford Smith and Pethybridge left Lympne once more, determined not to be forced back again. The weather along their route was not good, but they cleared Europe successfully and reached Allahabad in India in only three hours more time than Scott's twin-engined Comet had taken. The record could be theirs. They cabled Sydney that they planned to reach Darwin by midnight on 8 November, and would leave for Melbourne after only half an hour's pause for fuelling and refreshment. They took off from Allahabad.

A few hours later, another Australian flier, James Melrose, who had come second in the handicap section of the England–Australia air race and was now again making a bid for the record in his Percival Gull, saw the flare of twin exhausts above him in the darkness as he flew over the vast Bay of Bengal. The other aircraft was flying much faster than he; it could only be *Lady Southern Cross*. But no news of Kingsford Smith's progress reached the ground until that afternoon R.A.F. Singapore heard from Rangoon, Burma, that he had passed over there late the previous night. Nothing had been seen of him at Singapore where he was several hours overdue, and there were no reports of him from any other place. It seemed plain that he had met with some mishap.

R.A.F. landplanes and flying-boats were sent out from many stations to scour the Bay of Bengal and the jungle terrain of Burma and Siam. Melrose unhesitatingly gave up his record bid to turn back and search for his rival, himself having to force-land on a Malayan beach as a result. "Scotty" Allan, now a QANTAS pilot, flew thousands of miles during the next days in his company's emergency De Havilland-86 airliner, based on Singapore. But although he searched over jungles, mountains, sea and countless minute islands, he saw nothing he hoped to see; and neither did any other searching aircraft.

There were many theories. Kingsford Smith and Pethybridge could, for all anyone knew, be marooned in an endless fastness of Burmese or Siamese jungle, hearing and even seeing aircraft looking for them, but unable to signal to them. They could be on any of the innumerable islands off the Malayan coast, incapable of crossing to the mainland. The Viceroy of India, Lord Willingdon, was a notable subscriber to this view and so was a reassured Lady Kingsford Smith, who told newspapermen in Melbourne, "He has been in many difficult situations and his ability has always pulled him through. I have the utmost confidence in him and I am sure that if he has met trouble he has made a safe landing."

It was a belief shared by many others, both friends and strangers to the great airman. For all that fate had dealt him blow after blow, he had still been there afterwards, battered but not down. He had been wounded in his fighter in the Great War and had nearly crashed to his death, but had managed to recover and get back to base, an episode for which he had received the Military Cross. He had been lost before — and in circumstances attended by mystery — for twelve days in 1929; yet he, and Charles Ulm with him, had been found safe and well. On that occasion, thanksgiving services had been held in churches throughout Australia. His wife and many others were confident that they would soon be giving thanks again.

But many more, especially airmen who had flown over South-East Asia, were less sanguine. A well-known Dutch flier, Ever Vandyck, told how he had warned Kingsford Smith of the violence and relentless duration of the gales which could blow over the Burmese forests. In his opinion *Lady Southern Cross* had been struck by lightning.

The search continued for more than a fortnight. Hope lasted even longer. If they were in jungle they could still be safe, have reached some village or be trekking towards one. It might be weeks before they were brought out.

They never emerged. All that was ever found of them was a wheel from the Lockheed, washed up from the Bay of Bengal two years later. The immediate mystery ends with the supposition that their engine failed and that they fell into the sea. But we shall always wonder about those last hours and minutes; and that mystery will remain overshadowed by that surrounding the loss of Kingsford Smith's *Southern Cloud* four years earlier, a disaster which had played the prime part in driving him to abandon his principles of caution and hazard a flight he should never even have contemplated. Afterwards, the Australian Government increased their offer for the old *Southern Cross* from £1,500 to £3,000, and paid up at last. If they had done either of these things while he was still alive he would probably not have flown frustratedly to his death.

7: BALLOON OVER THE NORTH POLE

On 30 September 1930 a solemn crowd stood bareheaded along the harbour wall of Sweden's Göteborg. The ancient gunboat *Svenskund* lay at anchor. On deck were three coffins draped with the Swedish flag, a wreath on each. The polar explorers Salomon August Andrée, Doctor Strindberg and the engineer Fraenkel were coming home, posthumous heroes of their country. On the route to Stockholm they were accompanied by an escort of naval vessels and the tolling of church bells. Amongst the mourners stood men whose memories went back to a very different scene involving the same trio over thirty years before…

If the outcome had not been so tragic, it would be tempting to look upon the balloon expedition which set off for the North Pole from Danes Island, north of Spitzbergen, on 11 July 1897, as something of a farce.

To reach the Pole by balloon was an obsession that was to lead Salomon Andrée and his two companions to their deaths. A designer and constructor with a large Stockholm firm of engineers, Andrée had two passions which had little to do with his job. These were aeronautics and polar exploration. His colleagues and friends had no difficulty understanding the latter. After all, had not Scandinavia given birth to the magnificent Fridtjof Nansen who, while Andrée had to be content with his dreams, was making an attempt on the latitude record, and who had already challenged the frosty eminence of the ice in his ship, the *Fram*? But when Andrée began talking

ıs, good, down-to-earth Swedes shook their heads
ent.

sisted in his view that it was perfectly possible to
fly to the Pole, to skirt the barrier of ice which surrounds most
of the Arctic. Though in the early days only a few took him
seriously he was no enthusiastic crank with a bee in his bonnet
about balloons and only a vague notion of what the
undertaking implied. He knew perfectly well what such a trip
would mean — the shortest distance to the Pole from the
handy jumping-off point of Spitzbergen was 800 miles; a round
trip, therefore, of 1,600 miles, most of it over vast stretches of
white nothingness. What was more, no ordinary balloon could
possibly undertake the task. Something approaching a dirigible
was needed. Here was where Andrée's training as an engineer
would come in. He would be able to work out a highly
ingenious way to guide the flight of the balloon by numerous
guide-ropes and sails. He reckoned that when ropes were
trailed along the ground they lightened the balloon of their not
inconsiderable weight. When the ropes were pulled in, their
bulk brought about a descent. In this way a more or less
constant altitude — 800 feet, Andrée calculated — could be
maintained and the balloon could be kept on course at a speed
of around 20 miles an hour. It should be possible to fly along a
settled course of up to 30 degrees of the wind's direction, and
the North Pole could be reached from Spitzbergen in about 43
hours. Designers of the Zeppelins of the future would
doubtless have derived amusement from such crude notions of
flying. Andrée was convinced they could be made to work.

Test flights which he carried out over fairly short distances
were successful beyond his wildest dreams. One of the biggest
stumbling blocks was going to be shortage of money. To get
the necessary cash Andrée would have to convince the

Establishment of the exploring world, the Stockholm Geographical Society whose members included men with wide experience of exploration — not the type to show much sympathy with an idea that, on the face of it, seemed both ludicrous and dangerous. The approach would have to be handled with the greatest care. "All I ask," Andrée declared, "is for a fair hearing." In fact, he was asking those with polar ambitions to reject utterly their past thinking. The men who struggled over the vast wastes with sledges and dogs were, he was inferring, anachronisms in a balloon age. To travel over snow and ice and be at the mercy of the polar drift was slow and cumbersome. The whole thing could be done at much greater speed by harnessing the modern resources of flight.

To those who assembled to hear Andrée address a public meeting in the hall of the Stockholm Geographical Society on 13 February 1895 the proposition came as rank heresy. As he spoke, Andrée could sense the hostility around him. He persevered and outlined the type of balloon he needed. It would have to carry three people, needing ample food supplies and room to store them. There would be a burden of three tons. There must be a capacity of 63,000 cubic feet, and the balloon must be capable of staying in the air for a full month. He was well aware that no such balloon had previously been constructed, but this was no argument for not building one now. He had even fixed the month for the flight: July, since it was known that then the Arctic winds generally blew from south to north. He gave the results of his various tests. He had discovered, for example, that he could set a course which varied, in some degree, from the direction of the wind. He had calculated the effect of snow, rain and mist which would serve to make the envelope of the balloon heavier. He had worked out how the temperature in July would affect the expansion of gas within the balloon and give him the power of lift he would need.

The thoroughness with which he had carried out his research, and the persuasiveness with which he outlined his intentions, quite won over Andrée's sceptical hearers. By the end of the address he was confident that there was scarcely a single sage within the Stockholm Geographical Society who begrudged him every ounce of backing. He had exhibited an astonishingly profound knowledge of Spitzbergen, from where he proposed to start his trip. He knew all about winds, about precipitation. He had studied the Arctic minutely through books, plans and maps.

Yet some experts remained doubtful. Nobody had tried any such thing before; therefore, it was argued, it could not possibly succeed. Patiently Andrée answered all the questions and countered the criticisms.

All the sales talk and all the enthusiasm paled before the bleak fact there was no money to make a polar expedition feasible. Besides Andrée and his lifelong friend, the celebrated explorer Erik Nordenskiöld, one man expressed himself willing in principle to give tangible support. Alfred Nobel, the rich industrialist and inventor of dynamite, hesitated to contribute the entire 130,000 Swedish crowns required, but agreed that if there were substantial support from other sources he would think again.

By now Andrée's scheme had gone far beyond an idea to be mulled over in rarefied scientific circles; it was public property. Conscious of his subjects' sympathy for it, King Oscar became one of the first to help foot the bill, to the tune of 30,000 crowns. The effect was immediate: no one wanted to be left out. Soon the money was flowing in and the world's greatest constructor of balloons, Henri Lachambre, had received the largest order of his career. He had less than six months to do the job. The deadline was 24 December 1895. Lachambre would meet it, with twenty-three days in hand.

At this point a new figure enters the story. The 24-year-old Doctor Strindberg, a more flamboyant character than the rather withdrawn, phlegmatic Andrée, was as obsessed with meteorology and photography as Andrée was with polar exploration and ballooning. He had an insatiable appetite for adventure and a sound theoretical knowledge of the vagaries of weather conditions in polar regions, and was consequently beside himself with joy when he was chosen to accompany Andrée on this epic voyage. But Strindberg had one grave shortcoming in this context. He had never been up in a balloon in his life. It seemed to some critics that Andrée had made an eccentric choice of companion for what could not be other than a tough trip.

The *Oern* (Eagle) was by no means just a giant balloon with a basket slung under it. The crowd who saw the craft when it was first put on show in Paris gasped with astonishment. It was enormous. It had a diameter of 65 feet and the awestruck spectators were informed that there were 19,000 meshes in the vast expanse. The balloon's envelope was seen to be quadruple towards the top, triple in the centre and double in the bottom. It had a resistance varying between 2,250 and 4,500lb per square foot. The material encasing the envelope was made of different varieties of silk.

Three men were to trust their lives to it, in regions whose climatic complexion, despite all meteorological knowledge, was still unpredictable. From Spitzbergen the balloon would make for the Pole and return home via Alaska or Siberia. If it failed in its purpose, then its crew were prepared to pull themselves back by sledge, since obviously no dogs could be taken. Carrier pigeons would be the 1890s' equivalent of radio and would carry exclusive copy for a newspaper that had paid handsomely for the rights.

Andrée reasoned that the weather throughout the polar regions remained kind during July, a considerable assumption bolstered by his friend Nordenskiöld's assurance that a constant wind from the south would prevail. This was to be swiftly contradicted by Captain Sverdrup who had just returned from the icy wastes in Nansen's *Fram*. Sverdrup was adamant that there were no reliable south winds at this time of the year. With deep bitterness Andrée postponed his trip. At this news, the public, who had never ceased to be fascinated by the attempt, felt that they had been cheated. There was worse to come. One Doctor Erkholm, who had agreed to accompany Andrée and Strindberg on the trip, backed out, announcing that the enterprise was doomed to failure. Andrée concealed his disappointment and appointed an old friend, an aeronautical expert and engineer named Fraenkel, as replacement.

Andrée's troubles, though, were far from being over. The spring of 1897 once again found three men determined to make the attempt. They set off from Göteborg for Danes Island in a specially chartered freighter *Virgo* and its escort, the gunboat *Svenskund* — the same *Svenskund* that was to perform so tragic a function in Göteborg many years later. On 18 May 1897 the weather could not have been worse and the wind was blowing treacherously in the wrong direction. There was a sigh of relief when all at once gusts started coming from the south, but they were short-lived and soon changed to northerly. By this time Andrée was getting impatient and angry. The whole thing was becoming a farce; he *dare* not return home this time. Nearly a month passed. At three o'clock on 11 July there was a south-south-west wind with a ground-level strength of between 20 and 30 feet per second. Strindberg pressed his leader to make a start. Andrée insisted on a conference, from which the three men, after some two hours, emerged to tell the master of the *Virgo* they were ready. It was at this point that Andrée made a disconcerting statement; indicating his companions, he said resignedly, "I haven't that much confidence, I'm afraid."

The balloon was removed from the hangar. The inflation of its black envelope began. The gondola was fixed in place. The weather balloons indicated favourable conditions. At last all was ready and the *Oern* began to rise. Unfortunately, the solemn moment suddenly deteriorated into something resembling farce.

One moment the three aeronauts, momentarily poised in space, were shouting, "Long Live Sweden!" The next, the gondola was dropping like a stone, despite the fact that ballast had been jettisoned. With an almighty splash it struck the surface of the water.

Then the balloon started to rise again, to dart off on course at an estimated 20 miles an hour. But part of Andrée's ingenious guide-rope system had been left behind. The *Oern* was virtually out of control and could not be brought back for its vital equipment. Bumping and lurching through the sky, it passed at length from sight — for thirty years.

On the morning of the 16 July, the whaler *Alken* intercepted one of Andrée's carrier pigeons, bearing a message addressed to the newspaper covering the expedition. It read: "From the Andrée Polar Expedition to the *Aftonbladet*. 13th July at 12.30 hours. Position: Latitude 82.02 North; Longitude (Greenwich) 15.15. This is the third message dispatched by pigeon. All is well on board. Making good speed 10° South." No other message was ever received.

In due course, rescue operations were undertaken. When they discovered no trace of anything and when no information could be gleaned from returning whalers and seal-hunters, alarm spread throughout Sweden. The area around Spitzbergen was thoroughly explored. The American Robert Peary, who was to reach the Pole in 1909, searched around Smith Sound. The northern coasts of Siberia were scoured, all to no purpose.

On 14 May 1899 a damaged floating buoy was discovered off Iceland. It carried the note: "This buoy was dropped from Andrée's balloon at 10.55 hours G.M.T. in the evening of 11 July 1897. Latitude approximately 82°. Longitude 25° Greenwich."

The following month, the main buoy, originally intended for dropping over the North Pole, was found at Finnmark in Norway. It had drifted for 1,142 days. Such discoveries took no one any farther, except to the obvious deduction that the plight of the *Oern* had become so desperate that the jettisoning of normal ballast had proved insufficient. Expert examination of the second buoy revealed that its damage had been caused by some hard shock. It had been attached to the gondola by a cord and had evidently broken off violently. Search parties turned their attention to Greenland. Every rumour, however melodramatic, was fully investigated. An allegation of murder by Eskimos in Siberia was believed for a time, but never confirmed. It was not until August 1930, three decades after the disappearance, that a solution to most of the mystery emerged.

To the casual observer who might happen to find himself in Spitzbergen, a mere pimple of land called White Island would not seem of much interest. Bleak and uninviting, it was seldom rid of its crust of ice. But those on board the vessel *Bratvag* did not regard this inhospitable hump in that light at all. The men of the *Bratvag* were scientists of the Norwegian Society for Polar Exploration, on their way to Franz Josef Land, now patriotically renamed Fridtjof Nansen Land. Two members of the team, Olav Salen and Karl Tusvik, stepped ashore on the uninhabited island and went in search of water. They stumbled over the aluminium lid of a cooking pot. The two men explored farther and it was not long before curiosity had turned to excitement, as they found themselves looking at the tattered remains of a canvas boat. Salen and Tusvik dashed back for the captain of the *Bratvag*, who at once put under way a properly organized search. The boat with its cooking utensils, tins of food and various navigational aids pointed all too obviously to an expedition that had come to grief. It was a torn, nondescript canvas bag which gave the first clue to identity. The faded words read: "Andrée's Polar Expedition 1896." The men of the *Bratvag* had stumbled on the balloonists' last camp.

The captain stared around at the icy emptiness of White Island. Then his gaze returned to the boat, and it struck him suddenly that the half-melted ice and snow inside it seemed unnaturally lumpy. He and Gunnar Horn, another of the party, scratched away at the surface. They found themselves looking at the body of a man, his bare knees showing through ragged trousers. Tenderly they lifted the body of Andrée out of the boat.

A few yards away they found a stone cairn forming a crude grave. Here lay young Strindberg, a tab on his overcoat proving his identity. The body of Fraenkel was to be found later. Reverently, the bodies of the two aeronauts were conveyed to the *Bratvag* and hoisted aboard by the davits. The captain reasoned that since the bodies had remained hidden from human sight for over thirty years little was to be gained by abandoning his original mission and returning home. It was not until 2 September that the *Bratvag* steamed into Tromso harbour, Norway.

A ship packed with journalists, the *Isbjorn*, was the next to arrive at White Island. Their mission was simple: to find and bring back everything that had a bearing on the mystery. The team was to have greater luck than they had ever dreamed possible. The first discovery was Fraenkel's body. It was reasoned then that he and Andrée had probably died together, having earlier buried the body of Strindberg. But there were to be far more sensational finds. The journalists came across a notebook giving minute details of what had happened on that last voyage. It was damp and mildewed, but perfectly readable. Andrée's camera, only slightly damaged, was also recovered. If the plates were exposed and if they could be developed, here indeed was a find.

As soon as the *Isbjorn* returned home experts began to get to work to interpret the evidence. It was as if the three men had risen from their grave to tell their story. Andrée's log supplied a detailed account of what had happened almost up to the time of his death.

All had been well as the *Oern* passed over Dutch Point, the extreme northern landmark of Danes Island. But at about five o'clock the mist descended; below the three men was 1,600 feet of invisibility. To the accompaniment of gas hissing gently from the valves of the balloon and the sharp cry of the seabirds, the *Oern*, still not fully recovered from its uneven take-off, glided on its intended course. As the hours passed the exhilarating feeling of being alone in the air wore off and was replaced by one of hunger. Strindberg, appointed cook, prepared a delicious pasta meal in the special kitchen area aboard the gondola. Carrier pigeons were released from time to time, all with messages that were breezily optimistic. But Andrée was getting worried. He noticed that the balloon had steadily been losing height and that the weather was becoming worse. When the mist cleared drizzle took its place, and sometimes both came together. At 3 a.m., 24 hours after take-off, came the first portents of disaster. It was as if some giant foot had given the balloon a hefty series of kicks. Andrée knew immediately what this meant; they had struck the ice. The guide-ropes in which he had placed so much faith failed either to stabilize the craft or cause it to rise. All ballast was jettisoned, in vain. Over went the vast buoy, intended for the Pole as a symbol of triumph. The feeling of the trio as they heard it smash on to the ice can be imagined. When the balloon finally rose enough to skirt the ice, their relief was considerable, but short-lived.

One of the guide-ropes snaked round a block of ice and held the balloon as helpless as a puppy tied to a kennel. Even if he had been free, Andrée would have been no better off — the wind was blowing a vigorous north-west. As it was, the *Oern* could not budge an inch and remained stuck fast for 13 hours. The occupants' greatest fear must have been that it *would* break free, only to descend to renewed bumping and scraping and be battered to pieces.

Eventually the *Oern* was free again. Overboard at once went the ballast that could ill be spared, including tins of food. The mist, like a soggy flannel, descended yet again. Occasionally, there were notes of optimism in Andrée's journal, as spirits soared with the *Oern*, only to drop again when the balloon plummeted anew to the ice. When their flight had lasted 66 hours and 14 minutes they were 20 hours overdue at the Pole.

By the morning of 14 July they decided to abandon the balloon and risk taking to the ice for the journey home. They descended.

Andrée refused to be pessimistic. They still had a fair amount of food. There were bears to be shot. Strindberg was less happy, thinking wistfully of Sweden, of the girl to whom he had recently become engaged. Notes found on his body by the crew of the *Isbjorn* testified to his depression when faced with endless vistas of ice, bisected by rivulets of water. On 26 July the men calculated their position and found that the imperceptibly shifting ice had carried them east, instead of the intended west. They had originally intended to make for the food depot at North West Land but now hoped instead to make for one at Seven Islands, above North East Land.

Where there had been a time when they had cursed the all-enveloping mist, they were soon bestowing bitter comments on the blazing August sun which melted the snow to a cloying slush. It made dragging their sledge that much more difficult. Food supplies, never a serious problem before, were running short. The sight of land, if such a word can be used in the polar regions, revived their spirits. On their right was what they took to be White Island. It appeared none too soon, since Fraenkel was suffering from enteritis and snow-blindness. But the discovery proved a cruel illusion, only a stationary group of ice floes. A consolation was the sight of three bears waddling by; they were swiftly shot and cut up into valuable meat.

Grimly, the three kept on the march, camping in conditions that grew steadily colder as August advanced. The tent proved pitifully inadequate in nine degrees below zero Fahrenheit. The Arctic winter was tightening its iron grip. It was in the middle of September that they actually reached White Island — that vast, immobilized iceberg, part of whose surface could crumble away without warning. It seemed to offer hope of a sort. Here, the last act in this tragic drama was played out. Fraenkel, the most practical member of the party, built a snow hut and pathetically the three men crouched in it for refuge that was to prove an illusion. On 2 October, as Andrée's record testified, the hut split like a walnut at the mercy of nutcrackers. The walls disintegrated and the floor liquefied beneath them in their sleep. Waking in fear they desperately set to work to rebuild their ruined shelter.

We do not know what happened after that. Only a few more words were written in the log, odd snatches that tell us little: "Floating towards land" ... "transporting our things" ... "we returned in the evening." Had the party, in a mood of brave fatuity, attempted their trudge home anew and returned only to die? "Floating towards land...": this was the language of illusion, of dementia, for land there was none.

The log which had survived miraculously formed a remarkable record of what happened just before the death of these men. The photographs — of Andrée with a shot bear, of Strindberg and Fraenkel standing by the wrecked *Oern* — were developed and proved to be of astonishing clarity, a strange form of resurrection of men dead thirty years.

Strindberg, the tough young extrovert with a love of adventure and a girl back home, must have been the first to go. His companions buried him. Then Andrée, the superbly ridiculous, touchingly indomitable victim of "balloon mania", and Fraenkel, the meticulous, fussy technician, lay down near each other to die. Despair, the shattering of a dream, probably hastened death as much as the elements of the impersonally cruel polar region.

8: A ROYAL TRAGEDY AT EAGLE'S ROCK

Until her death in 1968, a royal war-widow made a yearly pilgrimage in August from London to a remote spot in Caithness, in Scotland. She would walk along the narrow roads which fractured the hillsides until she reached the tall, bleak outline of the 900-foot Eagle's Rock.

It was at a spot nearby that the then Duchess of Kent became a widow. On 25 August 1942 the 40-year-old Prince George Edward Alexander Edmund, Duke of Kent, was killed when the Mark III Sunderland flying-boat in which he was a passenger for Iceland crashed into the hillside. He was the first son of an English monarch to be killed on active service for five centuries.

In 1942 death had once again become a commonplace, its tragedy and consequences accepted as the essence of war. Nonetheless, the news of the death of the Duke of Kent, on active service but not in battle, came to everyone as a particularly sharp shock. Apart from anything else, the accident seemed as unnecessary as it was inexplicable.

As the Prime Minister, Winston Churchill, expressed it in a moving tribute in the House of Commons: "The loss of this gallant and handsome Prince has been a shock and a sorrow to the people of the British Empire, standing out lamentably in these hard days of war."

There had been a fairy-tale quality about the romance of the young Greek Princess Marina, daughter of the exiled Prince Nicholas and the Grand Duchess Helena of Russia. At the age of 28 she had come to England to marry a personable Royal

Duke in November 1934. An admiring people had taken the couple to their hearts. Yet if it had not been for the war the Duke would probably have passed out of the public eye in Britain. In 1939 he had been preparing to leave to assume the post of Governor-General of Australia. When war broke out he immediately requested a more active role. A career in the Navy seemed logical, since he had already seen ten years of pre-war service, but after a short time at the Admiralty he transferred to the R.A.F. and filled a Group Captain's post in the Welfare Branch.

Making his own contribution to the Royal Family's sterling work to boost wartime morale in Britain, the Duke of Kent did not confine his activities to semi-official visits in which he only met senior officers on R.A.F. stations. He scorned pomp and would drop in unannounced on flight crews all over the country, studied briefings, watched them fly off on missions and mixed with the ground crew they left behind. In 1941 he flew in an American B24 Liberator to Canada where he surveyed the work of the Empire Air Training Scheme. The Duke was a good mixer with a range of interests tending to be wider than those of his brothers, King George VI and the Duke of Windsor. He had a passion for music and other arts which far from making him more remote from ordinary folk blended with his affability to produce a well-rounded, easily likeable character.

On 4 August 1942 a family party took place at the Kents' family home at Iver, Buckinghamshire. It had followed the christening of the baby Prince Michael George Charles Franklin, born a month previously. The Duke had managed to combine the christening with three weeks' leave. When it was over, the Duke, wearing the inch-thick ribbon of an Air Commodore on the sleeve of his uniform, drove from Iver to

Euston station in London. Another welfare tour lay ahead, this time in Iceland. He was to travel to Inverness and then make for Invergordon, the naval base on Cromarty Firth from where he would travel in a Sunderland flying-boat of 228 Squadron, flown in from Oban on the west coast. The flight from Invergordon to Iceland, a distance of close on 900 miles, was scheduled to take seven hours.

The Duke and his party — private secretary, acting air equerry and batman — arrived at Invergordon on 24 August. The Sunderland which awaited the Duke was not one of the super-luxurious, executive-suite-style aircraft normally placed at the disposal of the Royal Family. It was a simply equipped service aircraft of the kind the pilot, Flight-Lieutenant Frank Goyen, was well used to flying on patrols over the Mediterranean and Atlantic. At 25, Goyen was one of the most seasoned of the Sunderland pilots. An Australian, his seemingly easy-going manner concealed superb professionalism. It seemed that the Royal passenger could not be in better hands.

There was a crew of ten including a second pilot, two radio operators, three gunners, a navigator, an engineer and a fitter. The sole acknowledgment of the status of the distinguished passenger was the presence on board of the squadron commander, another Australian, Commander T. L. Moseley, whose service in flying-boats dated back to well before the war.

The weather forecast for 25 August was not ideal. The whole of the British Isles was suffering intermittent storm and low clouds, though not severe enough in degree to make flying impossible. In the north of Scotland, which usually experienced the worst of such conditions, flying was still a practical proposition. The meteorologists spoke of cloud-base at Cromarty Firth of about 800 feet. Over the Faroes, direct on the Icelandic route, conditions were improving. There seemed no reason whatever why the Sunderland should not take off. The flight time was seven hours in an aircraft with an endurance of twelve hours and a cruising speed of about 110 knots. Its fuel tanks were fully loaded and it carried depth charges in case enemy submarines should be encountered on the route.

Cromarty Firth is an extremely narrow stretch of water with surrounding coastline shaped rather like a thumb and index finger crooked to face each other. After a longish take-off run, Goyen pulled the Sunderland's hull clear of the water. Ahead loomed the two precipitous Sutor rocks which marked the entrance to the inlet. The route now lay north-east, passing Tarbat Ness which jutted out on the edge of Dornoch Firth, after which the Sunderland would continue to follow the coast route, though keeping over the sea all the time. She would edge in closer to the land for the turn at John O'Groats, then make north-west for Iceland. The reason why it was not following the direct route overland lay in the Sunderland's size and weight. Its climbing rate, particularly when fully loaded, was not sufficiently dependable to cope with the sort of high ground to be found on what might otherwise have been the easiest route. The briefing stressed the following of the coastline for 85 miles before the narrow turn at John O'Groats which led to Pentland Firth, south of the Orkneys, from where there would be a straight over-sea flight to the destination.

The Sunderland had reached around 1,000 feet and was climbing. The Tarbat Ness promontory came into view. Behind it was the great bay of Dornoch Firth. For a time the prominent turrets of Dunrobin Castle, seat of the Sutherland family, could be glimpsed. Then the cloud banked up again. Anxious not to lose sight of that reassuring coastline for too long, Captain Goyen came down to 1,200 feet and lower. In the tail turret, 21-year-old Andrew Jack found himself wishing that the mist enshrouding the flying-boat like a cocoon would soon dissolve.

All would have been well if the Sunderland had not, in addition to losing altitude, drifted perilously near to the coast. She was soon flying directly over the high ground which it had been stipulated should be given the widest berth. With the sea now well to starboard, she flew over Langwell House, just south of Berriedale. As yet there was little danger. The terrain below was peaceful pasture where the inhabitants of whitewashed cottages had only stags and sheep for company. But ahead glowered a rugged chain of purple mountains, topped 900 feet above the rest by Eagle's Rock, reckoned by local people to be the most forbidding spot in all Caithness.

If it had only been necessary for the flying-boat to clear the summit, all would have been well. But on the far side was a separate shoulder, 100 feet lower than the summit. The pilot, perhaps not reacting quickly enough, failed to check his descent after clearing the top of Eagle's Rock. The Sunderland clipped the edge of the escarpment. The blow was sufficiently violent to fling the flying-boat upward and then over on to its back. It hung for a moment, then plunged shuddering into the heather, crushing the bracken with wreckage and flame. Death, so the experts were to reckon later, could only have been instantaneous for everyone. All, that is, who died.

The one survivor was Andrew Jack, occupant of the rear turret, who stated later: "All I can remember is being in the cockpit one moment and the next regaining consciousness in the heather." His survival was nothing short of miraculous. Luckily for him the tailplane had snapped off on impact and had been thrown clear from the rest of the wreckage. Like a man who is flung from a horse but is still entangled in the reins, Jack had been dragged, half in and half out of his turret. He could recall little of it himself. The position of the turret and the ripped soles of his flying boots enabled investigators to reconstruct later what had happened while he was too shocked to register the appalling pain that must have seared through his badly burnt face and arms. Mercifully, unconsciousness quickly followed. His last memory before he passed out was the sight, through mist and drizzle, of the scattered bodies of his comrades. When he came round again the burns were beginning to hurt, and when he tried to walk red-hot pains seared through his feet and up his legs. He did not know which was the more agonizing — trying to walk or to wrench off his boots. After many attempts he managed to jettison them, along with his ragged uniform trousers. He felt a little better, but more weary than he could remember. Even rescue seemed unimportant. He lay down on the bracken and thankfully surrendered to oblivion.

His memories of what happened when he woke resembled a series of hazy snapshots. There was a friendly cottage with a welcoming family. There were surgical dressings and kind soothing words and more sleep. Farmer David Morrison and his son Hugh had heard the Sunderland's engines as the flying-boat passed over Eagle's Rock. Then there had been two crashes — the impact on the lower peak and the brutal smash to the ground. The Morrisons possessed cool nerves and plenty of sense. They realized swiftly that looking for the aircraft by themselves would be fruitless. In the mist, they could not even guess at its position. Hugh Morrison raced down to the stormy track where he had left his motorbike, and rode furiously to the village of Berriedale for help. Everyone in the neighbourhood, estate workers, shepherds and crofters, converged on moors and hillside. The police with the local doctor, 71-year-old John Kennedy, joined in, but little could be done that day, for the mist was as thick as ever and darkness was approaching.

At lunchtime next day, pieces of shattered wreckage were spotted near Eagle's Rock. The searchers came upon eleven bodies. One lay apart from the rest. His face was peaceful and he did not look as if he had suffered much. On his uniform sleeve was the single thick ring of an Air Commodore. Below the sleeve was a platinum wristwatch. It had stopped 32 minutes after take-off.

What had happened during that time to cause the crew of the Sunderland to make so disastrous and so utterly incomprehensible an error of judgement we simply do not know. Frank Goyen had been ordered to keep to the sea route which had been planned for him. Even if he had, for some unknown reason, been forced to abandon it, there was no conceiving what had possessed him to fly anywhere near the vicinity of Eagle's Rock. There was one point above 2,000 feet in this part of the world, Mount Marven, a few miles inland, yet Frank Goyen, a veteran Sunderland pilot, had come down to a lunatic 900 feet. Even if he had momentarily taken complete leave of his senses, the rest of the crew could scarcely have been unaware of the danger. All were R.A.F. men on active duty in wartime, not green cadets.

The inquiry went minutely over the original briefing. The weather reports were studied, and the flight record of every member of the crew. On 7 October 1942 Sir Archibald Sinclair, Secretary for Air, announced the findings to the House of Commons. They were:

1. The accident occurred because the aircraft had been flown on a track other than that indicated to the pilot and at too low

an altitude to clear the rising ground. The responsibility for subsequent events rests with the pilot.

2. The weather should have presented no difficulties. There was no engine failure, since the propellers were under power when the aircraft struck the ground.

The question remained, why had all this happened? To many people it seemed unrealistic to place the entire blame on the pilot, in what should have been a case of collective responsibility. It was later suggested that the Duke of Kent had insisted on making the flight, despite the fact that weather conditions were not ideal. There was no evidence to support such an assertion which implied something quite out of character. In any case, few pilots — and certainly not Frank Goyen — would have been persuaded to fly if his professional superiors had not considered it safe, Duke or no Duke.

Did the answer lie in the Sunderland itself? The court had established that, as far as was known, there had been nothing wrong with it. But instruments and controls get damaged in air crashes and possibly vital clues are destroyed. The key question remains, now as then, why was the Sunderland near Eagle's Rock at all?

The body of the Duke of Kent was taken to Dunrobin Castle and from there travelled by train for the funeral at Windsor. The coffin was draped with the tricolor roundels of the Royal Air Force and the Union Jack. Four Kings — George VI, the King of Norway, the King of Greece and the King of Yugoslavia — saw it laid in the royal vaults.

Twenty-two years before her death in 1968, Princess Marina, the former Duchess of Kent, made her family promise that her husband would eventually be placed next to her. She felt that the Duke, who always loved the open air, would want to be in the beautiful park at Windsor. When she herself was buried at

Frogmore a mile away from there the Duke's coffin was moved to a spot nearby.

A few months after that tragedy at Eagle's Rock in 1942, King George VI made a quiet pilgrimage to the lonely spot. He gazed silently at the charred heather and the fragments of wreckage still lying there. A clutch of stones in the shape of a cross had been erected by those who lived in this remote corner of Caithness. It still marks the spot of a tragedy whose definitive explanation we have never heard.

9: THE DISASTER OF MOUNT TORMENT

A flight over the north-east of the Canadian city of Quebec passes over the dominating peak of Mount Torment which rises above hilly country on the route between Quebec and La Malbaie. Mount Torment is even more aptly and tragically named today, for on Friday, 9 September 1949, it was the scene of one of the most brutal acts of sabotage ever known to civil aviation.

The detailed and thorough examination of the wreckage which led to the tracking down of the killers has its own peculiar fascination; but the whole affair, brought to a head out of a tangled mess of human passions, has its interest for students of human nature too. Behind the crash of a DC-3 of the Canadian Pacific Airlines lay an extraordinary story worthy of the pen of a Zola.

On the morning of 9 September Captain Pierre Laurin joined the rest of his crew at Montreal-Dorval Airport for the eventual destination of Baie Comeau, a small township which lay to the north-east of Quebec. Take-off was at the scheduled time of 8 a.m., with 9 passengers aboard. The weather was fair and calm and there was no reason to suppose that here was not another entirely routine flight. At L'Ancienne Lorette Airport in Quebec the DC-3 picked up eight more adult passengers and two children.

When the aircraft left there at 10.25 it carried with it 23 people including the crew. The passenger list suggested that not very many of those on board were travelling for pleasure. There was a substantial complement of business executives, most of them American tycoons with big interests in oil. Of the rest, only one need really concern us: Rita Guay, a dark-haired woman who had announced that she was going to Baie Comeau to visit relatives.

The wooded, hilly country which bordered the St Lawrence River dropped away as the DC-3 increased altitude. Whatever subsequently happened aboard the aircraft was totally unforeseen because only one routine report was made, or, indeed, was necessary. Far below Patrick Simard, a young fisherman preparing to spend a peaceful day on the banks of the St Lawrence, did not bother to look up as he heard the drone of yet another aircraft. Seconds later he was gripping the edges of his boat in terror. The sky had cracked with a violent explosion. Involuntarily, he jerked his head upwards to see a pattern of flame, like a burning cross, shoot towards the earth, a succession of objects tumbling from it.

Two miles offshore, on a wide reach of the river, the Master of the S.S. *St Lawrence* also heard the explosion and saw the aircraft, hopelessly out of control, plunge towards the river. Workers on the Canadian National Railway tracks also saw it and came running to the likely spot of the accident. Sawmill workers at Sault-au-Cochon stumbled up the steep hillside to gaze with the rest at the scattered wreckage spilled along the slope of Mount Torment and into the surrounding woods.

It did not take an expert to guess that some highly unusual explosion had caused the destruction of the DC-3. The Quebec Provincial Police and the Air Services Branch of the Department of Transport were quickly able to go even further: no mechanical misfortune, no sudden unexplained breakdown could have had this savage result.

It was quite unnecessary to tell the investigation team what their very first move was to be. Everyone's attention turned automatically to the saboteur's favourite place for planting an explosive device — the forward luggage compartment. If the compartment were situated behind the cockpit, pilot and co-pilot would, given the presence of a bomb, have been killed instantly. Lieutenant-Colonel Leon Lambert, Chief of the Provincial Police in Quebec, listened grimly to the report of the experts — the centre of the explosion of this DC-3 of Canadian Pacific Airlines had indeed been in the forward luggage compartment. To make such a discovery so early was a distinct advantage. The authorities need waste no time looking for some mysterious mechanical shortcoming which might otherwise have been thought accountable for the crash. The earnest business of a full-scale criminal investigation could now be put under way.

In his essay *Murder Considered As One of the Fine Arts*, Thomas de Quincey states that the wisest thing any would-be killer can do is to murder a complete stranger. Once a man disposes of anyone likely to have had any connection with him, his chances of getting away with his crime become slimmer. A subsequent event, seemingly unconnected with the crime being investigated, can start a chain of happenings leading inexorably to the unmasking of the criminal. Yet at first sight there was no reason why the attempted suicide by sleeping pills of a woman in her Quebec flat should have had the slightest connection with the appalling tragedy of Mount Torment.

The woman, Marguerite Ruest Pitre, did not die, but was kept in hospital under observation for some hours after she had been discovered. The police took a statement from her- and so it happened that her name was in the forefront of someone's mind as the police went through the laborious business of checking the relatives of those who had perished in the DC-3.

It turned out that the husband of Mrs Rita Guay — the passenger mentioned earlier — was a Quebec jeweller whose infidelities were a rich source of gossip in the shabby neighbourhood where the couple lived. The name of a Mrs Marguerite Pitre was mentioned in this connection, and it was not long before someone remembered the would-be suicide in the Quebec hospital. The fact that a man is an adulterer may have nothing whatever to do with the unfortunate, if providential, death of his wife; but the more the police delved, the more substance there seemed to be to their shadowy suspicions that here was an exceptional instance.

Treading cautiously, the police were at first inclined to discount the malicious rumours about Mrs Pitre and Albert Guay. Outwardly, she was a respectably married woman who lived with her husband and their small daughter in depressed Gavreau Street, Quebec. But a report of a seemingly trivial event a month before the tragedy made the investigators think otherwise. Guay and Marguerite Pitre had gone out for a meal in a restaurant. Guay had become involved in an argument and had drawn a gun. Police had been called and Guay had been arrested and subsequently fined for carrying the weapon.

While the authorities were, naturally, keen to conceal the fact that they were building a dossier on Guay, the Press were free to speculate. Conscientiously deaf to rumour, the police quietly got on with sifting the evidence which would lead to the arrest and conviction of Albert Guay and two others for the murder of his wife. For the sabotage of the DC-3 was the successful conclusion of a number of sabotage schemes whose tragedy was that a psychopathic menace had not been restrained before his ultimate act.

It emerged that, the previous Christmas, a man named Lucien Carreau had visited Guay at his shop about some jewellery repairs. The jeweller had seemed considerably agitated and to the astonishment of Carreau, who knew him only slightly, suggested that they drive into the country. During the trip, Guay made a series of astonishing confessions and furthermore outlined a scheme which made his companion's blood run cold. In essence, Guay admitted to being tired of his wife and anxious to be rid of her. He had, he said, evolved a plan whereby Rita was to be lured into a taxi booby-trapped with dynamite. An alternative scheme was to blow up a boat bound from Quebec for Baie Comeau when Rita happened to be aboard. But, after careful consideration, Guay had come to believe that such measures were untidy and lacked finesse. Subtlety was called for. At last Albert Guay had conceived a foolproof scheme for getting rid of his wife. For a consideration, would Carreau be interested in acting as her executioner?

Too astounded to make any reply, Carreau could only listen to the details. "Poison is the obvious method," said the jeweller unemotionally. "You will make the easiest five hundred dollars of your life." With these words, he produced a bottle and small envelope, evidently containing poison. As if he were merely discussing the extermination of greenfly, Guay continued: "Rita is very fond of cherry wine. You can bring the bottle to my home tonight. You can slip it into her glass quite easily. There would be no reason on earth for her to suspect anything. As far as I am concerned, this conversation will never have taken place." Somehow, the dumbfounded Carreau managed to decline. He told the police later that he had thought Guay was joking. This explanation was accepted.

Denied Carreau as an accomplice, the would-be murderer was soon focusing his attention on his old love, Marguerite Pitre. Whether she was so infatuated with him as to lose all reason or whether she wanted to share in the insurance money that could be collected on Rita's death is not clear, but she proved a willing tool. After the tragedy, the police also questioned a labourer named Ovide Cote, a friend of Albert Guay. His part in this story is a small one, but his considerable knowledge of explosives was to prove fatal to every passenger aboard the DC-3.

On the morning of 1 September — eight days before the tragedy — Cote dropped in for a chat with a disabled watchmaker named Généreaux Ruest who was Marguerite Pitre's brother. Albert Guay was in the watchmaker's workshop and, recognizing an expert, professed an interest of his own in explosives. "Tell me," he inquired with studied casualness, "I'm thinking of blowing up the stump of a maple tree. It's about ten to fifteen feet in diameter. How would you do it? Do you find that it's useful to use a battery with dynamite?" Cote was pleased to air his knowledge and he had a willing listener both in Albert Guay and Généreaux Ruest.

There were numerous attempts later to suggest that Marguerite Pitre was a wholly innocent accomplice or that she had fallen under the influence of a Svengali to such an extent that she had been incapable of resisting his demands. Both propositions were to prove equally ridiculous.

After he had learnt more than enough about explosives, Guay dispatched his mistress on a significant shopping expedition: she was to buy 20 sticks of dynamite, some detonators and 30 feet of fuse. It might have been accepted that she innocently believed this was to be used for dynamiting a tree. If so, it seemed more than strange to the police that she had signed a receipt for the goods in a false name. Her subsequent actions confirmed that she was only too aware of what Albert Guay was up to. The twisted little backstreet jeweller with murder in his heart; a conniving mistress and her watchmaker brother — these seemed to be characters out of some nineteenth-century novel particularly strong in Gothic melodrama.

It is scarcely surprising that the arrest and trial of the terrible trio attracted close interest far beyond Canada. Right from the time of the preliminary hearings the courtroom was crowded with reporters from many countries. The evidence against Guay was so straightforward as to be deadly, but somehow the jeweller seemed to take no interest in the proceedings. Pale-faced and aloof, he appeared to accept the inevitability of the only possible verdict. Marguerite Pitre, on the other hand, was perfectly aware that she was fighting for her life. If her lover had fondly supposed that she would protect him, he was soon in for a shock. Certainly she knew of his interest in dynamite and that he had learnt how important it was to have a timing device for explosives. Certainly she had helped Albert Guay to send off a small express package on the DC-3. "Did you know what was in that package?" asked the prosecutor. At this point Marguerite Pitre plainly believed she had admitted enough. She flatly denied any knowledge of a bomb. She had, she said, no reason to suppose that the package contained anything other than what Guay had told her — a statuette to be delivered to a customer in Baie Comeau. By arrangement, she had met Guay at the Union Station late on 8 September. He had previously deposited in the left-luggage office a parcel marked "Fragile" which he handed to her with the urgent injunction that it must catch the plane upon which Rita was travelling.

How Marguerite Pitre came to be discovered in her flat suffering from an overdose of drugs was one question to which no definite answer could be given. If the accused woman's story was to be believed there was more than a touch of crude melodrama about it. A day or two after the crash, she said, a very agitated Guay had called on her, mentioned the crash and said that the police already knew of her connection with the parcel and that it was only a matter of time before they questioned her. With the same casualness with which he had spoken to Carreau about murdering his wife, Guay now told his mistress: "There is nothing for it. You will have to sign a confession and kill yourself. I suggest you take these tablets and turn on the gas."

The emotional state of Marguerite Pitre during this interview can only be guessed at. Was she so terrified that she swallowed the yellow capsules, only to regain enough sense not to gas herself? Or had she gambled on being found before the pills took effect? Far from showing herself to be a terrified neurotic woman in the dock, Marguerite Pitre's demeanour varied from hurt indignation to the sort of playful irresponsibility that led her, during the trial, to tweak a policeman's ear. The mystery of her complex personality remained after her guilt had been proved.

Généreaux Ruest's protestations of innocence were more straightforwardly ludicrous. He freely admitted that when Guay had bought him a clock he had drilled a hole in the face and added a special timing mechanism which would set off a dynamite charge. He had no idea, he claimed, that this was going to be used for purposes of murder.

The three prisoners attempted to throw the blame on one another. None succeeded. All were found guilty and subsequently executed.

The sabotage of this DC-3 of Canadian Pacific Airlines had, in many respects, followed the familiar pattern of such crimes. Like many saboteurs before him, Albert Guay had bought his wife flight insurance, and he had concealed the bomb in a package which he had gambled successfully would be placed in the forward luggage compartment. But behind the crime lay a strange story of passion that, in other circumstances, might have resolved itself quietly in the shabby obscurity of a poor corner of Quebec. Instead it spread to engulf 23 innocent lives.

10: THE COLORADO JIGSAW

Murder is an abhorrent act at any time; but it takes the form mostly of an impulsive working-out of something between two people, or a few, and does not much affect uninvolved "bystanders". Yet, just occasionally, there emerges one of that cold-blooded species who will kill by calculation; and, thankfully even more rarely, one who will make a sacrifice of any number of innocent lives in order to be sure of dispatching his single intended victim. Albert Guay, the subject of the preceding chapter, was one. Jack Graham was another.

It was already dark when the DC-6B of United Airlines Flight 629 from New York to Seattle left Stapleton Airport, Denver, Colorado, at 6.52 p.m. on 1 November 1955. On board were 38 adult passengers, a baby and a crew of five.

Eleven minutes later a flight controller, high in the airport tower, saw the dark sky suddenly light up with a brilliance that revealed clouds towering to 10,000 feet. In his relatively soundproofed domain he heard only a muffled explosion; but to startled watchers on the ground some miles east of the town of Longmont the detonation had the violence of a thunderclap. Streamers of fire streaked the sky like cascading rockets. An airliner was plainly seen in the glare, reeling like a savaged bird at 6,000 feet over the Colorado hills. The tail section was seen to break away from the fuselage, then both parts plunged to earth. When the main portion struck there came an even more violent explosion as the fuel tanks went off with bomb-like effect.

The control-tower official having seen it happen, it proved quickly possible to check by radio which of several aircraft had not met with disaster, thus leaving no doubt that the victim had been the DC-6B, whose position at the time was precisely known. Police and others sped towards the spot, helicopter pilots were summoned, and urgent calls went out to the Federal Bureau of Investigation headquarters, in Washington, and the Civil Aeronautics Board, which has representatives throughout the United States empowered to set afoot immediate investigation into any disaster or dispute involving aircraft occurring in their respective areas.

The Board's chief investigator for the Colorado region, Raymond P. Parshall, was fortunately at his home in Kansas City when the emergency call came through. He acted at once, ordering the disaster area — estimated at six square miles — to be cordoned off by police, not only to keep morbid-minded sightseers at their distance but to prevent the inevitable souvenir-hunters from misappropriating even one scrap of debris which might, in the event, yield vital evidence of the cause of the crash. CAB experts in several cities were ordered to get themselves aboard the first available flights to Denver to form an investigation team, and representatives of United Airlines and of Douglas and other companies, builders of the aircraft, its engines and components, were invited to join them. The organization was magnificently thorough. It needed to be; for it was clear from the outset to expert eyes that they were dealing with no accident.

To ensure that no item, however small, escaped attention, a large-scale plot was made on graph paper to represent the entire area in which debris would be found. The precise position on the ground of each piece recovered, whether it was a large piece of wreckage, an engine, a human body, or even the most commonplace remnant of a passenger's baggage, was recorded on the diagram. Much was missing or distorted beyond identification: the explosions had been terrific and the fire intense.

When the location of a piece of the aircraft had been safely recorded beyond the possibility of future doubt it was taken to Stapleton to form a part in a massive jigsaw puzzle. Upon a skeleton of wood a framework of wire-netting had been built to represent exactly the shape of the aircraft as it had been. Experts worked for days securing each new-found piece into its appropriate position on this frame. It was taxing work, but it succeeded. By a process of elimination, clearing section by section of any evidence of pre-crash damage, the investigators found their attention always returning to the shell of what had been No. 4 Baggage Hold where the disintegration was clearly greatest. Everything around this region was shattered: the fuselage shell burst outwards by some violent detonation within; the rear and forward bulkheads forced backward and forward respectively, the fuselage bottom and the cabin floor above burst downward and upward. Without doubt, this hold had been the seat of a cataclysmic explosion — and, despite the effects of the flames which had swept it, there persisted about many fragments an unmistakable odour of explosive materials. When those items of passenger baggage which were known to have been carried in this compartment were placed in the mock-up it was found that some of these, too, smelt distinctly of explosive and showed traces of a coating of a whitish grey substance not found in any other section of the debris. It was straightway apparent to the FBI what these signs proclaimed: there had been a dynamite explosion in No. 4 Baggage Hold.

Even the soot left by those consuming flames yielded its clues. Subjected to laboratory analysis, some of it was found to contain traces of sodium nitrate and of manganese dioxide, a constituent of dry-cell batteries. Five tiny scraps of metal, out of the tons of shattered debris, could not be identified as any part of the aircraft itself nor recognized as remnants of a person's belongings. One of them, however, bore a mere fragment of blue lettering on a red background. It was the combination of colours that attracted the investigators' interest: the familiar colouring of "Ever Ready" batteries.

While this incredible work of deduction and elimination was going on, other CAB and FBI investigators were following different lines of inquiry. The distressing task of trying to identify the human remains was being carried on with the aid of relatives who had either come forward of their own accord or could be traced through details in booking lists. Only 9 out of the 44 who had perished could be identified visually. Some others could be recognized from the records of fingerprints which many American companies keep of their employees. Just as the aircraft was being pieced together, so, as far as possible, was every passenger's belongings and baggage being reassembled, separately according to whether it had been carried in the cabin or stowed in a hold. Many items of lighter weight had drifted through the air to points miles beyond the main disaster area, but the thorough investigation led to the recovery of a large proportion, ranging from items of clothing to letters and papers. Among the latter was a small scrap of paper. It was a newspaper clipping four years old, describing the arrest of a youth on a charge of forgery.

This insignificant piece of paper was placed alongside another paper salvaged from the passenger-cabin wreckage — a letter also referring to the forgery. The youth, it appeared, was the son of a passenger who had been carrying both letter and clipping; and that passenger, as it was possible to deduce from other personal possessions, was a Mrs Daisie E. King, who had joined the aircraft at its last stop, Denver. Only the baggage of passengers from Denver had occupied No. 4 hold where the fatal explosion had taken place; and before long investigators were confirming the identity of a suitcase that had been Mrs King's. They had to do it from fragments, for the case had suffered more than any other and bore more traces than any other of the soot deposited by the explosion.

Although this discovery diverted none of the investigators' scrutiny from the remains and belongings of the other 43 persons who had perished, some of them now made it their keen business to find out all they could about Mrs King. They were soon rewarded. She was found to have taken out special insurance for the flight, naming as principal beneficiary her son — who had the forgery conviction against his name. The son, in fact, had bought the policy at the airport on her behalf before she had boarded her aircraft.

This, of course, proved nothing. But it led the FBI men to the more extensive record of the youth in question, whose name was Jack Graham.

His mother, this revealed, had been widowed when he was three. She had subsequently re-married, but Graham had found little happiness at home, once running away as a child but being brought back. His stepfather's death had done nothing to mend a bad relationship between son and mother. At 16 Jack Graham had left home permanently, to join the U.S. Coast Guard, serving for 10 months, 63 days of which he had spent Absent Without Leave. This was not what had caused him to be discharged, though: someone had found out that he was below the permitted age for the service. Then he had taken a job as a wages clerk with a Denver firm of manufacturers. He had soon got into the trouble recorded in the newspaper clipping, forging a number of his company's cheques, thereby raising enough money to buy a car and indulge in spending well beyond his usual means. He had decamped from Denver in the car and for a while had been sought widely by the police, eventually falling into their hands through driving a load of whisky in the "dry" state of Texas. It was a relatively technical offence, but Graham had shown criminal determination by trying to burst the police roadblock, forcing them to fire to stop him.

He paid back a large part of the misappropriated money — no doubt being enabled to do so by his mother — so received only a suspended sentence and probation, paying back the rest in instalments while working as a mechanic in Denver.

He married, became the father of two children, then "allowed" his mother to come and live with him and his family, though no doubt Mrs King, the well-off entrepreneur of a variety of business enterprises in Denver and elsewhere, called the tune with her money. She built a drive-in restaurant for him to manage for her. Customers there and neighbours at home overheard bitter quarrels between mother and son. Perhaps he was striking back at her, consciously or unconsciously, when he organized an explosion in the restaurant; he blamed it on breakers-in and tried to collect insurance compensation for the damage. By all accounts it was not his only attempt to work the insurance trick: a lorry of his had been found abandoned on a railway track in time to prevent its being turned into an insurance loss by the next train to come along.

Such a background was, of course, of the deepest interest to the detectives investigating the human element of the DC-6B crash. Without yet approaching Jack Graham they questioned his probation officer and went on to find out discreetly what they could about the period immediately before Mrs King's departure on her fateful flight. It appeared that Graham had driven his mother and his family to the Stapleton Airport and dropped them at the terminal building. Then he had driven the car over to the parking area and after a slight delay had arrived at the checking-in counter with Mrs King's baggage, which he had carried from his parked car.

The aircraft's departure had been delayed by some forty minutes. When it had gone the Graham family had taken a quick meal in the airport restaurant. Graham had appeared uncharacteristically tense; so much so that he had had to hurry into a cloakroom and be sick. As they left afterwards they learned that an aircraft that had recently left there had blown up in flight and crashed.

This was all the investigators could learn from third parties. It was enough, they decided, to justify questioning Jack Graham himself. His story proved plausible enough, tallying with everything they had already learned. He was generally frank about his past misdemeanours and made no pretence of his feelings towards his mother. As to practicalities, he told how he had carried her luggage at the airport and described the pieces, but denied with surprise the suggestion that he might have put anything into one of the cases. The FBI men closed their notebooks and left.

They were soon back. A woman neighbour had watched them come and go and had evidently been disappointed not to see them escorting Jack Graham. She had had her eye on him during the ten days that had now elapsed since the disaster, and thought he had been exhibiting extraordinary signs of nervousness and tension, forever wandering about his house, unable to settle. The agents returned next day, but this time it was Graham's wife whom they questioned. Her story matched his, except in one particular. She told them that Graham had put something into his mother's baggage. Mrs King had disliked anyone interfering with her packing when she prepared to travel, but this had been a surprise present in advance of Christmas, a gift-wrapped box of small tools designed for working seashells into objects of art, a hobby of hers.

Another day later, this time at the FBI office, Graham was again asked whether he had put anything into one of his mother's suitcases. He denied it. His wife's statement was put to him, but he was able to explain the discrepancy. He had talked to his wife of his intention to get his mother a toolkit, but had not succeeded in doing so. His wife must have assumed he had done and that he had put it in the baggage without showing it to her. He was told that he was known to have bought insurance on his mother's life, with himself as principal beneficiary. He admitted it, but said he had mailed the policy from the airport to himself at home — he could not exactly say why — and it had never reached him. Believing they had reasonable grounds for suspicion, the FBI frankly told Graham that their inquiries were centred upon him and asked his permission to search his house. He agreed readily; perhaps surprisingly, for an early discovery there was the "missing" insurance policy, hidden in a wooden chest. In one of his shirts they found wire of a kind used for detonating explosive. They knew already that Graham had sometimes used explosives in his work — his half-sister had told them of the zest with which he had described this to her and his mother, adding that both of them had been afraid of the violent streak in him.

The evidence, though circumstantial, all pointed inexorably to a link between Graham, explosives, insurance, Mrs King — and the disastrous end to Flight 629. Within a fortnight of the aircraft's destruction the FBI had Graham's confession on paper and he was being charged with sabotage. He was committed for trial and held in jail, unable to meet the high figure set for his bail. But the FBI inquiries were not over. One by one the dead passengers and crew were eliminated from connection with the plane's sabotage, leaving only Mrs King. A storage manager was found who could identify Graham as a man to whom he had sold dynamite four weeks before the disaster.

At first, Graham tried hard to save his life. Two insanity pleas were entered on his behalf and he made a token attempt at suicide in his cell, but psychiatrists who examined him pronounced him sane. He tried to repudiate his confession. There was enough evidence to damn him without it. Tried and found guilty, he ceased to struggle. He refused to allow an appeal against the death sentence and was executed on 11 January 1956, only ten weeks after his wholesale killing of 44 people in order to gain a little over £5,000, a crime which had been brilliantly and swiftly brought home to him by the co-operative skills of the Civil Aviation Board and the Federal Bureau of Investigation.

Graham's most memorable comment had been: "The number of people killed made no difference to me... When their time comes there is nothing they can do about it." Sane or no, such people as Jack Graham are blessedly rare.

11: FIRST ACROSS THE TASMAN?

For forty years the brimming record books of achievement in the air have shown the ubiquitous names of Charles Kingsford Smith and Charles Ulm as the first conquerors of the Tasman Sea, that lonely, treacherous 1,200 miles of storm-tossed water which divides Australia and New Zealand. They became the first men to fly it, we are told, on 10 September 1928 in 14 hours.

Yet, despite this long-established claim, there are New Zealanders — and perhaps even a few Australians — who prefer to believe that Kingsford Smith and Ulm were beaten to it by exactly eight months. It is not beyond possibility that evidence may some day be found to prove them right, and to clear up the mystery, getting on for half a century old by now, of what happened to George Hood and John Robert Moncrieff.

As 1927 ended, only one limb of the "All Red" air-route from England via Empire countries all the way to Australia remained to be flown for the first time — the Tasman Sea. The previous June, Alan Cobham and his mechanic, A. B. Elliott, had taken off from the River Medway in Kent in a De Havilland seaplane to blaze the aerial trail to Australia. It had been no barnstorming stunt, but a serious-minded survey, aimed at making it possible to annihilate the great distance between the two countries by regular air services.

Cobham, who had already made successful trials of routes to India and South Africa, had deliberately chosen to fly to Australia during the worst time of year for weather, the Indian monsoon season, so as to avoid over-optimism about the working of a regular service. In the event, it had not been the weather, but a bullet that had brought tragedy to the enterprise. While they were flying low over Arabian swamps striving to keep on course for Basra in a blinding dust storm, an Arab raised his ancient musket and fired what was perhaps the most accurate shot of his lifetime. It passed through the aircraft's fuel pipe and into Elliott's cockpit, smashing one of his arms, ripping his left lung and finishing up in his back. Cobham had got him alive to Basra, but he had died next day.

Shocked and disheartened at the loss of his inseparable companion, Alan Cobham considered abandoning the flight; but he went on, with a new mechanic, and after many difficulties reached Australia where unprecedented scenes of near-riotous enthusiasm greeted them at Sydney and Melbourne. Equal frenzy would have awaited them had they gone on to New Zealand. They flew back to London instead, leaving the Tasman to await some other pioneer.

In New Zealand, as in Australia at that time, aviation was the great topic. Almost every day the overseas pages of New Zealand newspapers carried reports of new aerial conquests in every part of the world. Meanwhile, New Zealand herself was waiting impatiently to be "discovered" all over again, this time in a way that would bring those far-flung islands into intimate contact with the heart of the Empire. Naturally, it was hoped against hope that the feat would be performed by a New Zealander; and as the New Year festivities for 1928 died away there came a surge of excitement at the news that New Zealanders were indeed going to "give it a go".

Three members of the Territorial Air Force comprised the team. Captain George Hood, aged 35, had pioneering in his blood: his father had been a pioneer-settler in the Wairarapa region. A fine shot, George Hood had served at Gallipoli and in France with the Wellington Mounted Rifles, transferring to the Royal Flying Corps towards the end of the war. A subsequent peacetime crash had cost him a leg but had done nothing to cool his enthusiasm; he attended a refresher flying course every year as a reserve officer, earning his living as a motor mechanic. Captain I. Knight was a motor mechanic, too; as also was 29-year-old Lieutenant John Robert Moncrieff, a New Zealander by adoption who had come to live there from the Shetland Isles as a boy and bore the nickname "Scotty". All three were "flying mad", the type of men popularly associated with aerial trailblazing.

They planned their Tasman crossing from Australia, so as to give their own people the satisfaction and excitement of seeing their arrival with the feat achieved. Moncrieff who was to be chief pilot argued for a seaplane to be used — the odds on a forced landing at sea in the course of so long a flight in the size of plane they would be able to obtain were quite considerable — but they decided they could not afford one. They bought instead a high-winged American Ryan monoplane and named her *Aotearoa* ("Land of the Long White Cloud"), the Maori name for New Zealand.

Her single Wright Whirlwind engine would give them 200hp. With the extra tanks they had installed to give them a total fuel capacity of 200 gallons, they calculated they could cruise between 92 and 100mph, using just over one gallon every ten miles. Depending on the winds they would encounter, the flight would take them roughly nineteen hours. The plane had specially built-in air chambers, to increase its buoyancy in case of a forced landing at sea, floats, a collapsible rubber boat, and a supply of emergency rations.

So much for the emergency arrangements. Those for the actual flying were not quite so adequate. The aircraft had no dual-control system. In experiments they carried out on the ground, the men found that it would be impossible for anyone to change places with Moncrieff at the controls, so cramped was the cockpit space. Moncrieff would have to handle the plane, through whatever conditions they might meet, for 19 hours without relief. In fact, it was now clear that all three of them would not be able to make the flight: the third man's weight would compel them to cut down on fuel supply. In a Sydney hotel, Hood and Knight tossed a coin for the privilege of going. Hood won, and danced a jig, wooden leg and all.

Another shortcoming of their plans was that neither Moncrieff nor Hood could use a Morse transmitter. They had their monoplane equipped instead with an automatic transmitter of a type which sent out a "whining" signal every 15 minutes. So long as the whines continued to be heard, listeners ashore would know that the plane was still flying. If it came down, only the absence of the regular signal would indicate as much; there could be no opportunity to transmit a distress signal or to indicate a position.

The aircraft had not long been assembled and tested at the intended starting-point near Melbourne when the fliers were shocked to receive an order from the Australian Prime Minister, S. M. Bruce, that they must not proceed. He invoked a regulation forbidding landplanes to fly more than 50 miles out to sea, but it is possible that expert reports had reached him that the expedition was ill-advised. When the disappointing news reached New Zealand her Prime Minister, J. G. Coates, personally interceded to urge a change of mind. New Zealand experts had examined the aircraft, he said, and found it and its equipment adequate. Bruce rescinded the ban; but it is interesting, in the light of events, to find Coates declaring later that he had spoken to the airmen and formed the impression that their plans were ill-prepared. Perhaps the mounting excitement in New Zealand for the flight tipped the balance of his judgement in favour of helping it to go ahead.

That excitement began to approach fever pitch as last-moment preparations for the flight went on. To have stopped it now would have been to dash the spirits of almost the entire population of New Zealand. Report after report appeared in the newspapers about the latest forecast of trans-Tasman weather conditions. Even today, weather over the Tasman is tricky to forecast. Forty years ago the task was even harder. Arrangements were made to broadcast the news of take-off as soon as it was received. A flag would be hoisted on the General Post Office at Wellington, and another on the Wellington Harbour Board's flagstaff on Mount Victoria, overlooking the capital. Printed slips bearing the news would be placed in tramcars, and the Mayor of Wellington suggested that employers might like to give their workers the afternoon off when the great day came, to enable them to join the expected exodus to Trentham racecourse near the city, where the aeroplane would land.

Such was the intensity of enthusiasm in those early days of flying, which were, after all, not so very long ago. In fact, so unused was the New Zealand public to the spectacle of an aircraft landing that solemn cautions had to be issued by the authorities, pointing out to all who proposed being at Trentham that the plane would land at high speed and would run for a long distance before coming to a halt. (Many of the Melbourne crowd who had greeted Alan Cobham had had to flee precipitately to avoid being scythed down by his propeller.) Appeals were made for the landing area to be kept clear; would-be handshakers were discouraged; a strong force of police was told off for duty.

"Aviators hopped-off for New Zealand 2.44 this morning," came the sudden Press Association message on 10 January. It was followed by a dispatch, sent through the *Sydney Morning Herald*, from the fliers jointly to their wives in New Zealand: "I am confident that we shall be able to carry the journey through to success. Best love. I shall be home tonight."

At 2.04 a.m. Hood and Moncrieff had climbed into their plane at Richmond aerodrome, near Sydney. They had tested their transmitter and found it working perfectly. Starting up the engine, Moncrieff had found the windscreen being spattered with excess oil; this had soon been corrected, but reporters seeking last-minute interviews had delayed the departure. Then the engine had been started again, the wheel chocks whisked away at a wave of Moncrieff's hand, and they were off, at 2.44 Australian time, 5.14 in New Zealand.

Some thirty minutes later lookouts on the S.S. *Maunganui*, about fifteen miles off the Australian coast, saw the plane dimly as it passed over the ship, its engine running smoothly. At 6.48 New Zealand time the whine from the plane's transmitter was picked up at Sydney. It was heard more strongly at 8.40 and louder still, and continuous, at 8.45. By mid-morning, radio listeners in Wellington were being told that signals were still being received continuously in Sydney, but of low pitch and dropping in strength. At 10.33 a station operated by a "ham" in Christchurch picked up the whine and held it until 10.43. He got it again from 11.13 to 11.44. Then there was silence.

From about 4 p.m. great crowds converged on Trentham. By six o'clock there were between ten and twelve thousand people lining the racecourse enclosure and packing the stands. On surrounding hills every vantage point had been taken by watchers.

Just after seven someone in the crowd jumped up, pointed towards the setting sun and raised a cheer. It was echoed automatically by thousands of throats as the crowd peered eagerly into the glowing sky. But the cheering soon stopped; there was nothing to see. The hoax was not repeated. The crowd waited in patience, becoming progressively quieter. Even the flag sellers and the newspaper boys stopped moving about and stood still to watch the empty sky.

Darkness began to fall and now the throng began to move again. Many had hurried out from Wellington without their evening meal, and hunger began to thin the ranks. Thousands stood fast, but by ten o'clock the last of the special trains had left, packed to its doors.

Ministers of the Crown and the Mayor of Wellington joined the homeward trek, but had not gone far when a rumour reached them that the aircraft had been spotted over Paekakariki, on the coast near the capital, over an hour before. Many of the official cars turned back to Trentham and the vigil began again.

That was the start of the inevitable rumours. Circulated among the crowds, they came to the ears of the radio commentator, who passed them on to a bigger audience. Thus they attained some semblance of official reports, until, one by one, they had been checked and denied. The plane was said to have been seen at numerous points, on the coast and inland. It had been flying steadily; coming in low to land; about to force-land in difficulties. It had crash-landed on a beach, in a lake, and in a forested valley. It had been seen far south of its destination, passing near Picton in the South Island; the master of the ship to whom this report was attributed denied it emphatically when he reached port. Then there were stories of flares being dropped, and of an aircraft circling endlessly near

Wellington, clearly hoping to stay aloft until daylight. Just in case this were true a makeshift flarepath was prepared at Trentham and a bonfire lit.

It was well past midnight when Moncrieff's wife, waiting with Mrs Hood and a group of their relatives, looked for the last time at her watch and said quietly, "Their petrol is out."

By 2.30, even the rumours had ceased.

The excited optimism that had gripped all New Zealand now became universal anxiety. People going to work later that morning automatically glanced skyward without knowing they did it. The action could only have been spontaneous, for there was no longer the slightest possibility that *Aotearoa.* was still flying.

New Zealand at that time possessed few aircraft. One was dispatched from the South Island to search the Wellington vicinity. The warships *Diomede* and *Dunedin* and a tug were sent to scour the area from where the last signal was judged to have been picked up. A storm whistled up with sudden violence and made methodical searching impossible, also ending any hopes that the aircraft might be afloat on the sea. A message from Captain Knight, in Sydney, suggested that the plane must have come down in the densely-bushed Tararua or Rimutaka Ranges, with which Hood was well familiar, and that the two men were sleeping before trying to make their way out. Dozens of men formed parties to enter those inhospitable areas, knowing too well that it would be like looking for the proverbial needle in a haystack. A plume of smoke encouraged them at one point, but it turned out to be from an innocent fire.

Meanwhile in Sydney reports circulated that the flight had been a success. Special editions of newspapers were rushed on to the streets and audiences in theatres and cinemas cheered when the news was announced to them. An ominous note was sounded, though, by a man in Melbourne who had the true information. He was Sir Keith Smith, who knew all about hazardous flying enterprises, having been one of the team of four who had made the first England–Australia flight in 1919, which itself had been a whole sequence of perils. From what he knew of the missing men and their arrangements, he declared, their flight should never have taken place.

A week after the event, with the searching ships withdrawn, Captain Knight returned by sea to New Zealand. One comment of his provided disturbing news for those with hope left. He said that the fliers had not expected to leave Australia until at least forty-eight hours after they had actually gone. Their decision had been a sudden one; consequently, right until leaving they had continued to go about their other activities and had even taken a long harbour cruise on 9 January, so that, at the time of take-off, neither of them had had any sleep for twenty hours. For Moncrieff to sit cramped at the controls for nineteen hours on top of that was perhaps too much to ask of human endurance.

The last of the searchers gave up. Funds were opened for Moncrieff's and Hood's dependants. Yet people still asked the question, what had become of them? The two men who claimed to have seen *Aotearoa* over Paekakariki were found to be reliable types who would not budge from their assertion in the face of official questioning. Certainly, no other aircraft could have been in that vicinity at that time. In due course, spiritualists claimed to have got into contact with the missing men, but they could not, as has sometimes been done, find out where they had met disaster.

New Zealand, like Australia, still has great areas of dense bush which have not been penetrated thoroughly. The *Southern*

Cloud (see chapter 5) lay undiscovered in the Australian bush for 27 years. Even in overcrowded and overdeveloped England, someone found, in the vicinity of the Battle of Britain fighter station at Biggin Hill, a crashed Hawker Hurricane which had lain undetected in woodland for about that same length of time.

It may be that some day, penetrating a little farther in a different direction, a hunter or tramper in the New Zealand bush will come across the twisted remains of an aeroplane that met an ill fate before he was born.

The case of Hood and Moncrieff rests until then, and the first Tasman crossing is one of the many achievements recorded against the illustrious names of Kingsford Smith and Ulm. But the *Aotearoa* tragedy had posthumous effect on another pair of fliers who "vanished" during an attempt to break the Australia–New Zealand record, but whose story, in agreeable contrast to most of their kind, has a happy ending.

On 8 December 1934 Raymond ("Ron") Galbraith Whitehead and Ernest Rex Nicholl appeared in Auckland Police Court, charged with making a flight from the northern peninsula of New Zealand to Auckland the previous month in an unregistered aircraft without a Certificate of Airworthiness and without carrying the documents prescribed by regulations. They pleaded guilty. If the law had provided for them to be charged with flying the whole way across the Tasman as well their plea would have been just the same. They had.

The Tasman had been crossed a number of times by November 1934. All that was left for adventurous airmen to do was to beat their predecessors' record, an enterprise which, in those pre-blasé days of aviation, could be sure of its share of public attention and excitement. The Whitehead–Nicholl attempt would create more sensation than most and divide public opinion, on both sides of the Tasman Sea, into "for" and "against" daredevil exploits in the air. We include it here, not so much for the small "mystery" that briefly attended it, but because it reflects so aptly the attitude of airmen, officials and public to bold undertakings in the name of aerial pioneering of the kind which are the substance of the preceding Hood–Moncrieff mystery and of those dealt with in several other chapters.

Whitehead, aged 24, was a Wellingtonian; Nicholl, 26, a Sydney man born at Ballarat. Their aircraft was the oldest De Havilland Puss Moth in Australia, bought for Whitehead by his businessman-father and used by him and Nicholl in the public joyriding trade in Australia. Having suddenly decided to break the trans-Tasman record, then standing at 10 hours, the two proceeded to work for several weeks on the old plane, removing the three seats to make way for extra petrol tanks which would increase the fuel capacity from 35 gallons to 117. What was left of the cabin was festooned with petrol pipes. A compass and an aircraft chronometer were the only instruments. There was no room for radio, which in any case Whitehead and Nicholl agreed would be a pointless accessory, since shipping in the Tasman was so sparse that a crash in mid-ocean would leave them no chance of rescue, radio or no. The engine would be supplied with oil by pouring by hand from a can into a pipe, by way of a funnel. When not in use the pipe would be stopped up with a plug of cotton-waste.

All that these arrangements left in the way of seating was a small board, placed across the control box, with a cushion tied to it with string. On this one man could just sit, his legs wide apart. His companion would have to sit on his lap — such as it was in this position. There would not even be room for the fliers to wear their shoes; bare feet could be curled into smaller space.

Not surprisingly, after taking one look at the conversion the Australian civil aviation authorities withdrew the machine's Certificate of Airworthiness. 'A flying petrol tank', it was termed. Well knowing that, after the Hood–Moncrieff disaster, they could not hope for an intervention by the New Zealand Government — even had their plane been nearer to standard — the two young men decided to flaunt the law. Pausing only to paint on the fuselage the name *Faith in New Zealand*, an adaptation of the name of Charles Ulm's old warhorse Avro, they had the plane smuggled at night out to Gerringong Beach, hoping for a take-off before anyone could prevent them. They found the tide in and the sand under water. While they waited for it to recede they prepared their only flight-chart by drawing a straight line from Sydney to Auckland and marking the Australian half of the Tasman "water" and the New Zealand half "still more water".

The last-minute rush to get away had deprived them of any sleep the previous night, so that by 1.25 a.m., Australian time, 22 November 1934, when they took off from the beach by the combined light of the moon, a few flares and some well-wishers' car headlamps, they were badly in arrears with their rest. They were overloaded by some 600 pounds. One wheel just tipped the crest of a wave and might have turned them over; but they staggered clear. Not daring to turn sharply nor wishing to climb much, for fear of wasting petrol, they eased round towards New Zealand at a height of about one hundred feet.

Whitehead occupied the cramped pilot's position for the first spell, sitting on Nicholl who pumped petrol and, every hour, poured a quart of oil into the funnel connected to the hose. In due course fumes from the oil thickened almost to suffocating point. They found that a leak had sprung in the waste-bung of the hose. Nicholl was able to make a new stopper out of a flashlight battery bound in adhesive tape.

They flew over the convoy of ships accompanying the Duke of Gloucester on his tour of Australasia, but apart from one other small vessel saw no shipping: their feelings about the value of radio seemed to that extent justified. One discovery cheered them: the warmth from the engine kept their bare feet comfortable.

After about six hours' flying the plane was becoming lighter and easier to handle as the fuel load decreased. The two cramped men decided the time had come to change positions. It required a fantastic manoeuvre, in about the space of a barrel. Nicholl, behind, had to rise into as much of a standing position as he could, keeping his legs wide apart for Whitehead to press himself backward between them and squirm into the "passenger" position, so that Nicholl could subside on to his lap and take the controls.

Several hours later, sustained meanwhile only by a packet of sandwiches, a flask of coffee, chewing gum and some caffeine tablets, they changed places again. They now knew that they had no hope of breaking the record — not by many hours would they equal it. In time, the first indications of approaching dusk became apparent. They had flown throughout a long day in a fantastically cramped posture and without the backing of a night's sleep. Dusk came closer. They spotted seagulls and some driftwood. Land must be near. With about four hours' petrol left they flew on.

Word of their unlawful flight had soon reached the Sydney authorities and been transmitted to New Zealand, where it had been made public. Whatever the official sentiments, that of the

175

man in the street in both countries was of unmitigated excitement and, initially, of fervent good wishes towards two intrepid youngsters. People in New Zealand began to crowd to possible landing places — for, of course, no one could know where the aircraft might arrive. Flares were prepared as darkness dropped down. Then, after several hours' vigil, the watchers dispersed into the night. It seemed plain enough this was a case of Hood and Moncrieff all over again. The aircraft's petrol supply must have been exhausted several hours ago. The only question now would be one for the authorities — where to search? And as the dejected watchers went homeward the arguments began to rage — had it all been a reckless stunt by a couple of irresponsible fools; or a brave demonstration of the inborn courage of New Zealand and Australian youth? Whichever way, it had all the attributes now of another mysterious aircraft disappearance.

When it became light next morning, planes from many airports took to the air to begin a search, including ones flown by visitors to New Zealand — competitors in the England–Australia air race which had just been concluded. Shipping had already been alerted. Search parties were being mustered to go into the bush at the first indication of which part of the country the fliers might have reached.

Having searched all morning as far south as New Plymouth, pilots from Mangere, Auckland, returned to the aerodrome heavy-hearted — only to see, as they came in to land, a Puss Moth such as they had been seeking standing in front of the hangars. Each man as he landed went hot-foot to the airport offices to hear the story which was already circulating New Zealand and Australia.

With dusk approaching, Whitehead and Nicholl had sighted land, lying both north and south of them. They had allowed themselves plenty of margin for drift, so turned north to correct this. After flying on for a while they had seemed to be losing the land again. Then, in the deepening gloom, Whitehead had recognized the disappearing small islands beneath them as the Three Kings, north-west of the North Island. With no idea how long it would take them to fly back towards the mainland and find an aerodrome, they had decided to land there and then on an inviting stretch of beach; and so *Faith in New Zealand* had reached the land after which she was named.

After easing their cramped limbs, Whitehead and Nicholl had walked off in the hope of finding a house with a telephone and giving the news of their arrival to Auckland. They had spotted a dwelling at last, but it proved to be separated from them by a creek. Rather than swim, they decided to return to their plane, light a fire and get a night's rest before taking off again in daylight. As it turned out they had had to endure yet another sleepless night. Their experience had left them too worked-up to do anything except talk away the hours.

In the morning they had taken off without difficulty and easily flown the 200 miles to Auckland, where only a handful of aerodrome staff had seen them arrive.

They sparked off a controversy which raged for days. A New Zealand Aero Club conference damned them outright, one member suggesting that they should be ignored socially, as well as officially. This drew a letter to a newspaper from an unnamed pilot, pointing out that nearly all trans-oceanic flights up to that time had been made in overloaded aircraft that had contravened the law. He castigated the N.Z. Aero Club (many of whose members, he inferred, were armchair airmen only) for picking on two unknown pilots after accepting and applauding well-known ones for taking similar risks.

In Melbourne, the Controller of Civil Aviation labelled the flight "very foolhardy". In Sydney there was talk of possible legal action against the men if they returned. From such evidence of public opinion as remains in print, it seems from today's viewpoint that, after the first enthusiasm, public feeling in both countries tended to be against the men. One notable voice raised more impartially than most was that of Squadron-Leader J. D. Hewett (later a senior officer of the Royal New Zealand Air Force) who had flown a twin-engined De Havilland Rapide aircraft across the Tasman only a week earlier. From the point of view of one who knew at first-hand what he was talking about, he stated: "In a way one cannot decry stunts of this sort. You must encourage people to take risks. If you did not have fellows willing to take risks you would not get anywhere. At the same time, a stunt of this kind is not doing aviation any good. If you get across with a single-engined machine you get a pat on the back, and if you fail — well, you are just a darned fool. But even if you succeed under such conditions, you are not really demonstrating to the world that the Tasman is a suitable stretch of water to fly across with only one engine."

Whitehead and Nicholl removed the extra fuel tank from their plane, so that once again it conformed with official requirements. But before they could undertake their intended barnstorming tour of New Zealand they were relieved of their flying licences. In what has all the appearance of a sheepish gesture they were issued with driving licences instead. A sympathetic Auckland businessman put a car at their disposal.

At least they were able to drive to court. They faced a penalty of six months' jail or a fine up to £200. The magistrate, convicting them, fixed no penalty but hastened to add, "That does not mean that anybody else will get off so lightly."

Although they had pleaded guilty — they could hardly do otherwise — the two men were unrepentant. With disarming logic they viewed their plane's age as its virtue: it had flown over one thousand hours without a single mishap, and was therefore thoroughly reliable. They had reached their destination with fuel to spare, hence their wisdom in installing the extra tankage. Personal comfort was, surely, a lesser consideration; and if they had risked anything it had only been their own lives.

New Zealand's Governor-General, Viscount Bledisloe, a man of much shrewdness, whose son and heir would in the course of time include in his list of recreations in *Who's Who* such hazardous pursuits as "mountaineering, skiing, tobogganing and flying", allowed himself to express an opinion. Classing Whitehead and Nicholl with the leading names in the country's aviation history, he observed, "Their revelation of the possibilities of aviation in this part of the Empire should stimulate the imagination and zeal of many youthful New Zealanders to emulate their skill."

When we recall the kind of deeds youthful New Zealand and Australian airmen were performing in fighters and bombers only five years later, we may well believe that Lord Bledisloe had the truth of the matter.

12: "A RED EAGLE FALLING"

The mist that had been prowling along the low ground near the Somme canal in Northern France on 21 April 1918 had risen by early morning to steam across to the airfield at Cappy. Here, at the base of *Jagdgeschwader* 1, a unit of the German Air Force, a group of young fighter pilots, rubbing their hands and jumping up and down to keep warm, were passing the last minutes before taking off in search of more Allied aircraft to destroy. The sun made a half-hearted attempt to break through, as if to confirm the forecast that the day would become brighter as it wore on.

Conversation ceased abruptly at the sudden appearance of a strikingly handsome man whose Prussian stockiness made him look somewhat older than his 26 years as he strode in hurried determination towards the group of airmen. This was the most successful, most famous fighter ace in the world, Rittmeister Manfred Freiherr von Richthofen. With the enormous total of 80 "kills" to his name, he was still eager for more. After a good night's sleep he felt in excellent health and was in the best of humours.

There was some derisive laughter as someone with a camera stepped forward and asked permission to photograph the Rittmeister playing with his big dog, Moritz, beside his red Fokker triplane. The laughter gave way to a hush of surprise when it was seen that Richthofen was allowing his picture to be taken. German flying aces were as vain as any actors, but they were also as superstitious. It was considered bad luck to be photographed just before a flight, hence the general surprise to see Richthofen haul Moritz on to his hind legs and good-humouredly tell the photographer to go ahead.

A few minutes later the all-red Fokker DR 1 425/17 was airborne, followed by others, and heading westward along the Somme canal towards a mystery which remains, more than half a century later.

Manfred von Richthofen began his service career as his father had done, in the cavalry. After passing through the War Academy at Berlin he joined the 1st Regiment of Uhlans. But the cavalry war of 1914 was nothing like those of the past. Richthofen soon became bored with a branch of the army that seemed to offer an uncertain future. He became fascinated with the new air-machines, frail canvas and wood structures, used for the first time as a weapon of war and promising more than a share of danger. Soon after the outbreak of war he was putting in for a transfer to the German Air Service and began his career as an aerial scout over the Russian lines. In March 1916 Richthofen had his first taste of active service over the Verdun front.

Even in the early days of his career he was renowned among his comrades for bravado and dash, combined with a distinct liking for the good things of life, notably oysters and champagne. Everything he did was in the grand manner, even the celebration of his "kills". By tradition, fliers were usually presented by their fellows with silver cups for their early victories. Richthofen went further — he presented himself with a silver cup for each kill. A Berlin jeweller made and inscribed them especially to his order. Richthofen kept him busy. A fine pilot, and a good shot since childhood, his tally of victories mounted rapidly. In little over a year he had command of his own squadron and was approaching the record of 40 kills set by the late Oswald Boelcke. He passed

Boelcke's total and still went on notching up victories. No German air-ace was to be so highly decorated and so lionized. The pilots of the German Air Service were the pop stars of the Great War, their photographs widely distributed in Germany, stories of their exploits filling the newspapers and accounting for a brisk trade in picture postcards. It helped the war effort and kept the spirit of patriotism alive.

Honours were heaped upon Richthofen. He received the Saxe-Coburg Medal for Bravery, the Bulgarian Order of Military Valour, the Hungarian Order of the Holy Crown, Order of the Royal House of Oldenburg, Pour le Mérite, Turkish Star of Gallipoli, Turkish Imtjah Medal and the Iron Cross (First-Class). The silver cups proliferated and the walls of his room disappeared under a covering of trophies, pieces of aircraft he had shot down and patches of fabric inscribed with their serial numbers. Ludendorff declared him to be "worth three divisions of infantry". Far from lapsing into self-satisfaction he remained insatiable for more conquests. He had first distinguished himself as an aerial duellist when for his 11th "kill" he shot down Major Lanoe G. Hawker, V.C., D.S.O., one of the most daring of Royal Flying Corps fighter pilots and commanding officer of the first British squadron to be equipped completely with fighter aircraft.

In 1917 Richthofen was given the command of a wing of four squadrons. It was also a year which brought disaster. In one of his many dogfights his red Albatros was shot down. He received severe head wounds when a bullet, fired at long range, struck his head. The aircraft plunged thousands of feet. It was not the fear of being smashed to pieces on landing which Richthofen was to remember. He recalled that he had remained fully conscious but unable to see: "I kept tearing at my goggles and saying over and over again 'I must see! I must see!'"

Eventually he managed to wrench off the goggles and could see fields, trees and a road careering towards him. He pulled back on the stick, levelling the aircraft just in time for it to rip along a road surface. He was unable to leave the cockpit. Soldiers lifted him gently out, the white of his skull showing in the wound.

It was characteristic of him that he spent his convalescence hunting, impatient to get back into action. His dedication was absolute, even to the extent of ignoring the entreaties of Kaiser Wilhelm II to take a less dangerous part in air battles and devote himself to training others. Probably no one else in the whole of Germany would have dared to make a public reply to the Emperor which ran: "I should indeed consider myself a despicable person if, now that I have achieved fame and wear many decorations, I should consent to exist as a pensioner of my dignity and to preserve my life for the nation while every poor fellow in the trenches ... has to stick it out."

But those who flew with him now noticed an odd streak of fatalism in his character. True, he worked on the training of his pilots with even more zest, but for the first time he seemed to feel that perhaps his luck was running out. He began to talk about providing for his parents should he be killed, and wrote a book to raise money. He tramped Germany meeting those close to the Kaiser, as well as politicians and statesmen. It was as if he wanted to learn as much as he could about his country in the time left to him. Yet he continued to fly an aircraft whose unique all-red colouring marked him out as the most desirable quarry for an Allied fighter to pursue.

On the same morning that von Richthofen left Cappy on what was to be his last flight — 21 April 1918 — Captain Roy

Brown, a Canadian of 209 Squadron, took off in a Sopwith Camel fighter from Bertangles on a routine flight at 1,200 feet over the front between Hangard and Albert. Richthofen's formation of Fokker triplanes was flying westward along the Somme valley and was joined in the air by the full strength of *Jagdstaffel* 5, some 18 aircraft.

At this point, some slow-flying British reconnaissance aircraft on a photographic mission west of the village of Hamel, which lay far to the south-west of Cappy, put in an appearance. Four German triplanes peeled off to attack them. Brown's patrol of Camels saw the one-sided encounter and dived to the rescue. It was a dogfight in the true style of the First World War, with aircraft wheeling and pouncing on one another at close quarters and cartridge cases raining down on soldiers watching from trenches below.

One of Brown's men, Lieutenant F. J. W. Mellersh, managed to get in a burst of fire on a blue-tailed triplane which limped away in a sorry state towards Cappy. Mellersh's satisfaction was short-lived. A pack of the enemy was on his tail. He twisted and turned and altered height to confuse his pursuers. Out of the corner of his eye he saw a red triplane scream earthwards and testified later that he had noticed Brown's Camel near to it.

Richthofen, looking for his 81st victory, had suddenly veered off after an obvious novice, Second-Lieutenant May. Easily, he had taken up his customary position on the other's tail, forcing the Camel to twist and turn in a vain effort to shake him off. Each evasive manoeuvre lost the Camel a little distance ahead of the relentless Fokker triplane. May was forced almost to ground level and into a trap from which it seemed he would never emerge: he found himself flying above a river, between its banks which were too high to allow him to fly in anything but a straight line.

Suddenly, Roy Brown's Camel swooped on the unsuspecting triplane. The Canadian was not able to see the immediate effects of his bullets because he had to flatten out his machine to avoid diving on into the ground, but he claimed later to have seen Richthofen turning his head as if to peer over his shoulder. It could have been merely a backward glance at his opponent. It might equally have been the effect of bullets in Richthofen's back causing his spine to stiffen and his head to be jerked round. With a last impression of his victim slumping forward in the cockpit, Brown turned his concentration towards getting home.

Brown was later credited with having shot down the triplane, but the R.A.F.'s terse communique on the engagement made no mention of Richthofen. It ran: "The enemy's machines were seen in large numbers … 11 machines were brought down in air fighting and 6 others were driven down out of control… Our anti-aircraft fire brought down 2 other hostile machines and 5 of our aircraft are missing."

Richthofen's Fokker fell near the Bray-Corbie road in the area of Vaux-sur-Somme. A heap of wurzels broke its careering progress. The undercarriage was completely wrecked and the petrol tank collapsed, the wings remaining unbroken. Australian troops who dashed to the wreckage unfastened the dead man's safety-belt and lifted him out. The stripping of enemy aircraft for souvenirs was a commonplace practice and this occasion was no exception. The machine was literally hacked to pieces. Anything useful that might have been learnt from the position of bullet holes was lost.

The pilot's face had suffered superficial injuries, probably caused by its impact on the butts of his Spandau guns. Someone removed a gold watch from his wrist. It was stamped with the initials "MvR". Papers in his pockets confirmed that the "Red Baron" or "Red Eagle" had met his match at last.

There seemed no reason to doubt Brown's claim to this notable victory until a post-mortem on Richthofen revealed a strange anomaly. Brown had reported that his bullets had caught Richthofen in the back. Medical examination now established beyond doubt that a bullet had passed obliquely into the chest, struck the spinal column, then glanced off in a forward direction and emerged on the left side of the chest. The angle of the wound suggested that the bullet had come from a gun on roughly the same level that the German machine had been flying; yet it was known that Brown had only straightened out from his dive *after* shooting at the Fokker.

Brown's claim, in any case, was already in dispute. A Lieutenant Quinlan of an artillery battery at Vaux, who claimed to have followed the flight closely from the ground, swore that at no point had Brown's aircraft been near enough to have shot Richthofen. Second-Lieutenant May, whom Brown had saved from certain death, was unable to throw helpful light on this. He said he had been too busy trying to dodge Richthofen along the river line to pay much attention to anything else. May recalled: "I felt he had me cold. Then as I looked round I saw Richthofen do a spin and a half and hit the ground." He could not say who had shot the pilot of the scarlet machine.

An anonymous Australian rifleman, writing to a newspaper back home, was to claim that he had shot Richthofen from the ground at a point when the Fokker had come into the path of 53rd Battery, Australian Field Artillery. His weapon had been a ring-sighted gun mounted for anti-aircraft work. The rifleman described the manoeuvres of the two machines accurately and there was no reason to doubt that he genuinely believed he had shot down the Fokker. Other gunners also claimed to have hit the aircraft from the ground.

They may well have been right. The immediate stripping of the wreck by the souvenir hunters made it impossible to determine how many bullets had hit it from below or above.

Over the following years, people fascinated by the mystery have tried to see if a re-examination of what is known will produce a possible solution. Enthusiasts have flown where May, Richthofen and Brown pursued one another. The battle has been re-enacted countless times over Hamel and many of its students agree that Brown could have got in a second burst of gunfire at closer quarters which he did not recall having fired. Furthermore, a study of military maps of the period, together with observations on the ground, have led a number of people to doubt whether it would have been possible for all self-styled eyewitnesses to have seen the crash of the Red Baron quite as easily as they claimed.

The mystery of his death is a part of the appeal of the legend of Manfred von Richthofen. He was given a hero's burial by the Allies. After the war his body was returned to Germany. The R.A.F. maintains a permanent tribute to him: the motto of 208 Squadron — Roy Brown's squadron — is "A Red Eagle Falling".

13: THE ACE WHO FLEW TOO HIGH

The mysterious case of Georges Guynemer, France's strangest air ace in the First World War, should never have arisen at all, for by all the rules Guynemer should never have been a pilot in the first place. The son of a French lawyer, he was chronically tubercular and spent most of his early years a semi-invalid. Of retiring, rather donnish personality, he showed considerable gifts for Latin and mathematics, and but for the war might have ended his days as, say, a tutor in some provincial university.

It is highly probable that he would have been exempt from military duty, if it had not been for a fascination for aircraft amounting almost to an obsession. His suggestion that he should become a pilot was greeted with tolerant laughter, but some kind soul did get him a job sweeping up at a training field at Vauciennes, near Villers-Cotterets, outside Paris. Whenever he had a spare moment he would dart into the mechanics' workshops and beg to be given something to do. Usually he was chased out, but his persistence was such that he was eventually allowed to tinker with engine parts at the workbenches. No one who met him could fail to be impressed by his astonishing knowledge of aircraft and their capabilities. He could identify any type of aeroplane in use by either side in the war, an accomplishment which, together with other evidence of exceptionally keen eyesight, brought him to the attention of senior officers at the airfield. Word began to circulate that the weedy youth of whom no one had taken any particular account was about to be singled out for special attention. It was true. There were a few jealous remarks, but on 26 July 1915 Georges Guynemer became a student pilot.

His success in the air was immediate and phenomenal. Here was a born aviator. His family did not rejoice to learn of it. Worried almost to distraction by this sudden, totally unforeseen development in their far-from-robust son's career, they shuddered with apprehension every time he swooped down over the Guynemer château in a Bleriot or Nieuport trainer. One of his instructors in high indignation sought an interview with the precocious young man's commanding officer. "Someone is playing a stupid joke," he spluttered. "Nobody can convince me that young Guynemer has never flown before." In the same July as he started flying, Guynemer went into action and achieved his first kill, bringing down a German Aviatik after fierce combat. He was awarded the Médaille Militaire.

Like England's Albert Ball, Guynemer was given the hazardous duty of flying intelligence agents across the line and landing them in what everyone optimistically hoped were isolated areas. Skirting enemy gunfire, he would return to pick up his charges again, and, with his heart in his mouth, ferry them back to his own lines. He is on record as saying that these little adventures scared him far more than combat. Yet he seemed to lead a charmed life. On the ground he was colourless and moody, his obvious frailty making those who did not know him laugh in open disbelief at accounts of his bravery. Once in the cockpit of a Nieuport or Spad he was transformed into a fearless killer, callous and altogether professional.

On 12 March 1916 he was badly wounded and almost lost his life. He had been given a new 120hp Nieuport and, with characteristic impulsiveness, had taken off without fully testing the new toy. While out on this extended joyride he encountered two German aircraft. Delighted at such apparently easy prey, they swooped in to take him from behind. Guynemer spotted them just in time and quickly swept the Nieuport up and out of the enemy's path. The unaccustomed speed of the aircraft was nearly his undoing. He was zooming over the Germans before he had time to draw a bead on the target. He had put himself in a perfect position for one of the gunners to plaster him, riddling the engine's accessory grouping and sending two bullets through his left arm. Pilot and plane were lucky to get back to their lines, where the Nieuport ploughed into the ground near some trenches.

If anyone suggested to Guynemer that this escape should serve as a warning not to be overconfident, he paid no attention. He followed up the nearly fatal experience with a whole succession of dazzling victories, many of them achieved against the odds. By the end of 1916 he had chalked up 25 "kills", a tally which made him France's top ace; in the next year he was to double his record.

It seemed to his friends that Guynemer had a strange, demonic compulsion that led him to spend every available moment in the air killing Germans. Few of them knew that he was riddled with the tuberculosis with which he had been born. He could not expect to live very long, hence the urgency of his mission.

The keg of gunpowder which Georges Guynemer straddled during his short and bloody aerial war exploded on the foggy morning of 11 September 1917. He took off from the airfield at Villacoublay in his pet Spad, affectionately dubbed "le vieux Charles". He was followed by one of his closest friends, Lieutenant Bozon-Verdurez. Not long after the two French fighters had passed over the damaged railway between Ypres and Thourout and were approaching the German lines Guynemer spotted a German two-seater. Once again he manoeuvred his aircraft into the position which had stood him in such good stead countless times before, losing height gradually to bring him directly behind his quarry's tailplane. Then "le vieux Charles" was hurled into the attack, zigzagging to prevent the German observer from getting in an accurate burst of fire. Behind Guynemer followed Bozon-Verdurez, but both men missed the enemy with their initial bursts and had to wheel away to begin another pass at him.

Just then Bozon-Verdurez noticed a formation of German scouts closing in. So that Guynemer could be free to down his prey, his accommodating friend offered himself as bait to the pack and drew them away after him. He had time to see Guynemer lining up the solitary German again, but there was no time to stop and watch for the result.

The scouts fired a half-hearted burst at Bozon-Verdurez, but then, seeming to sense that they had fallen for a decoy, began to peel off and make for Guynemer's Spad. Bozon-Verdurez instantly made up his mind that his place was back alongside his friend. Banking quickly to look for the Spad he was astonished to see only empty sky, except for the homeward-going German planes

Bozon-Verdurez made many wide sweeps in search of his friend, scouring sky and ground for as long as he dared. At length, with his petrol supply almost exhausted, he turned sadly homewards, trying to cling to the hope that Guynemer might somehow have landed safely at their aerodrome, but knowing in his heart that this was at the least unlikely. He would surely have spotted the Spad heading for home. As he stepped from his cockpit back at base, anxious faces confirmed his fears. "He's not back yet," someone told him.

Telephone calls were made urgently along the French lines. Plane after plane took off to scour the area, but not a trace of a shattered machine was to be found anywhere. In the Officers' Mess that night Guynemer's chair stood empty amongst a downcast company, still hoping against hope that their improbable hero would return after all. The likeliest source of news now would be the Germans themselves. Anyone who had managed to shoot down Guynemer would scarcely keep quiet about it, for here would have been a prize indeed. For several days there was silence. Then, when the Germans did proffer some information, it served only to deepen the mystery. Notes were dropped on British airfields reporting that a number of English fliers had been shot down at certain dates and places. One name on the list riveted attention: "Captain Guynemer, 8 a.m. 10th September." This could only be a mistake or a fabrication. Time and date were both wrong: Guynemer had not disappeared until 24 hours later. At 8 a.m., on 11 September, he had been gulping down his breakfast, before taking off 30 minutes later.

The village of Poecapelle, above which Guynemer had vanished, fell eventually to the British after changing hands many times. Following up a rumour that some time earlier an aircraft had been brought down on the village from 12,000 feet, some of Guynemer's colleagues visited the cemetery, looking for freshly dug graves. There were no traces of recent burials. There was talk of three German soldiers who had found the wreckage of a Spad and in it a badly injured pilot, but attempts to trace the men met with no success.

All kinds of fantastic legends grew up around Georges Guynemer. The Germans alleged that he had in fact died of tuberculosis and that the story of his death in action had been invented by the romantic French, determined that a hero's death should be recorded for their ace. It was even suggested that Guynemer's tubercular body had been propped in the seat of his machine and that the Spad had been made to take off, carrying its dead pilot to an eventual crash in the depths of the countryside.

Pilot and Spad had vanished like phantoms at the approach of daylight, and at this remove of time it would spoil a legend-touched mystery to learn what is no doubt a prosaic truth. We prefer the explanation given many years after the war to French schoolchildren who had been taught to regard the brave Guynemer as the very ultimate in heroes.

"Georges Guynemer," it was said, "flew so high that he could not come down again."

14: THE MYSTERY OF THE *ITALIA*

Across an enormous table in a cavernous state apartment of Rome's Palazzo Venezia, General Umberto Nobile faced the squat, pugnacious figure of his Duce, Benito Mussolini. The Duce listened attentively to the proposal the general put before him — to fly the airship *Italia* over the North Pole from King's Bay, Spitzbergen.

Under Mussolini's steady gaze, Nobile gave full details of the preparations which had been made for the flight. The Duce was not at all interested in aviation or polar exploration, but he reasoned that such a journey, if successful, could only reflect credit on his Fascist state. He pronounced himself satisfied with Nobile's scheme. "You seem to have worked out everything in advance," he commented. "That is surely the way to succeed. The scientific world will be impressed, particularly abroad. This is important for our country." Nobile sighed inwardly with relief, doubtlessly reflecting that in these strange times it was just as well to have the blessing of the Duce.

Neither of them could foresee the disastrous effect the flight was to have on Italy's prestige. The whole enterprise was to cause the deaths of a great explorer and several other men, and disgrace, instead of glory, for Nobile.

A hot-tempered man, Nobile had not endeared himself to the world of aviation and science by picking a quarrel with one of the greatest living polar explorers, the legendary Norwegian Roald Amundsen. In 1926 Umberto Nobile had commanded a flight of the airship *Norge* to the Pole. Amundsen and the American Ellsworth had been aboard. They had crossed the hitherto unexplored basin of the Arctic to Cape Barrow and landed at Teller on the Bering Sea. For Nobile it was a considerable achievement. The volatile general seized on the occasion to make a virulent attack on Amundsen: "Some of us spent the entire time gazing out of the gondola. The real explorer was the pilot."

Amundsen retorted: "You are a military marionette, a braggart and a boaster." He pointed out that on several occasions Nobile had nearly wrecked the airship, that his knowledge of navigation was deplorable. "He knows nothing about the Poles and can't even ski. He should confine himself to rowing boats."

"Shameful, disgusting lies!" screamed Mussolini's enforcedly subservient Press. "The honour of Italy has been insulted."

The truth was that one of Italy's sons had been deeply insulted. His attempt to make a name for himself in polar exploration had left a legacy of bitterness and hurt pride.

Nobile felt that he must make the flight again; but this time it would be an all-Italian affair: an *Italian* airship and an *Italian* crew. There would be no insulting foreigners.

On 14 April 1928 the dirigible *Italia* slipped her moorings and passed over Milan. On board were six mechanics — Arduino, Carati, Alessandrini, Pomella, Ceccioni and Ciocca. The two wireless operators were Pedretti and Biagi. The Italian Navy was represented by Lieutenant-Commander Mariano, Lieutenant-Commander Zappi and Lieutenant Viglieri. The engineer was Trojani. The knowledge of the expedition's scientist, Pontremoli, became a godsend for copy to the two journalists, Tomaselli and Lago, who had been invited to accompany the expedition. It is unlikely that Nobile particularly relished the presence of foreign scientists, even as observers, but it would have been difficult to exclude such influential men as the Czech Franz Behounek and the Swede Finn Malmgren.

For all his declared approval, Mussolini's practical help to the expedition was remarkably parsimonious. A decidedly creaky cable ship, the *Citta di Milano*, was based at Spitzbergen. On board were placed eight military skiers; they would have been of limited value in an emergency. The lack of co-operation by the government was puzzling. Possibly Mussolini was cute enough to avoid giving the expedition publicized support. It would be prudent to wait for success to be achieved before attributing it to the newly aroused spirit of the Italian nation.

The *Italia* was a long way from her first stopping point, Stolp in Pomerania, when she flew into a violent storm. Thunder threatened to blow her out of the sky. It looked as if lightning might slice her in two. Several times she dipped towards the earth, only to be saved by swift manipulation of the rudder by Nobile himself. It was a very tired and battered *Italia* that touched down at the end of her first leg. But after a couple of weeks' stay in Germany, she set off gamely for Spitzbergen.

Only the weather was worrying. Spitzbergen was veiled in mist, and Nobile thought seriously of postponing the trip. It was then that Malmgren dropped his bombshell: he said he had to be back in Sweden by August and would not be free for any polar trip after that. To have excluded even one foreign member of the crew would have delighted Nobile, but Malmgren was the only man on board with all-round experience of the polar regions. The ultimatum gave urgency to the project, so when the weather looked up a little on 22 May Nobile decided to take his chance. At 4.38 a.m., sped on her way by the cheers of some 150 spectators, the airship roared into life and made for the Pole.

All seemed well at first. Wireless operators aboard the elderly *Citta di Milano* picked up reports of the smooth progress of the *Italia*. The distance to the Pole narrowed — 200 miles; 150 miles; 100 miles. Then came a blow: some 60 miles from the objective a curtain of black cloud made its menacing appearance. It was a brave decision to carry on in the hope that the cloud would lift. The *Italia* was sucked into dark nothingness, then at about midnight the clouds parted and the sun smiled. The latitude was 89.30°; the North Pole should be twenty minutes away.

As Nobile and other survivors were later to testify, he was beside himself with joy. With Latin fervour he declared: "We *shall* triumph." A member of the crew was more taciturn: "Latitude 90°," he announced. There were congratulations all round; then all went to the windows to stare down at the icy Polar vastness.

A gramophone was solemnly produced; the Italian National Anthem was played; the crew toasted each other in egg-punch. The Pole had been reached, and Italians had done it. The glorious name of Italy — the Duce's Italy — had been vindicated. Nobile had triumphed. Proud, flowery messages were dispatched — to the Duce, to the King of Italy, to the Pope. A symbolic cross, presented to Nobile by His Holiness, was dropped on to the ice.

At some point in these celebrations, someone pointed out mildly that a mist was beginning to gather around the *Italia*. Nobile felt thwarted. He had dreamed of descending on to the ice and of bringing back pictures and technical data to confirm his feat. Now the weather was robbing him of the chance. The engines of the *Italia*, which had hummed gently above the Pole, throbbed with power and, through the encroaching mist, the airship swung away on its return journey. The sun vanished abruptly.

A sharp wind began driving the *Italia* off course to the east. Nobile started to worry about his position. The friendly voice of the *Citta di Milano* was audible enough, but it could only aid him approximately in calculating his whereabouts. Nobile was urged to move as quickly as possible to shake off the appalling weather conditions. Now there was no more self-congratulation, as everyone realized that the mists and winds should have been anticipated. Valuable time had been wasted over the egg-punch. Ahead, at King's Bay, the wireless team picked up a string of urgent demands from the *Italia*: "Where are we?" "What is our position?" It was clear that Nobile had lost his way. He and his crew stared ahead into the inky blackness.

Nobile kept repeating, "We *must* be over Spitzbergen. Why can't I see it?"

The very last degree of power was wrung from the engines of the *Italia*. Even at 30 miles an hour the wind, now at storm intensity, held her almost stationary in the sky. Every so often buffets of wind would throw her even more violently off course.

Odd cracklings and mumblings reached the wireless men at Spitzbergen. Then there was sudden silence. At first no one was worried but reasoned that Nobile might not be answering for the simple reason that he had nothing to say. As the hours wore on the anxiety developed and grew. Something had happened to the radio of the *Italia*; and that could so easily mean that the airship herself was in trouble.

It was exactly what it did mean. Despite the foul weather conditions the *Italia* was in reasonable mechanical shape. But on 25 May her elevator suddenly jammed. At 9.25 she began to lose height, until the ice stretched a mere 500 feet below. At any moment jagged crests could slice through the base of her hull. Then miraculously the airship checked her descent and even rose a little. But it was a temporary respite.

Umberto Nobile stared hypnotized at the variometer which told him the extent to which the *Italia* was rising or falling. She was dropping rapidly — and there was nothing anyone could do to stop her.

The survivors testified to a great roar which filled the airship as she struck the ice. Nobile, a devout Catholic, recalls stretching out his arms in supplication. Instead, he encountered cold so intense that he cried out in agony. Was this the cold of Death? He opened his eyes and gingerly moved forward. Unspeakable pain lanced through him; the limpness of a broken leg and arm told him why. And the great cold was explained — he was clinging to the ice. Yet, despite broken limbs, he was alive.

To his astonishment the *Italia* was still in the air above him. *It must be an illusion! Perhaps he was dead after all...*

Then he realized that she was a very sad airship indeed, her tail dragging low as she drifted eastward, rather than flew. Her envelope was all slack and creased. A sinister collection of cables and spars hung from her, making her look rather like an untidy giant ball of wool.

Nobile could not conceive what had happened. As he could hardly move, he could only guess the fate of those of his companions who lay scattered around him on the ice. Trojani, the engineer, his face pouring blood, was barely recognizable as he staggered towards his Commander. Later Nobile was to recall Lieutenant-Commander Mariano moaning over and over again, "Where is Nobile? Where is Nobile?" Dimly through his pain Nobile was able to distinguish Ceccioni, Behounek, Malmgren and Viglieri. He could see no sign of the others.

Then the truth dawned. The *Italia* must have been sliced by jagged ice and then risen again, in the process decanting some of the crew as if they had been coal from an upended sack. The rest must still be aboard.

Nobile's attention was distracted momentarily by the news that the dead body of Pomella, one of the mechanics, had been found. "At least it was a quick end," he commented. What Fate had in store for the rest of them, either on the ice or helpless in the crippled airship, seemed less decisive. It seemed they must all surely die, but less mercifully — they had no shelter, no food and no wireless. Then came a delighted shout from Biagi. Amongst a scattered pile of wreckage, he had discovered a wireless set. Fevered examination showed it to be in perfect order. Immediately an appeal was sent to the *Citta di Milano* in Spitzbergen.

Back came the reply: "*Italia* keep up your courage. We are coming to your assistance."

Encouraged, Biagi began giving details of their plight, to which he received the identical reply: "*Italia* keep up your courage. We are coming to your assistance." Again and again this stereotype message was repeated. It was clear that Biagi's transmissions were not being received. This was confirmed later by transmissions heard from European radio stations. All were asking anxiously: "Why has no message of any kind been received from the *Italia*?" Patiently, Biagi repeated their predicament; that they were on drift-ice, that they needed food and clothing. Every hour their message was repeated, only to fall on deaf ears. To keep their mind off things, the little group of survivors continued, during the days that followed, to listen to the set on which for some unknown reason they could not transmit.

It was a gloomy experience until, on 6 June, Biagi, who was listening idly to a short-wave station in Sao Paolo, suddenly began to scribble, in trembling excitement. He told Nobile, "We are in luck. Some Russian radio ham has heard us. The Italian Ambassador has been told." Nobile, still in severe pain, was overjoyed. Then Biagi had another bit of luck. He managed to make contact with *Citta di Milano*. It looked as if everything was going to be all right after all. But for three of Nobile's companions the future was still uncertain. The Swedish scientist Malmgren and the two Italian Naval Officers, Zappi and Mariano, had set off on foot in search of land. No one knew where they were.

Whether deliberately or by sheer mismanagement, the Italian Government was remarkably inconsistent when it came to informing the public about what was happening. Contradictions were frequent and bewildering. "The *Italia* is no more, but all members of the crew are safe," one report declared. Another announced gravely that the *Italia* had vanished with most of the crew and that Nobile and his companions faced death on drifting ice.

The most sensible way — perhaps the only way — of rescuing those marooned in the polar reaches seemed to be by air. A number of aircraft took off from Spitzbergen, but although they made extensive flights they saw not a trace of the conspicuous red tent which Nobile had found and managed to set up precariously on the drifting ice. It was certainly ironic, but entirely understandable, that would-be rescuers should turn to Roald Amundsen for advice.

Amundsen did not hesitate. He and Nobile were fellow explorers. The quarrels of the past counted for nothing.

Amundsen set off to search in a Latham hydroplane — duly to disappear himself, a mystery within the mystery of the *Italia*. So the initiative for rescue operations passed out of the hands of the Italians and into those of the Russians.

The Soviets did not send an aircraft to the polar regions. They sent an ice-breaker, the *Leonid Krassin*, reckoned to be the best in the world. This inelegant, lumbering hulk, with long twin funnels, rounded hull and sharp bows resembling a hatchet, happened to be in Norwegian waters and was swiftly directed towards Nobile. She could, if necessary, count on the assistance of the *Malygin* which was at Novaya Zemlya, the boomerang-shaped island which lay between the Barents Sea and the Kara Sea, due south of Franz Josef Land. As it turned out, the position of the *Malygin* rendered her useless in rescue operations.

The *Krassin*, with the goodwill of the world speeding her, soon became engulfed in wispy curtains of mist which were never-absent sentinels guarding the polar regions. Fortunately this was not as bad as it had been during Nobile's aerial journey, but progress was slow. On 30 June the distinguished Soviet scientist Professor Samoilovitch, in charge of the operation, was handed a message by the *Krassin*'s wireless operator. To his amazement, it proved to be from Nobile, begging permission to board the *Krassin* and continue the search for his marooned comrades.

The message was no hoax. How on earth Nobile had managed to escape on his own, and why he had abandoned those with whom he had been imprisoned on the ice floe, no one could understand. The message had been transmitted from the *Citta di Milano*, aboard which Nobile had been for the past four days. When the news reached Italy it threw Mussolini, already furious at the loss of the *Italia*, into a towering rage. For a commander to leave his crew, for however short a time, was regarded as inexcusable. The Duce ordered that Nobile was to be placed under arrest aboard the *Citta di Milano*. There the chastened aeronaut heard over the radio grim news from Samoilovitch; the *Krassin* had encountered unyielding ice. Each movement forward had to be followed by at least two retreats to build up the power of the engines, so that endless manoeuvrings were needed to cover the shortest distance. On 3 July a blade of the starboard screw snapped. The *Krassin* was immobile and useless.

Aboard the *Citta di Milano*, Nobile raged helplessly. Amidst all the emotionalism, he explained why he had abandoned his men. His red tent had eventually been spotted from the air and supplies had been dropped. Rescue had seemed to be imminent. Eventually, a single aircraft with skis had landed, piloted by a Swedish airman named Lundborg who had told Nobile, "It is your duty to help us find your comrades on the *Italia*. I am taking you off and then coming back for the injured men." This was easy enough to say, but none of the other aircraft taking part in the search could land or take off on ice. On one of his trips following the rescue of Nobile, Lundborg crashed, finding himself a prisoner on the ice with the rest. Things now looked bad indeed. Both the *Krassin* and the most promising of the rescue aircraft were out of commission.

The *Krassin* had an aircraft on board. Nobile begged Samoilovitch to use it for a general reconnaissance. Pilot Tchuknovski took off on the morning of 10 July. All day Samoilovitch remained on watch in the ship's wireless cabin, to be rewarded by two messages. The first stated that the "Malmgren group" had been sighted in the neighbourhood of Charles XII Island; the second, that Tchuknovski had force-landed near Cape Wrede. Rescue from there, Samoilovitch knew, would be relatively simple, and Tchuknovski could be safely left for subsequent rescue while the problem of forcing a passage to Charles XII Island was tackled. Samoilovitch vowed that so long as he commanded the *Krassin* this clumsy hulk would be bullied on its way. Repairs had her mobile again and the usual procedures followed — a frontal attack on the ice, making a crack, a retreat, then a run-up for the final breakthrough, the ship's whistle sounding a constant message of hope for the survivors' ears. The hours wore on without sign of them. Had the pilot mistaken birds for men? Had he *imagined* he had spotted Malmgren and the others? Every available crewmember was on deck, eyes aching from hours of staring through binoculars.

Eventually two scarecrow figures were spotted, one of them pathetically waving a ragged makeshift flag. The *Krassin* lumbered alongside. A party was landed. The inevitable questions, *"Are you Malmgren?" "Where are the rest?"* were greeted with blank stares. The Italians could not understand a word that the Russians were saying. But the name "Malmgren" brought a grim reaction. The two rescued men — they were Zappi and Mariano — pointed to the sea and made a thumbs-down gesture.

They were interrogated aboard the *Krassin*, a thankless business, since no one had more than a smattering of Italian. It appeared that Malmgren had become totally exhausted, insisted that he was prejudicing the chances of his companions and had begged to be left.

"Did you leave him?" the interrogator asked sternly.

"We felt that saving General Nobile was our first duty," was Zappi's reply. "Malmgren begged us to dig his grave and finish him with a hatchet. He couldn't bear to suffer any longer."

There was a horrified silence. "We refused to kill him," Zappi continued. "We simply left him and he waved at us frantically to go on."

Like a hound on the scent the *Krassin* broke her way through the ice with renewed vigour, depending on the *Citta di Milano* to guide her direction; and at 8.15 p.m. on 14 July, the rescue party of the *Krassin* warmly embraced the smiling survivors whom Nobile had left behind. Their spirits had remained high. An aircraft had arrived a few days before to take off Lundborg, so everyone had known that rescue was at hand.

It was a story that could in the nature of things only have a partially happy ending. The mysterious death of Malmgren remained a sinister mystery. Reports that the *Italia* herself with the rest of the crew had been recovered, proved to be false. Other ships continued the hunt, but in vain. Meanwhile, the Swedish Government, concerned over the fate of Malmgren, demanded an impartial inquiry into the whole affair. The Fascist Press, as quickly indignant as ever at the slightest hint of criticism, described Zappi and Mariano as "men of honour whose word cannot and will not be doubted". The Italian Government rejected all requests for an independent inquiry, though Mussolini offered to set up one of his own. The results were predictable: everyone had acted with supreme conscientiousness; none was to blame; Zappi and Mariano had behaved like true patriots. A scapegoat was, however, necessary. General Nobile was held responsible for neglecting his airship and causing it to crash. He resigned his rank and became a recluse, eventually leaving Italy to live and work in the Soviet Union.

Neither the *Italia* nor any trace of her occupants has been found to this day. At the time, determined and experienced Polar explorers searched widely, many of them impelled to do so not only out of compassion for the eight men of Nobile's expedition who might be awaiting rescue somewhere in the ice, but from anxiety for the safety of Roald Amundsen.

The great explorer had vanished without trace; yet there seemed more hope for him and the crew of his Latham hydroplane than for the *Italia* survivors, if any. Amundsen was one of those men who seem to be invincible, indestructible. No matter what had befallen him, it was believed, he would overcome it. If his aircraft had been forced down he would lead his companions confidently to safety. As likely as not he had found the *Italia* but had been unable to convey the news by wireless. A whole crop of rumours sprang up about his having been sighted, having actually returned, having been in radio contact — but all proved false.

On 5 September a fishing smack sighted what its master took to be a floating oil barrel. It was a hydroplane's wing float. It was hurried back to Tromsö where a mechanic who had worked on Amundsen's aircraft identified it by a small copper patch he had put on it to stop a leak. The float was undamaged, suggesting that there had been no crash: perhaps it had been used as a raft, or to convey a message. It was opened, but there was nothing inside.

The Polar winter set in and prevented further rescue attempts. More were made the following year — Amundsen's countrymen were determined to spare no effort to find their hero. They never succeeded. The eventual finding of the Andrée expedition's remains, with its diaries and photographs (see "Balloon over the North Pole") gives us some little hope that we may yet know what became of the *Italia* party and of Amundsen. Meanwhile, the Polar vastness keeps its secrets to itself.

15: THE LESSON OF *YOKE PETER*

Referring to the 490-passenger Boeing 747 "Jumbo Jet", an American civil-aeronautics official is reported as having said, "If one of these goes down it would be a disaster like the *Titanic*."

Aircraft are designed and controlled so as *not* to go down, and people travel in them on the assumption that the statistics which show flying to be the safest of all means of transport will not suffer a setback while they themselves are involved. Unlike the early days of aviation, when a pilot's individual skill and the doubtful adequacy of an engine decided whether a flight would be accomplished safely or not, there are not many chances left to be taken today. The aircraft designer knows pretty well to a certainty that what he has planned will succeed, and exhaustive testing of his product confirms or denies this. Meteorologists have the weather fairly well taped. Ways of communication that would have staggered the pioneers do everything but fly the aircraft (to a large extent they do that, too), making the pilot and crew human adjuncts to a machine in a highly sophisticated system.

Yet, rarely though they do, things can go wrong through error, criminal interference, or freak circumstance. One of the greatest attributes of the aircraft industry has always been its determination and ability to learn its tragic lessons and ensure through them that every mishap which could have been avoided with more skill, more knowledge, more precaution, leaves flying that much safer than before it occurred. Perhaps the classic example of this is the case of *Yoke Peter*.

Yoke Peter was a Comet, registration number G-ALYP; hence its name, the phonetics for YP in the old Civil Aviation Organization alphabet. (It would be "Yankee Papa" today.) When the Second World War ended the lead in air transportation was America's without dispute. Her shorter involvement in the war and her industrial might had enabled her to end hostilities the possessor of vast numbers of military transport aircraft of the latest types. Recognizing that these would otherwise soon be left redundant on its hands, the U.S. Government released thousands of them as surplus to requirements. They were snapped up by established airlines and by countless small-time operators, many of them Air Force veterans, determined to be in at the beginning of what looked like being the greatest boom-time aviation had known.

Yet, although some of these aircraft were perhaps the best of their kind in existence and were eagerly sought by airlines throughout the world including Britain, they merely represented improvements upon existing concepts of design. This was true, too, of brand-new types about to emerge. The Douglas DC-6, the first new type of airliner to be introduced in the United States after the war, and revolutionary in being the first commercial aircraft to have reversible pitch propellers, could carry just over fifty passengers at a cruising speed of only something over 300 miles per hour, for all its size and power. The fastest U.S. transport aircraft, a modified military type, was the 400 miles per hour Republic Rainbow; and in 1946 supplies were not yet available.

It did not represent all that much of a step forward from what had gone immediately before. American designers were, of course, looking beyond the present, though along vistas whose end was yet far beyond their sight. Their minds were occupied with means of applying to civil aircraft the gas-turbine engine developed by Sir Frank Whittle in England and Heinkel in Germany. The new American P-84 jet fighter set up a national speed record of 611 miles per hour in California in 1946 and brought the jet age a stage nearer; but, more significantly in that year, a Lancastrian bomber in England suddenly began flying 100 miles per hour faster than any other Lancastrian could. Two of its four reciprocating engines had been replaced by jets.

With vision matched by courage, the de Havilland company determined upon a bold course. It would throw in its lot with the jet age by designing and building the world's first commercial jet aircraft. It would "put a girdle round the earth", if not in forty minutes, then at least twice as fast as any airliner in existence. No one doubted the implications of this: it would take flying into new realms, face it with unexplored hazards perhaps more suddenly than was prudent.

But all pioneering requires some risk-taking. The only alternative is to plod along with the rest and watch some more ardent spirit dash first to the goal. De Havilland preferred to take the risk and took it brilliantly, backed, to their great credit, by British Overseas Airways Corporation and the Ministry of Transport, both of whom risked millions of pounds ordering Comets straight from the drawing board. In July 1949, just under three years after the design team had begun its work, the prototype Comet, *Victor George*, flew for the first time. When it was first shown to the public, flown by test-pilot John Cunningham at the Farnborough Air Display that year, it staggered experts and laymen alike by its superb lines, its exciting new take-off technique, and the possibilities it revealed. It was the future brought to the present in one superb gesture.

The building of more Comets went ahead fast. BOAC took delivery of the first few of its fleet and began proving flights at once. On 2 May 1952 *Yoke Peter* took off before big crowds at London Airport, to inaugurate the world's first turbojet transport service, between London and South Africa. Three weeks later the Queen Mother and Princess Margaret became the first royal passengers since the Comet had come into service — the Duke of Edinburgh having characteristically managed to get a flight while proving was still in progress.

An increasing fleet of Comets began to earn back the huge investment BOAC had made. They were flown by a new elite amongst airline pilots, specially chosen and trained for an exacting role — for the Comet was not an easy aircraft to handle. By the end of 1952 there had been a number of accidents at take-off and landing. One Comet had been written off, fortunately with only one slight casualty, and the operating instructions had had to be revised. The following year was only a few weeks old when a more serious crash occurred, at Karachi, killing all aboard. On 2 May, the precise anniversary of the Comet's triumphant first commercial flight, disaster came again. Near Calcutta, *Yoke Victor* flew into a violent monsoon storm and disintegrated, killing 43 passengers and crew. A French-owned Comet overshot a runway at Dakar in West Africa and became a write-off. There were several minor mishaps as well in a tally which by now amounted to a disturbingly bad record. It was soon to be far worse.

Yoke Peter left Rome's Ciampino Airport for London at 9.30 a.m. on Sunday, 10 January 1954, piloted by Captain Alan Gibson, a former R.A.F. pilot with several thousand hours of flying to his credit, much of it on Comets. The aircraft passed over the Orbetello beacon at 26,000 feet, Captain Gibson radioing progress reports all the way towards the planned cruising altitude of 36,000 feet. As the Comet headed out to sea in the direction of the island of Elba at 9.51, Captain Gibson called up a colleague piloting an Argonaut airliner which had left Ciampino shortly before. His message, about a routine matter, had barely begun when it broke off abruptly.

Two Elba fishermen, Giovanni di Marco and Luigi Papi, heard from their boat the whine of an aircraft. Then there were three explosions in quick succession. After a pause, a "silver thing" rocketed towards the sea, smoke billowing from it. By the time the fishermen had reached the spot there was little they could do beyond, with the help of other vessels which joined them, take aboard some 15 of the bodies. It was obvious that there would be no survivors from *Yoke Peter*'s crew of six, and 29 passengers.

There was no obvious explanation for what had happened. The aircraft had been at the correct height, the weather calm and clear. There was no reason to suspect sabotage. The unpalatable conclusion was that if faulty repairs or servicing had not been responsible — as some were ready to contend they had — then there must have existed some structural fault. BOAC grounded all Comets immediately. An investigation committee, after intense deliberation, announced that an electrical failure was the probable cause and listed some sixty suggestions for modification. By 23 March the Comets were operating again.

Then, on Thursday, 8 April 1954, came a fresh disaster. The BOAC Comet I, G-ALYY, on charter to South African Airways, crashed into the sea off Naples after leaving Rome for Cairo. It seemed the end of the road for Comets. Their Certificate of Airworthiness was withdrawn. For de Havilland it was a crippling blow. The company had been in the forefront of British aviation since the dawn of flying. It had taken very real economic risks in developing jet travel, and now stood to lose £40 million worth of orders for the discredited Comet. For the entire industry it was a crisis situation; but the Government was not inactive. After the January disaster the Prime Minister, Winston Churchill, had called an immediate Cabinet meeting and dispatched the Minister of Transport and Civil Aviation, Mr Lennox-Boyd, to Elba to investigate.

Clearly, no decisive conclusions could be reached until as much as possible of *Yoke Peter* had been recovered from the bottom of the Mediterranean. This implied an elaborate salvage operation. The nearest British naval base to the disaster, Malta, was contacted promptly. Victor Campbell, Senior Admiralty Salvage Officer, was keen to help but had to point out that neither his divers nor any available equipment could get down farther than 200 feet. *Yoke Peter* lay in water that varied between 450 and 600 feet deep. Malta could be useful in the salvage work, but considerably more help was obviously needed.

Following the principle of going unhesitatingly to the top for major assistance, Mr Lennox-Boyd was soon asking his secretary to connect him with a telephone number near Romsey in Hampshire. In the study of his country home, Broadlands, Earl Mountbatten of Burma, Commander-in-Chief, Mediterranean, was soon hearing all about *Yoke Peter*. His reported reaction was, "Let my salvage firm handle it." If he did use the expression, it was an elaborately casual term for the Mediterranean Fleet. There was nothing even remotely casual about the order the C-in-C issued. He wanted *Yoke Peter* found — and quickly.

The undertaking was by no means easy. The aircraft lay not only in twice the depth of water that any available gear, however sophisticated, could tackle, but could be anywhere within 100 square miles south of Elba. The fishermen had been quite unable to pinpoint the position of the crash. Lord Mountbatten put the ball firmly back in Malta's court, but made it plain that Victor Campbell, now Director of Operations, could have all the help he wanted from Britain. Malta herself could provide the salvage vessel *Sea Salvor* for which the Boom Defence vessel H.M.S. *Barhill* could lay moorings. It was a start; but underwater salvage is an intricate trade and its tools are a load of highly technical ironmongery, many of which, such as observation chambers, a grab, and underwater television, Malta did not possess. Contact was made with the Director of Boom Defence and Marine Salvage back in Britain, with the result that an imposing and efficient salvage force was quickly assembled. This included, besides *Barhill* and *Sea Salvor*, Captain C. M. Parry's H.M.S. *Wrangler* and Lieutenant-Commander Stern's *Sursay*, which would lay marker buoys on any contact. In addition, the two trawlers *Ravilla* and *Carmelina*, chartered through the Anglo-Mediterranean Salvage Company, were assigned to trawl in a northerly direction over the search area. Each vessel was armed with all manner of detecting equipment, including an observation chamber from which an observer, sitting on a revolving seat, could have an all-round view of the marine depths. The Admiralty took on the job of hunting for suitable underwater-television equipment and operators and many other items on this money-no-object shopping list.

As luck would have it an aircraft of Skyways Ltd had flown over the disaster area at the time of the crash, en route for the Middle East. It had photographed boats picking up bodies and wreckage. The salvage people were interested to see a print showing a corner of Elba which made the fixing of an approximate position possible. The search was begun there, but was hampered when *Sea Salvor* and *Barhill* became storm-bound for a week and then had to contend with a gale that made further work impossible. The underwater TV could only record what it saw and this, in many cases, turned out to be a muddy nothing, as gales made the ocean bed look like a London pea soup fog. Camera cables became tangled with marker wire which meant minor but irritatingly expensive waste of time.

There were moments of exhilaration, followed by groans of disappointment as the relic of some wartime sinking was dragged to the surface. Things looked up considerably, though, when on 10 February *Sea Salvor* was positioned on a full set of moorings. She carried with her an enormous toothed grab which seized on a large piece of begrimed wreckage from the aircraft's rear and, amid cheers, deposited it on deck. It was only a start, followed by days of utter frustration when nothing was discovered at all. Then *Sea Salvor* scored more triumphs with the plane's pressure dome and some passenger seats.

Storms of a kind that are never to be seen in the more seductive travel posters lashed the Mediterranean mercilessly, forcing most of the salvage fleet into harbour. But there was no putting off *Sea Salvor*. She worried on, her crew hourly expecting her already battered moorings to be cut to ribbons. During a lull she lowered the observation chamber and spotted the centre section, wing spars and two engines of *Yoke Peter*. After several further days of small finds and unidentified debris, the undercarriage and the other engines were hauled up. The real triumph came, though, when the powerful grab, guided slowly and laboriously by the man in the observation chamber, fastened on the biggest catch of all. It was a long, slow haul to the surface, but the prize was the Comet's forward components including the entire cockpit. With the finding of smaller items like sections of wing, flaps and flight instruments, Lord Mountbatten's faith in his "firm" had been amply justified. By the time "Operation Elba Isle" had completed its main phase, three-quarters of *Yoke Peter* had been salvaged.

The stage had now been reached where de Havilland had to give an account of itself, as the Government demanded on behalf of the public a full analysis of what had happened to this and the other crashed Comets. Most of the pieces of the jigsaw were to hand; it was a question of fitting them together. This task was assigned to Britain's leading aeronautical engineering body, the Royal Aircraft Establishment at Farnborough.

At this point a remarkable figure makes his entrance. During the war Arnold Hall had, as a highly skilled "boffin", kept out of the limelight and worked feverishly on research into new weapons. All his life he had exhibited a healthy, if sometimes alarming curiosity. Even as a child he had that curious indifference to the safety of himself and others which scientists sometimes exhibit: he had blown up his mother's kitchen while testing fireworks in an oven. The son of a furniture dealer, he had gone up to Cambridge on a mathematics scholarship and had fitted effortlessly into a career in aeronautical science. At the age of 36, a precocious and brilliant talent had been awarded with a knighthood. And now Sir Arnold Hall, F.R.S., Director of the R.A.E., Farnborough, was the man chosen to probe the mystery of the Comets. He had with him some of the finest aeronautical scientists in the world.

He began by announcing that every single fragment of *Yoke Peter* would be examined thoroughly. No part of the structure was free from suspicion and nothing would be discarded until the experts had given it complete clearance. Instead of theorizing they would work on an actual Comet. *Yoke Uncle*, an exact counterpart of *Yoke Peter*, was provided, probably the most expensive guineapig in history.

The experts had already suspected that metal fatigue had led to a pressure explosion of the aircraft. At sea level the pressure of air upon the human body is about 14.7lb per square inch. The higher one ascends, the less the air pressure becomes, until there arrives a point where the body cannot tolerate the difference. In an aircraft flying at, say, 30,000 feet pressure must be artificially increased, or crew and passengers could not survive. The effect of thus raising the pressure inside the aircraft greatly above that of the atmosphere through which it is flying, is to transform what is basically a tube of metal into a flying "bomb" of compressed air which a flaw could cause to "explode" with disastrous results.

To find out whether this had, in fact, happened in the case of *Yoke Peter* it was necessary to see how much punishment from pressure *Yoke Uncle* could take. A steel tank, over 100 feet long, 20 feet wide and 16 feet deep, was constructed at Farnborough and *Yoke Uncle* was placed inside it, wings protruding. For the Comet's Certificate of Airworthiness the de Havilland company had been required to design for a minimum pressure differential one-and-a-half times that to be experienced in flight. They had carried the margin even further in the interests of extra safety and had carried out pressure tests on cabin mock-ups. Now, Farnborough proceeded to test *Yoke Uncle* to a point where something must give. The question was, what would give first?

When *Yoke Uncle* had been placed in the tank, both tank and aircraft interior were filled with water whose pressure could be controlled. The use of air, obviously the ideal, would have been too dangerous. But an object damaged by water subjected to internal pressure could usually be repaired and used again. *Yoke*

Uncle had made something like 1,200 pressurized flights before she took on her new role and this wear had to be taken into account in all calculations. Over several weeks, pressurization tests up to 11lb per square inch were conducted. Nothing dramatic happened, yet reams of data were compiled, studied and filed. Nothing yet answered the vital question of what had caused *Yoke Peter* and the other Comets to explode with such suddenness? The Government badgered Farnborough for results, but the patient scientists worked calmly on.

Suddenly, during one test, metal on each side of a tiny rivet near a cabin window began to crack. This was the first confirmation of their belief that metal fatigue had, like some deathwatch beetle, been eating into *Yoke Peter*. But no expert at Farnborough yet knew at what precise point metal fatigue had proved fatal to the crashed aircraft. If at this point the Navy felt relieved that its gruelling salvage marathon was over it was mistaken. The experts demanded still more debris. They suspected it must exist, because as well as conducting the experiment in the tank Sir Arnold Hall had ordered that tiny wooden models of Comets should be built and then deliberately exploded. This had enabled Farnborough staff to calculate that fragments of wreckage must have been strewn over a greater area of the Elba waters than had hitherto been supposed. The Navy was instructed to find them.

All Comets were still officially grounded, but Sir Arnold persuaded the authorities into letting his team have one to fly. At appalling risks, of which they were in the best position to be aware, the scientists flew the aircraft in all conditions, even in the most dangerous weathers. The exercise was useful, but still did not get to the root of the problem, which lay inescapably in examining more bits of *Yoke Peter*. Meanwhile, the Navy combed a wider area of the ocean floor. By 12 August several pieces of cabin roof had been recovered and there was more useful information gleaned from the results of dredging by an Italian fishing vessel. The Farnborough tank trials and tests with model aircraft were intensified.

During the weeks that followed, scientists working on these various investigations became more and more interested in a section of *Yoke Uncle* near to the direction-finding aerial (ADF) in the forward end of the fuselage. Could this be the cause of the explosion, with the damage to the cabin rivet, discovered earlier, merely a foretaste of what was to come? The question was academic until such pieces as survived of the ADF section of *Yoke Peter* could be recovered, so that the two parts might be compared. Eventually the Mediterranean yielded up the ADF part. Its state matched that of its counterpart in *Yoke Uncle*, damaged during the tests. Here was the weak point.

Even before the Comet disasters, the effects to be expected from sudden decompression had been known. Tests had been carried out with dummy passengers seated in mock-up cabins and recorded by slow-motion photography. The results had been grim, showing that a passenger sitting next to a window which suddenly failed would be sucked instantaneously out of that window. Brilliant work by Italian medical specialists who had examined the bodies from *Yoke Peter* had confirmed that they had suffered violent decompression and had been hurled helplessly upward from their seats. The scientists at Farnborough had to know beyond the slightest doubt the full particulars of the disaster; and now they discovered what had not been known before — that the failure of part of a pressurized fuselage, whether due to metal fatigue or any other cause, could result in a great gash running instantly from that point along the entire fuselage. From the tests on *Yoke Uncle*, from their examination of the fragments of *Yoke Peter*, and the

218

Italians' findings from the victims' remains, they saw at last what had occurred; and literally saw it by making it happen to models.

The complete evidence was presented to a public inquiry and accepted. Able to recognize its enemy, the de Havilland company was enabled to return to its work of producing a new, safer breed of Comets which, four years later, inaugurated the first pure jet passenger service across the North Atlantic, an historic link-up which, but for a classic of plodding investigation and deduction, might have been many more years delayed.

16: THE LOST TYCOON

It would doubtless have pleased Alfred Loewenstein, late of the Belgian Army, to know that the exact cause of his death in July 1928 would still be a source of perplexity today. For Loewenstein, czar of big business, the very ultimate in tycoonery, was a man who lived his whole life at a high pitch of drama; so it was fitting that his end should be of a kind that might have appealed to a thriller writer.

He boarded an aircraft on 4 July at Croydon to fly to Brussels. At a certain point on that journey he vanished, leaving only a flapping door as a clue to what happened to him.

It should be added that even these brief facts may not be facts at all. It may be that Loewenstein, who indisputably arrived at Croydon Airport for the flight, was at the last minute impersonated by someone else who climbed aboard in his place and who was cunning enough to vanish without trace, while the real Loewenstein stayed behind and made good an ingenious escape. In short, it is worth mentioning at the outset that nothing much in this extraordinary story can be accepted on trust. Very little about Loewenstein himself is straightforward.

Like many of his kind, he began with literally nothing. True, his father had been a rich Belgian banker, but the family business crashed when Alfred was still in his teens. The young Loewenstein, however, had finance in his blood. He was certainly not the type to bow to misfortune. He had a genius for investment and speculation and even before the First World War had made himself an exceedingly wealthy man.

The Europe in which he operated after 1918 was in complete economic chaos. Elephantiasis afflicted the currencies of just about every country, a fact which Loewenstein was quick to exploit for his own ends. He would buy handsomely on credit and rely on currency depreciation to ensure him enormous profits when the time came for him to pay up. He backed his own judgement and knowledge of the markets to the full and was seldom disappointed. There are still enormously rich men in the world today, despite the fact that Europe is decidedly more socialized than it was in the time of Loewenstein; yet it is unlikely that even a man with the fortune of a Paul Getty could become quite such a formidable creditor as did the Alfred Loewenstein of 1926.

Until then, most of his dealings had been with individuals or with rich banks and giant corporations. Now he branched out and offered to cushion the resources of entire nations. The Belgian franc was in dire need of support? Very well, then Loewenstein was prepared to supply a prop to the tune of ten million pounds without interest. The French were in even worse straits? Loewenstein was prepared to be of assistance. Thirty million pounds could be quite easily forthcoming and at the beggarly interest of 2 per cent.

These countries were in extreme financial difficulties. They could not afford to disregard such an offer, even though it entailed Loewenstein himself investing the money through his syndicate and pocketing profits that could result in any increase of the market value of securities. One might ponder the moral as well as the economic climate of European nations that allowed themselves to be placed in hock to one man, however powerful. Perhaps we can only really understand their willingness to submit to Loewenstein in the context of a time when Europe had emerged tired and depressed (in every sense) from a dreadful war.

Alfred Loewenstein was not one of those wealthy hypocrites who pretend that money can afford no pleasure. He was prepared to be seen to be rich. He made enormous sums with extreme relish and spent them with an equal show of enjoyment. When Loewenstein swept down on Paris, London or New York, the World knew it. He lived well and with maximum ostentation: villa at Biarritz, a palace in Brussels, whole floors hired at the Ritz and Claridge's.

Yet no human is all of a piece. Alfred Loewenstein was no exception. One might reasonably have expected him to be of impressive appearance, a type to awe men of lesser achievement. Instead he was of modest, even nondescript, appearance. He dressed quietly and was as devout a Roman Catholic as he was a family man. He was approachable and genial, ruthless with inefficiency but generous towards those who served him well. Only a superabundance of energy gave a clue to his extraordinary success.

He had his enemies, of course. There were those who looked upon him as a contemptible parasite who battened on lesser nations and bled them dry. Amongst those who attended his superb parties he was understandably popular. He was a sportsman, entering a horse in (but not winning) the 1927 Grand National. His business methods made those who lacked his nerve positively blench, but at least everyone felt sure he was honest. Or was he? In common with many other international financiers, Alfred Loewenstein was frequently either about to launch or close a deal and, as often as not, was dangerously short of hard, if not paper, resources. So long as the international market held up he could survive handsomely. Then the money markets of the world were stunned by the

Wall Street crash. Countless companies, robbed of any space in which to manoeuvre, went into liquidation. Many of Alfred Loewenstein's associates were ruined. He himself was badly shaken and announced that from now on he would concentrate on stable financial enterprises; there would be no more speculation. Cynics said that he had lost his nerve — either that, or he realized that if he continued with his usual business methods certain unpleasant facts might be revealed.

Certainly some of Loewenstein's enemies were prepared to engineer his downfall. The Dreyfus brothers, founders of British Celanese, a company whose board Loewenstein had once controlled, were the financier's bitterest enemies. Both sides accused the other of conducting personal vendettas. It was alleged that Loewenstein was out for revenge after being dismissed from British Celanese. The company hinted — they could do no more — that they had enough evidence of Loewenstein's illegal activities to ensure that, if this were published, he would not be in a position to continue in business anywhere.

If this was true it could explain a good deal of what happened subsequently. Certainly someone knew a great deal more about Loewenstein than the financier considered healthy. Rumours began to circulate that there was in existence an extremely damaging dossier, disclosing that he was seeking to oust the Dreyfus brothers from British Celanese by share-juggling, showing him thoroughly incompetent when it came to advising would-be shareholders where to invest their money, and drawing a portrait of an utterly heartless business automaton, driven by an insatiable thirst for wealth and power. All this was unpleasant enough, but less successful businessmen were often just as culpable without anyone being particularly indignant with them. Nothing criminal was alleged.

Ah, but, it was whispered, the dossier contained a statement that was nakedly libellous and that, if true, would spell the finish of Alfred Loewenstein. There had been a jewel robbery in the financier's Biarritz villa to the tune of some £200,000. The robbery, claimed the dossier, was nothing but an elaborate swindle deliberately planned by Loewenstein for the insurance money. There were whispers that the financier was being blackmailed.

Even the most confident and extrovert of men might well have shown outward signs of worry with such rumours centred upon him, but when Loewenstein granted an interview to a journalist just before take-off at Croydon Airport he was his usual ebullient self. Asked about his feud with Dreyfus he replied belligerently: "I'll deal with him on my return."

Wherever Alfred Loewenstein went, his employees, if they wanted to keep their jobs, had to be on their toes constantly. There was an atmosphere of bustle as he strode determinedly into the entrance hall at Croydon and prepared to board his Amsterdam-built Fokker VII. This was one of a fleet of private aircraft, flown by crack pilots seconded from Imperial Airways. Loewenstein could never resist a touch of the dramatic and would frequently swoop down on unsuspecting crews after a terse telephone call announcing that he expected to be in the air within hours. He courted secrecy with an ardent devotion, adding to the image of awesome power that he was always seeking to project.

On this occasion Loewenstein was to be piloted by his favourite aviator, Donald Drew, of Imperial Airways. The financier did not seem to be in any particular hurry. He chatted for a few moments to the crew and airport officials and kept them waiting while he made a private business call. He made his usual great play of consulting the pilot and co-pilot on the flight ahead, and was told that weather conditions were good, that the flight at 4,000 feet would take about two hours. Loewenstein expressed himself satisfied and made to board the Fokker. Like a medieval monarch, secure and important while surrounded by his court, he was flanked by secretary, valet and two shorthand typists.

The layout of what was in fact a flying executive suite is important if we are to understand what followed — or what is believed to have followed. Loewenstein entered the aircraft by mounting a set of strutted metal steps, which remained in place outside the fuselage during flight. Immediately opposite, as he entered, was a mirror and washbasin, just aft of a toilet door which opened towards the aircraft entrance. This door which hinged forward also closed on the cabin, thus shutting off the cabin from the rest of the plane in flight. Its only use otherwise was to conceal the lavatory seat during embarkation and disembarkation. In flight it remained closed on the cabin, leaving the toilet and washbasin area clear.

Loewenstein took his place in the front of the aircraft, on the port side (the left), a table in front of him. Opposite him and facing aft was his secretary, Arthur Hodgson, who also had a table. The two men could thus give each other close attention during flight. Behind Loewenstein was the valet, Fred Baxter, and on his right were the two typists with a single table between them. Co-pilot Bob Little stayed beside the port engine until it roared into life. Then he climbed aboard, carefully securing — but not locking — the external door: if an aircraft had to be evacuated quickly after, say a forced landing, it could have been fatal to lose time by grappling with a locked door. The pressure of air on it during flight would be sufficient to keep it shut securely.

Bob Little believed that the man he saw when he entered the cabin was indeed the untidy, bulky figure of Alfred Loewenstein. A boyfriend of one of the secretaries was waving from the airport building, and swore later that he had recognized the financier looking out of one of the windows. There is no reason whatever for doubting that it was indeed Loewenstein who climbed aboard for the intended flight to Brussels. It was perfect flying weather, a beautiful summer's evening, as the Fokker VII, codename *York Ink*, climbed above Croydon, heading for Purley, Sevenoaks, Maidstone, Ashford. Bob Little took over the controls from Donald Drew. It was going to be a peaceful flight...

Alfred Loewenstein was indifferent to the form of transport he used and air travel had long ceased to hold any novelty for him. An aircraft, a train, even the back of a limousine, was simply another office. Typewriters clacked, documents were hastily scrutinized and signed. Hodgson was at the receiving end of a string of orders given in Loewenstein's Continental-accented, staccato tones.

Lympne Airfield picked up "Hello Lympne. *York Ink* calling. I am leaving the coast at South Foreland at 4,000ft, heading for Dunkirk. Destination is Brussels."

Soon the coast was slipping away and the Goodwin Sands came into view. Like a contented bird, the Fokker flew on calmly through the sun of a summer evening. When Alfred Loewenstein got up without coat, collar or tie and made for the toilet at the back of the aircraft, no one looked up or had any particular reason for doing so. To have removed so much clothing was perhaps unusual for him, yet there was no thought that the flight was causing him any discomfort. Loewenstein was big and middle-aged and, in common with many professional men who drive themselves hard, was said to have a weak heart. He simply might well have felt more at ease without his jacket. Co-pilot Little also recalled seeing Loewenstein poke his head out of the sliding window at one point, but this need not have indicated any feeling of illness. The unrestricted view was well worth seeing: Cap Gris Nez lay across the smooth carpet of the Channel. To the north was Harwich, south lay Le Treport and Dieppe. Alfred Loewenstein, however, was little concerned with views. They were not a source of profit.

Whatever the reason, Loewenstein went to the back of the aircraft and no one paid any attention. It was the secretary, Hodgson, who became mildly apprehensive after about ten minutes. He was endowed with a healthy sense of self-preservation and had no intention of incurring Loewenstein's undoubted wrath by disturbing him unnecessarily. This was a job for Baxter. The valet rapped on the door leading to the toilet compartment. The expected impatient rejoinder did not come. There was only the imperturbable beat of the Fokker's engines. An awful premonition gripped the little valet. Hodgson was beside him now, grasping the door handle and pushing... The compartment was empty.

This fact was terrifying enough, but what rooted the attention of Hodgson and Baxter was something else. The outside fuselage door was open, quivering ominously in the slipstream. Stupidly, no doubt — but with an involuntary action that was perfectly natural — both men swung round to look at Loewenstein's former seat in the cabin. That was empty, too.

No one in that aircraft could later recall how long the mood of panic lasted. Fear gripped them all. Baxter crumpled into his seat, his eyes staring with sheer terror. Hodgson, unable to grasp the truth of what he had seen, flinched at the hysterical screams of the secretaries. As if in a daze, he found himself groping for pencil and paper. He stumbled to the cockpit and shakingly thrust a message under Drew's nose. It read, "The Captain's gone." Drew stared at it in mildly irritated incomprehension for a moment, then, whispering something to Little, went into the cabin. The grotesque tableau remained for him to witness. The two secretaries were quieter, but sobbing uncontrollably. The valet seemed on the verge of imbecility.

Only Hodgson had recovered himself. Coolly, he explained the discovery. Drew's decision on what to do next was to be criticized later, though it is difficult now to see what else he could have done. It would have been madness to continue to Brussels when he had in his care four emotionally shocked passengers. The two secretaries in particular might very well be overcome again by hysteria — a dangerous condition aboard an aircraft. Drew was determined that the Fokker must make an immediate landing. Fortunately, this presented little difficulty. He simply headed the plane for the firm beaches between Gravelines and Dunkirk. Once the Fokker had landed safely crew and passengers were able to sort out the facts for the inquiry which inevitably lay ahead. They also examined the plane from nose to tail, just in case there was the remote chance that Loewenstein had hidden himself away in some other part of the aircraft. There was no trace of him.

The questions they asked one another and themselves at that time have remained unanswered. Did Loewenstein board the aircraft at Croydon, stage the whole scene of the flapping door at the rear of the aircraft, hide in a secret compartment, and then make off as soon as the plane landed on the Dunkirk beaches? Had the man who boarded the plane at Croydon not been Loewenstein at all, but an impersonator? Had

Loewenstein, knowing that ruin could be staring him in the face, decided to end his own life by jumping from the aircraft? Had he been murdered by his rumoured blackmailer who had been aboard? Or had the whole affair been an accident? Nothing much can be proved or even taken as fact. The idea that Loewenstein could have arranged his disappearance by hiding in some secret compartment is, to say the least, unlikely. It is possible that he could have had one built, but this would imply that Captain Drew was his accomplice, since he must, as one of Loewenstein's regular pilots, have known of the existence of any modification to his aircraft, however secretly carried out. Drew was a man of unimpeachable honesty and this theory can surely be discounted. Besides, there is something ludicrously unbelievable about the notion of a middle-aged, corpulent businessman making off across the Dunkirk beaches, coatless and collarless, one fine summer's evening without someone spotting him.

The impersonation theory seems to belong to the realm of thriller-fiction rather than to reality. It calls for considerable suspension of reason. At Croydon, Loewenstein had kept the crew waiting while he made a business call. This was to an associate, Sir Herbert Holt. Supposing that, having done so, he simply left the airport and his accomplice, a man who resembled him in looks, gesture and speech, took his place, it argues that the aircrew, Loewenstein's secretary, valet and two typists were all completely taken in by the substitution.

The suicide theory is certainly more plausible. To open the door of an aircraft in flight is no easy task, requiring terrific pressure. None the less, this particular Fokker was later tested by the Inspector of Accidents for the Air Ministry and it was found that its door could be opened slightly, given the necessary pressure. Loewenstein could just have ended his life in this melodramatic fashion.

As to murder, nothing remotely disreputable was known about Loewenstein's staff. In any case, the murderer would have had to get rid of his victim by following him in full view of the other passengers to the toilet. Then he would have had to grapple with the powerfully-built Loewenstein, forcing him towards a door which could only be opened with a good deal of strength. Loewenstein would have been sucked into the slipstream, right enough; but might he not have taken his killer with him? Even if he did not, would the assassin not have shown signs of the struggle? For a while Baxter was looked upon with suspicion. His behaviour after the discovery of Loewenstein's disappearance had been the most marked. But he was a small man whom Loewenstein could easily have overcome. (Baxter, incidentally, committed suicide four years later while working for Loewenstein's son.) Someone suggested an alternative: Hodgson *and* Baxter had committed the crime when they went to the lavatory door, ostensibly anxious about their master. It was theoretically possible, but most improbable.

Rumour and speculation about the real fate of Alfred Loewenstein were inevitable. Curious questioners wanted to know what Captain Drew had been doing: why he had landed his aircraft away from prying eyes on a lonely beach. After all, here had been a Belgian national travelling in a Dutch aircraft registered in England which had landed in highly suspicious circumstances in French territory. Perhaps people cannot be blamed for wondering whether or not there was an international conspiracy to get rid of Alfred Loewenstein.

Loewenstein's body was recovered by a trawler in mid-channel fifteen days after his disappearance. Medical evidence revealed that death had been by drowning and that he had been alive when he hit the water. Little else is known. Big business circles throughout the world took the view that Loewenstein had committed suicide because he was on the verge of exposure as a swindler. The panic took the form of nosediving Loewenstein shares; there was hardly a corner of the stock market that did not somehow suffer. Loewenstein had been as powerful as that. But Loewenstein — if it was he — had shown no signs of depression either before or during the flight. On the contrary, he had been in high good-humour, looking forward pugnaciously to his coming duel with the Dreyfus brothers.

What is the truth? Loewenstein *could* have pushed impatiently at the door opposite him imagining that it led back to the cabin. If the door was not properly fastened he may have stumbled into the slipstream and been sucked out, all of which presupposes that he did not know the geography of his own aircraft. There seems no satisfactory explanation. It would appear that we can accept that Alfred Loewenstein *did* board the Fokker VII on 4 July 1928 and that he and no one else fell out of it. How? And why?

17: DISASTER ON "RED 19"

The flight from London to Greece had been uneventful for the 38 passengers aboard *Charlie Oscar*. At Athens, the Comet which had flown 15,470 hours in just over six years' service, was refuelled and serviced for the flight on to Nicosia, over which stage of the journey her British European Airways owners would be operating on behalf of Cyprus Airways. The flight crew remained the same, but Cyprus Airways provided its own cabin staff. More passengers joined. When *Charlie Oscar* took off again at 2.31 a.m. on Thursday, 12 October 1967, she carried in all seven crew and 59 passengers. She was allocated the air corridor known as Upper Airway Red 19 for the Mediterranean crossing.

The Comet's captain, 45-year-old Gordon Blackwood, who lived in Berkshire, was one of BEA's most experienced pilots, having joined the airline from the R.A.F. immediately after the war. He had more than 14,000 flying hours in his record, including 2,637 on Comets. The two First Officers with him, Michael Thomas, 34, and Denis Palmer, 36, had Comet experience almost matching his. *Charlie Oscar*, in the prime of life, could not have been in better hands.

Yet disaster struck out of a clear night sky — and struck too suddenly for any "Mayday" distress signal from the crew. The last moments, as far as they can be determined, went like this.

At 3.18 a.m. a message was picked up by Nicosia Tower, "Bealine Charlie Oscar, Over," to which was given the reply, "Charlie Oscar, go ahead, Over." The invitation was never followed up and that was the last ever heard from Captain Blackwood. It would seem a sensible assumption that he intended to give a routine position check or perhaps inquire after the weather. If there had been anything more urgent he would surely have come to the point more quickly. A little earlier, in cheerful form, he had radioed Captain John Emerson, another BEA Comet pilot and a close friend. The conversation had been about nothing in particular: "I am fine. How are you? See you in London." Emerson, who was flying in the opposite direction to *Charlie Oscar*, signed off with a request to Blackwood to tune into Nicosia airport control. Captain Blackwood replied: "O.K. Thank you. I have already done it."

The rest was silence...

The disappearance of an aircraft out over the sea is an extremely rare event today. Thanks to radar and the elaborate network of ground control, a pilot can usually keep everyone informed of the progress of a flight and in turn is "watched" by many unseen eyes. The days of a pilot battling against the elements with little contact beyond that supplied by a shortwave radio are very much of the past. Disaster, when it occurs, happens eight times out of ten on take-off and landing. The exceptions are as likely as not attributable to something having happened that is rare enough to class — for a time at least — as a mystery. Before he left London to investigate the loss of *Charlie Oscar*, British European Airways' flight manager, Captain William Baillie, declared that here was "a most amazing type of accident in this day and age. It happened from a cruising altitude of 29,000 feet."

But that came later, when the scene of the crash had been located. Meanwhile, as soon as the Comet became overdue at Nicosia the first stages of an accident-alert had been set up. An R.A.F. Hastings aircraft and two C47 transports of the Greek Air Force began a search. It took only some two hours for wreckage to be sighted about fifteen to twenty miles south-east of the island of Kastellorizon, ten minutes' flying time from Nicosia. Conditions were far from favourable to a rescue operation. There were storms in the skies above the wreck of *Charlie Oscar*. The captain of the Hastings, Flight-Lieutenant Denis King, found he had to fly over the wreckage for close on five hours before he had anything concrete to report, with restless seas so hampering visibility that it was impossible to confirm that here indeed was the wreckage of the Comet. Some bodies were eventually spotted and doubt was ended.

Announcements by the official Greek and Cypriot Press services reflected the barely concealed hostility between their peoples. Cyprus was accused of negligence and of delay in sounding the alarm until 7.45 a.m. local time, nearly two hours after the time the Comet had been scheduled to land. This and other allegations helped to force the inevitable crop of rumours. With understandable caution British European Airways refused to comment at so early a stage and rumour and speculation prevailed. Some held that *Charlie Oscar* had simply fallen victim to bad weather, always a risk over this route at this time of year. But it was also contended from unnamed Cypriot sources that an engine had exploded. There was talk of structural failure. One whisper was that Russian MIG fighters had been seen in the area and that there might have been a collision. A damaged drop-tank from an American F100 aircraft, recovered from the sea near Rhodes, bore traces of red paint which, it was held, might point to a collision having occurred with the Comet with its red BEA livery. Analysis of the paint showed, however, that it was of quite different type to that used on BEA aircraft and the tank was found to be one of a pair dropped by a U.S. plane several months earlier.

General George Grivas, Commander of the Cyprus Armed Forces, was at one point believed to have been a victim. Then Grivas himself turned up alive on the evening of the accident. He had been in Athens discussing Cyprus defence affairs with the Greek Government. It was later revealed that Grivas had indeed booked on Comet *Charlie Oscar* but at the last moment had decided to take another flight. Had someone, one of his many political enemies, not known of the switch and gone ahead with plans to sabotage the aircraft? Soon the word "sabotage" was being openly mentioned in Greece, Cyprus and London.

At this point there was very little for investigators to go on. The theory of heavy turbulence as a cause of the crash was, however, ruled out very early on, for another Comet pilot had reported seeing *Charlie Oscar* in perfect flying weather shortly before the disaster. A team of British investigators set up their headquarters at Rhodes, their task to find out what had caused the aircraft to plunge 29,000 feet to the sea. In terse language the official Board of Trade report on the inquiry commented: "The accident was not survivable." Some bodies were recovered. There were 24 Britons among the dead, including two children and the flight crew of three, while the remaining passengers had included American, Greek and Cypriot holidaymakers and businessmen.

The best friend of any flight investigation team is the aircraft's electronic flight recorder. *Charlie Oscar* had been equipped with a Plessey-Davall model which would have been invaluable in providing details of behaviour in the last few minutes prior to the crash; only it was never retrieved from the 6,000 feet of water in which the wreckage was lying. Flotsam and bodies were recovered by Turkish ships to the north of the wreckage. To the south of the accident area, some one hundred nautical miles east of Rhodes, German, Greek and American ships and an R.A.F. rescue launch found kerosene-soaked flotsam, consisting mainly of seat cushions, carpets and parts of the galley.

One of the first puzzles to face the investigators arose from indications that passengers had inflated their lifejackets. If this were true, it meant there had been some prior warning of disaster; but in fact, many of the lifejackets recovered from the sea had broken from their containers, unfolded themselves and become inflated. The report concluded that "there was no evidence that any lifejacket had been donned in the air". Thus, another rumour had been disposed of.

The whisper of sabotage could not be dismissed so easily. Indeed, the idea that some explosive device had caused the crash of the Comet seemed, with each day that passed, likely to harden into certainty. The British Press revealed that the search for possible saboteurs had switched to London and Scotland Yard detectives combed the Paddington area of London in search of a number of known Greek Cypriot extremists who might have been capable of sabotage.

It was not long before there was more concrete evidence for the crash investigators. A superficial examination of the seat cushions recovered from the wreckage showed that at least one had been punctured by slivers of metal of a kind that could not be identified immediately and which the experts in Rhodes could say did not appear to have come from any part of the Comet. The cushions were sent home to Britain for scientific examination, together with three small pieces of metal recovered from bodies during examination by pathologists.

Scientists working at the Home Office branch of the Royal Armament Research and Development Establishment found the cushions very interesting indeed. Forensic experts who work at the scene of robberies are accustomed to finding cushions that have been used to muffle explosions in cases of safe-breaking. One cushion from *Charlie Oscar* in particular, identified as having belonged to the tourist cabin, was singled out for special treatment. In it, tiny particles of metal and fibres were found embedded and it was perforated with some twenty holes from the lower to upper surface. Scientists built a mock-up of the cabin of the Comet and fitted cushions of a similar kind to those which had been aboard *Charlie Oscar*. Charges were then exploded and their effect on the cushions compared with what had happened to those found amid the flotsam from the accident. The cushions which had been recovered, like those used in the mock-up, were seen to have their surfaces severely blackened. Microscopic and X-ray examination confirmed this to be due to amorphous carbon, without much doubt attributable to some high explosive. The cushion which had first attracted the scientists' attention was given separate tests, while in a series of laboratory experiments small particles of metal were projected at measured velocities into other cushions and their degree of penetration recorded. The inescapable conclusion was that only an explosive device could have accounted for small fragments of metal travelling at such high velocities.

The next stage was to examine the metal particles themselves. Scientists were able to prove that all of them showed characteristics of having been part of an explosive device — they had suffered "detonation shock". The next question was, what kind of "bomb" had this been?

It soon became obvious that here was no crude act of sabotage. Whoever had carried out the mass murder of 66 people had not depended on anything so crude as gelignite or any of the more common industrial explosives. The high velocity of the explosion seemed to point to some form of military device. At this point the investigators came up against a stumbling block. Bombs of any kind need something to set them off; timing or detonating equipment is essential. None of the light-alloy fragments pointed to any British or known foreign type of detonator. This was but one aspect of the mystery which has never been cleared up.

Submitting a number of seat cushions to a series of small explosions had helped to gain a good deal of information. The experts now believed that a single explosion had occurred aboard *Charlie Oscar*. To confirm this and to ascertain the effect it must have had on the aircraft a further mock-up of the passenger cabin, complete with seats, was assembled, this time made of light alloy. Sixteen ounces of an explosive charge known as P-4 and thought likely to have been the type used in the sabotage was encased in a thin steel tube, fitted with a detonator and exploded. It tore a hole some three to six square feet in one of the cabin walls. The damage to the cushions and to sections of the cabin closely matched that done to their counterparts recovered from *Charlie Oscar*. The explosion aboard the Comet was deduced to have happened at below floor level. The fact that the bomb punctured a large hole in one section of the fuselage is not believed to have caused the aircraft's immediate destruction. Experts believed rather that the Comet had immediately spun out of control in the general direction of Rhodes, plummeting from 29,000 feet to around 15,000. The fuselage remained intact for a few minutes and then, as was inevitable under such stress, snapped.

Although cabin debris and bodies scattered over three miles of water were recovered, the amount salvaged from the rest of the Comet was pitiably small. The sea was extremely deep at the point of the crash, in some cases as much as 1,583 fathoms. The bed, though mainly silt and gravel, was believed to consist of many clutches of rocky outcrops, implying great difficulty in achieving anything like total salvage. Besides, when an aircraft explodes in mid-air, bits of debris are flung over a wide area and there is no one place in which to search. Once scientists were armed with the knowledge of the power of the probable explosion, they felt certain that shattered and useless fragments would be the only haul. Further salvage attempts would yield little of value. The Mediterranean was allowed to keep its disintegrated hoard.

Sabotage had been established beyond doubt; so, who was responsible and what had been the motive? Had the passengers of Cyprus Airways flight CY 284 been the innocent victims of political crossfire; or had this been a case of the planned murder of one passenger or someone's desperate suicide? It has never been established. The theory that a bomb had been placed aboard the aircraft by political agents, possibly Turks who had intended to kill General Grivas, still holds strong sway. One of the general's bodyguards was a victim of the disaster.

It is perhaps scarcely surprising that no enlightening statement by any of the countries which might be harbouring the intended murderers of Grivas has been forthcoming. The identity of the saboteurs, whatever the motive, is unlikely ever to be known. It was not the business of the official Board of Trade report to indulge in theories. It merely commented: "The aircraft broke up in the air following detonation of a high-explosive device within the cabin." Yet, for all the strong presumption of political machinations, there is a distinct possibility that 66 people died on account of one of their own number, and for reasons not connected with politics at all. When it became likely that sabotage was the cause of disaster

239

to an aircraft with a certain man — we will call him X — aboard, a team of Scotland Yard detectives under Detective Superintendent Percy Brown flew to Rhodes, in response to a tip, to look for a possible connection.

This X had been a man with a dream. To new acquaintances he presented himself as a successful businessman who was about to make a fortune. His wife was under the impression that her devoted husband was being sent by his firm on a series of high-powered business trips. The truth was sadly different. He was an employee in a shop, with financial obligations well beyond his means, who had turned to gambling in an attempt to raise the wind. But he was fighting a losing battle and needed much more money than the uncertainty of gambling could produce. While continuing to play the table vigorously in Athens and Corfu, he began to look around for new sources of cash.

There is no shortage of smugglers in Cyprus and, as in every community the world over, no shortage of weak, pleasure-loving individuals prepared to do their dirty work for them. It is probably flattering this man X overmuch to call him a smuggler; he was more of a smuggler's carrier. As such, he was the complete fall guy, sure to be left holding the goods if he were ever caught. He was of undeniable value to the smugglers — a subject ripe for blackmail, he was hardly likely to let them down.

He seems to have been born unlucky. His smuggling activities brought him nothing but misfortune. On one of his last trips he was almost caught red-handed at Athens airport with a consignment of watches worth £950 when his contact man, believed to have been a customs official, failed to show up. The airport authorities were suspicious and opened the brown leather suitcase he was carrying. By a miracle of fast-talking he managed to hoodwink the customs investigators into believing that the suitcase was not part of his luggage; but the consignment was confiscated. He now owed his masters, for whom he had been carrying the watches, close on a thousand pounds.

A few days before his death — or, to be more exact, before his name appeared on the passenger list of the doomed Comet — X was having a depressing and self-pitying drink in a Larnaca bar. To a friend, subsequently interviewed by Scotland Yard detectives, the wretched man confided: "It is better for me to die. My whole life has turned into disaster." It can be imagined that, with each new inquiry, the interest of detectives in this passenger began to quicken. His financial state was examined more closely, revealing that for years he had kept only one personal accident policy for a not very large sum, excluding aviation risk. In September 1967 he had walked into the Larnaca office of the company and taken out increased personal accident cover, valid only for the month of October and covering a single journey abroad to Greece and England. In the next few days, X took out yet another policy, this time with another company; then a third new policy, for an even higher amount, with another.

Two weeks later Comet *Charlie Oscar* exploded. This X, so it appeared, had been aboard. One insurance company, with no reason to suspect anything untoward, paid out the sum assured to his widow. The other companies, though, were less accommodating and held up the money. Clearly, news of their client's reputation had spread.

Had a desperate man decided to do away with himself after arranging belated financial amends to his wife? Men driven to the very edge of desperation will do a great deal — and that has occasionally included mass murder — in order to encompass their own suicide. Would this small-time crook have had the sheer nerve to place a bomb aboard an aircraft and sit waiting for a time-device to trigger off the mechanism, even though he would have known that his death could leave his family well provided for?

Detectives wondered and investigated other possibilities, other theories. One alternative casts the man as a thoroughly subtle villain who cleverly tricked an acquaintance to make the trip for him using his name and carrying his ticket. Possibly he had spun a story of not being able to get to Cyprus, but desperately needing a certain briefcase to be delivered there. Doubtless he would have made it well worth the while of the substitute passenger, who, not suspecting that the briefcase contained a bomb, would gladly have carried out so simple an assignment. The briefcase theory is tenable in the light of evidence that the bomb is believed to have exploded from floor level — beneath the cabin seats, perhaps. His purpose accomplished, X's plan would have been to lie low for a time. His wife would have paid his debts out of his insurance money and he would have been free to start a new life elsewhere in the world.

Another theory is that he had been associated with an organized gang who took out insurance policies with various companies under different names in order to collect the proceeds. His role was to arrange for some unsuspecting carrier of the bomb. Naturally enough, all insurance claims from relatives of crash victims were investigated, but no enlightening discrepancies were revealed.

Scotland Yard will not discuss its enquiries into the disaster. The Board of Trade report deals only with the facts of the accident as they can be ascertained from the record of the aircraft's flight, weather conditions at the time, the state of the recovered wreckage, and the texts and research which revealed that an explosion had taken place. We do not know if the rest of the truth will ever be revealed and we cannot be sure that somewhere, certainly under a different name and very probably in a different country, exists a man who knows more than anyone about the fate of *Charlie Oscar.*

18: EXIT A HEROINE

By the mid-1930s, America was gradually emerging, battered and tired, from cruel depression. The country was in the mood for an escapist spree. There was a feverish sense of optimism. While politicians elsewhere winced at happenings in Europe, the United States was far more interested in its latest folk hero. Already in 1928 Amelia Earhart had, in a three-engined Fokker, flown the Atlantic, the first woman to do so. On 1 June 1937 she planned to go around the world.

Amelia Earhart was an updated version of the frontier adventurer — a peculiarly American phenomenon. She was a refreshingly uncomplicated person, standing for stable values in an unstable world: a university graduate, a competent linguist, happily married to a New York publisher, and — of particular appeal to influential American matriarchy — a bustling social worker. A woman, in fact, who was a credit to her country and a shining example to youth. For months before she began her marathon of the air, Amelia Earhart occupied the front pages of most newspapers. There wasn't an aviation enthusiast who did not know her around-the-world route. She and her co-pilot, Fred Noonan, were to start at Oakland, California, and go east to Miami. From thence it was south-east to Brazil, snaking across South Africa, and then to Karachi, Rangoon, Singapore, Sourabaya, Port Darwin and New Guinea. Finally, it would be back across the vast Pacific. This was the self-imposed journey of 33-year-old Amelia and Captain Noonan, in his forties and recently married. He was one of the country's best aerial navigators.

The pair were destined never to return to Oakland. The world does not know what happened to their sturdy little twin-engined Lockheed Electra. The big question remains: how did Amelia Earhart and Fred Noonan die? It is unlikely that the real truth will ever emerge now. It could be that there are no sinister secrets to hide. Even so, there are those who believe that somewhere buried in Washington archives is a particularly grim explanation of the disappearance.

In these jet-flying days when an ocean-crossing is regarded as no more remarkable than hopping on a bus, one might perhaps wonder what all the fuss was about when the trip was mooted. By modern reckoning the Electra would be more at home in a suburban flying club than out over vast ocean wastes. Even in the days when it was an up-to-date machine it required excessive courage to think of flying long distances in it. Amelia Earhart possessed that abundance of courage. No part of her long journey would be particularly easy, while one section would be especially difficult and dangerous.

The task facing her when she set out on 2 July 1937 on one of the last legs of the trip might be likened in mundane terms to finding a pin that has been dropped on a patterned carpet. Flying from Lae, New Guinea, she was making for Howland Island, half a degree north of the Equator, a stepping stone to Hawaii and San Francisco.

Comparing Howland to a pin is perhaps no exaggeration. It is one and a half miles long and half a mile wide — just enough land to stick above the level of the sea. A runway had just been built but it had never been used. One suspects that pilots were not exactly impatient to put their wheels down there. Clearly, searching for this dot was going to be a difficult proposition, next to impossible without some help from below. It was arranged that a coastguard cutter should anchor near Howland and guide the Electra in by radio.

Already Amelia had made one abortive attempt to reach Howland on the way out; the Electra had crashed on take-off. Now she and Noonan were ready to try again en route for home. It meant a flight of 2,500 miles, which might not have been so difficult if the route had been pimpled only with the Gilbert Islands which the Electra had to cross and which were on about the three-quarter mark of the journey. But to the north of the Gilberts lay the Marshalls and south of them the Ellice Islands, and from the air these island groups and atolls would look very much the same. Fred Noonan was a brilliant navigator, but even he could make mistakes. It was all rather like a giant treasure hunt, with helpful clues mixed in with tantalizing red herrings.

The day dawned for the New Guinea take-off. The thick, tangled vegetation of the jungle seemed to resent the space that had been cleared in it for a runway. It seemed to crowd in on the oddly vulnerable-looking Electra which was preparing to turn into the wind and leave Lae for the millions of acres of ocean ahead. A knot of natives and Europeans saw the Electra, her tanks brimful with fuel — she would need every precious gallon — ride the cliffs that dropped sheer to the sea. Then she climbed high above the Pacific and was gone. It was 10 a.m. New Guinea time.

Although no pilot today would fancy flying an Electra across the Pacific — let alone around the world — Amelia Earhart and Fred Noonan were by no means trusting their lives to something that dated from the Wright brothers. Their aircraft was sophisticated for its time, specially equipped with just about every navigational aid. They were well provided with safety gear. The radio had a range of several hundred miles over water and was of the most modern type. The weight of the extras added a problem, so on the Howland leg Amelia and Noonan carried as few personal possessions as possible — little beyond toothbrushes and changes of clothing — in keeping, in its way, with the American frontier tradition.

The pair had been delayed in New Guinea for twenty-four hours because of excessive headwind, but the weather had now calmed a bit. For the next eight hours radio reports from the Electra could be picked up back at Lae. Then, quite suddenly, the sky became ugly again. But whatever buffeting the Electra received in the hours after take-off did not deter them. One can picture Noonan, interpreting, with the calm exactitude of the scientist, his comforting instruments, while Amelia peered ahead trying to keep above the banks of cloud, at the same time straining for a sound from the *Itasca*, the cutter waiting off Howland Island. It was there, all right. Its giant high-frequency radio direction finder was like some enormous net, greedy to pick up any shoal of sound.

Back at Lae they were getting the staccato routine reports. By now New Guinea had no clear idea of the Electra's position, so when radio communication eventually failed this was put down to the aircraft getting out of range. No one worried. Amelia and Fred Noonan were now in no man's land, too far away from Lae for communication and not near enough to the cutter. Modern science could do nothing to help. They were on their own, with the elements and the approaching darkness.

Radio messages were transmitted frequently from the Electra in the early hours of the following morning, though they were hopelessly muffled by static. The most coherent call came at 6.15 Howland time: "We are about one hundred miles out. Please take a bearing on us and report in half an hour. I will transmit in the microphone." It was brief and to the point;

rather too brief. It gave the *Itasca* operators little to go on. For the moment, there were no more signals, no possible way of determining exactly where the Electra was. In frustration, the experts traversed their direction-finding ironmongery, only to encounter silence.

Then at 7.42 Amelia's voice came through loud and clear: "We must be right on top of you, but we can't see you. Our gas is running low. Have been unable to reach you by radio. We are flying at an altitude of 100 feet. Please take a bearing." Then the static started again, blotting out any use the message might have had in establishing the aircraft's position. Amelia then evidently decided that morse signals would not suffer so much from static and decided to try her radio compass on transmissions from the *Itasca*. Her next message was: "We are circling but cannot hear you. Go ahead on 7,500 kilocycles, either now or on the scheduled half-hourly time." The *Itasca* obligingly transmitted her call sign in morse, but it was still not possible to get a definite bearing. "We are receiving your signals," Amelia confirmed, "but we are unable to get a minimum. Please take a bearing on us and answer with voice on 3,105."

The *Itasca* was destined to get only one more clear message from the Electra. It was certainly not in Amelia's cheerfully adaptable nature to panic and the dominant element of scientist in Fred Noonan would have been a sufficient barrier to despair. But there must suddenly have been a feeling of utter loneliness, of futility. Here were two people searching for something ludicrously called an island, and doing so in the knowledge that their fuel was running dry and that through some fiendish twist of fate useful radio contact seemed impossible to achieve.

The cutter received just one more message: "We are in a line of position 157-337. Will repeat this message on 6,210 kilocycles. We are running north and south. We have only half an hour's fuel left and we cannot see land."

These were the last known words of Amelia Earhart. After that came the silence of the grave. The *Itasca* did not give up. For three more hours her crew tried over and over again to re-establish contact. It was no use. The so-nearly completed world flight was over.

Although the *Itasca*'s captain had no illusions about the plight the aircraft was in, he was very far from giving the pair up for dead. True, the Electra had very likely come down in the ocean. Even if this were so, it need not be especially serious. The radio would not work, but the fuel tanks could certainly keep the aircraft buoyant for hours and even days. Nevertheless, Captain Thomson had to wire to Washington: "Amelia Earhart missing." It is hard to appreciate the consternation caused by these words. It would be an exaggeration to say that Amelia exuded glamour; yet she held something approaching Hollywood status and was regarded as some species of goddess to whom the normal rules of mortality did not apply. That anything should have happened to this fine symbol of a supremely confident America was unthinkable.

Although the stretch of the Pacific over which Amelia and her companion had flown was now menaced by storms, through some strange dispensation of nature Howland Island was exempt. Around the tiny spot of land all was clear. Therefore, if the couple were near the island and made use of the Electra's flares and signalling pistol there was every chance that they would be spotted. They had emergency rations and water. There were lifebelts and a collapsible lifeboat on board.

There was no shortage of available help, and the U.S. Naval Department lost little time in mustering it. Although the British cargo steamer *Moorsby*, bound for Sydney, was the only vessel within tolerable distance of the *Itasca*, the aircraft carrier *Lexington*, accompanied by six destroyers, put to sea from San Diego over 4,000 miles away. Her planes were to sweep a total area of 151,556 square miles. But the *Itasca* had the biggest search task of all.

It was highly unlikely that the radio of the Electra was functioning, but there are few breeds in this world more enthusiastic than the radio "ham". In every Pacific country they sprang into action, twiddling knobs, listening intently, some of them keeping round-the-clock vigil. The professional operators in the searching aircraft and ships picked up from time to time strange, incomprehensible messages which could just be mumbled snatches of desperation from Earhart and Noonan. One of these seemed to say, "281 North Howland ... call KHAQQ ... don't hold with us much longer ... above water ... shut off." KHAQQ was the Electra's call sign. The message suggested that the aircraft had overshot Howland. Ships and planes now had somewhere to make for. Then came: "We are on a coral reef just below the Equator... We are O.K. but a little weak." The use of wireless in such circumstances puzzled experts, but it was argued that Noonan's ingenuity might have brought their salvaged set into use.

More and more craft converged on the likeliest sea area, as everything that could possibly be done to find the pair was implemented. There were two enemies with which rescuers had to contend. One was the really vile weather. Terrible storms kept aircraft at Honolulu grounded. Howland, previously exempt from it all, was lashed with violent storms which brought snow and sleet. The other enemy was even more unspeakable, because human: that despicably familiar figure at any time of tragedy, the hoaxer. Even when the storm was over, desperate wireless appeals continued, as though from the missing fliers, some of them giving positions which were clearly ridiculous. Sometimes, days of valuable time was wasted in following up improbable clues. The searchers had no time to waste on disgust. They gritted their teeth, cursed the hoaxers and pressed on. Other islands near to Howland were searched, but with no result. At length, on 18 July, after 4,000 men had carried out a fortnight's search at a cost of a million dollars, all attempts to find the Electra were abandoned.

The disappearance of a celebrity can, with a fickle public, mean that the personality concerned is forgotten instantly. Or the reverse can happen: there can be growth in stature as the missing person develops into legend. All manner of strange stories gain currency and immortality is sometimes claimed on the strength of qualities others have imposed but which never wholly existed.

Poor Amelia Earhart! There was nothing particularly legendary about her. She and her attitude to her work were quite straightforward. Flying was fun, a satisfying challenge. It is unlikely she would have claimed any more for herself. But once she had gone her image became transformed. It was whispered that she was an American spy, sent by the President to carry out a mission against the Japanese. Could she have been abducted by them?

There were those who were convinced that this was the exact opposite of the truth. She had, they averred, been a *Japanese* spy. The State Department, wanting to eliminate her and arouse the least suspicion in doing so, had given orders for the Electra to be shot down. Naturally, stolen secret documents had also been aboard.

Those who fancied a connection between tragedy and scandal suggested that Amelia and Noonan had been having an affair and had made a love nest on some uninhabited island. Actually, Amelia's marriage had been perfectly happy. Noonan had only been married recently. His twenty years' experience as a navigator and his great technical skill, which permitted him few rivals in aviation, had been the true reasons for his choice to make the flight.

The searchers themselves reckoned there were enough mysteries already without creating fantasies. Perhaps the biggest question was, *why* had the Electra lost contact with the *Itasca*? The radio was one of the latest models. True, there had been other landmarks near to Howland which might have confused the pair and sent them off in the wrong direction. Could Fred Noonan really have been so deceived? In any case, nearby was the Gilbert group, a clutch of easily identifiable islands and atolls.

But another preoccupation was at hand to divert the attention of serious inquirers and rumour-mongers alike. The whole Earhart affair was soon overshadowed by the Nazi menace in Europe. The world drifted into war. Inevitably, the vanished Electra was all but forgotten. It was not until the return of peace that interest was revived, though no one had any fresh ideas where to look for bodies and the remains of an aircraft. A lead came by accident. Intelligence investigators from the U.S. Army, sifting through naval files in Tokyo, came across a dossier on the entire life and career of Amelia Earhart, including an account of her disappearance. None of this told the Americans anything new, but inevitably it started speculation: Why would the Japanese have compiled such records? It is a question neither Washington nor Tokyo has ever answered.

A sensational development came in 1946. A naval dentist, Dr Casimir Sheft, in practice on the island of Saipan in the Marianas, which lie north of Howland Island, was discussing the Earhart affair with a colleague. Sheft's Japanese assistant, Josephine Blanco, overheard the conversation, and something stirred in her mind. A crashing aircraft … a woman pilot and a male passenger… For a moment nothing added up, until Josephine remembered a bizarre incident from her wartime childhood. As a schoolgirl, she used to take her brother-in-law's lunch on a bicycle to the island's Tanapag harbour where he worked. One day in the summer of 1937 (she couldn't recall the month or the date) she was riding to the harbour as usual when she heard an aircraft overhead. It swooped low and flopped on its belly in the waters of the harbour. Curious, the girl waited. Eventually, she saw a man and a woman, both dressed in fliers' clothing, being taken into nearby woods by harbour guards. Two shots rang out… The guards returned alone. Josephine claimed she had seen the aircraft force-land at midday. If it had been the Electra it was possible. There could have been enough fuel to last until then.

But why Saipan? Amelia *could* have reached there. The distance from Lae in New Guinea was almost the same as that to Howland. Josephine Blanco could have had no discernible motive for inventing it. She examined and readily identified photographs she was shown of Amelia and Noonan, although the event she described had happened eight years earlier.

Delving deeper, investigators came up with a plausible explanation why the two unexpected arrivals should have been summarily executed. In 1937 the Japanese had begun work on a small airstrip on Saipan, in violation of all international treaties. The pilot and her companion might be presumed to have spotted it. Yet still the mere fact of the Electra's having been at Saipan at all was puzzling. It presupposed a serious navigational error. Those who believed the Saipan story — and many still do — pointed out that the mistake could have happened if the Electra's crew were dead tired, even though this had been a navigator of no ordinary calibre. They could have taken the wrong clutch of islands as their identifying point. The Gilberts were the correct landmarks, but the Carolinas were of similar shape and they lay on the route to Saipan.

Saipan was favourite for a time after Josephine's story; the harbour was dragged for remains of the aircraft she said she had seen. An electric generator was salvaged, but it had not belonged to the Electra. Then the remains of two unidentified bodies were found, also on Saipan. In high excitement, they were flown to the States for pathological analysis. It did not take long to discover that the bones and teeth belonged to those of Asian descent.

Were Amelia Earhart and Fred Noonan — or perhaps Amelia alone — engaged in spying? It is not impossible that Amelia had been persuaded to enter this seamy, twilight world; but to do what, precisely? Take photographs of Saipan? Try to undermine Japanese influence in the Pacific in some way or other? It all seems highly unlikely; a not-very-subtle plot from fiction. Yet, how significant is it that no one in authority has ever offered to explain the existence of that Tokyo dossier?

Then there is the personality of Amelia herself. Hers had been a healthy, uncomplicated life. She was the brand image of a clean America. One doesn't see her as a pawn for espionage, though that could be precisely why she was recruited.

It is to be hoped that Amelia and Fred Noonan died quickly and cleanly when the Electra crashed into the Pacific. This is how both would have wished it. Such a death had always been "on" from the beginning of their flight, and they would have accepted it resignedly — perhaps even cheerfully. To have had to face a firing squad — even if there had been something to be guilty of — would have been a different matter.

19: SUICIDE BEHIND SCHEDULE

It is all too tempting to cast Albert Voss in the role of a mass murderer. On quite dubious evidence, society was prepared to condemn this shadowy figure as a drug trafficker, a smuggler, a currency swindler and, inevitably, a womanizer: so why, it is sometimes asked, should he not have been guilty, in March 1933, of sabotaging the Imperial Argosy airliner *City of Liverpool?*

Voss, it is true, was not a particularly likeable individual and some of his business associates were distinctly disreputable. But there lies a considerable gap between a predilection for fiddling and the capability of committing wholesale murder. Evidence is the telling factor, and this is one of those cases in which evidence is in short supply.

The Argosy airliner left Brussels for Croydon at 12.36 p.m., on 23 March, having started from Cologne at 10.22 — 22 minutes behind schedule. Used regularly on the route between London, Belgium and Cologne, it was piloted by 35-year-old Lionel Leleu who had been with Imperial Airways for seven years and had an excellent record. The journey from Cologne was uneventful; so much so that Leleu was able to make up time and bring *City of Liverpool* into Brussels on something approaching normal schedule. However, there was a good deal of freight to be loaded and this took up rather more time than had been anticipated. Not that this sort of thing was particularly worrying in the aviation world of the mid-1930s when timetables were not adhered to quite so rigidly and when commercial flying was a far less complex business than now. Admittedly, present-day pilots have much of their "flying" done for them by automatic controls and navigational aids, but this in itself implies preoccupation with numerous technicalities and mastery of many advanced skills. The loading of freight and luggage, too, was less methodically managed and a lot of time was wasted at Brussels redistributing the weight of the aircraft's load. Most of the passengers' luggage was stacked in a rack at the cabin's rear. So it was not until 12.36 — 36 minutes behind schedule — that *City of Liverpool* was airborne again, now carrying 12 passengers, eight of whom had joined at Brussels. One of these was Albert Voss.

Before it reached the Channel the aircraft had to cross the Belgian plains south of Ghent. After the Channel, the route lay across Kent to Croydon, then Britain's principal airport. The estimated flight time was two hours and the aircraft would be flying at 95 miles an hour.

By one o'clock, some 24 minutes after take-off, *City of Liverpool* was due south of Ghent, flying at 4,300 feet in excellent weather conditions. Her radio transmissions confirmed all as being normal. After a further 20 minutes Croydon was picking up another routine message and the Channel was a mere quarter of an hour away. Yet, at about 1.25 something happened to the Argosy — just what will never be known.

According to the testimonies of some Belgian peasants the aircraft had appeared to be passing over normally until, suddenly, a wisp of smoke was spotted from the top of the hull's after end. This was followed by flame near the tail and *City of Liverpool* went into a slow dive. As it did so the after end of the cabin compartment seemed to have become a trap for an intense sheet of flame. It was clear to the watchers that at any moment a blaze would spread through the aircraft, though the front part had so far escaped and there was no sign of damage to the wings and the three engines. Some more knowledgeable witnesses believed that, given a cool head and a certain amount of luck, the pilot would manage to bring down the aircraft before it wholly disintegrated. They watched it fly at a steadily decreasing height towards the Eesen road, two miles south of Dixmude and reckoned that the pilot was making for a large open field beyond a group of poplars, a well-chosen spot for a forced-landing.

The Belgians watched anxiously. *Three hundred feet* ... surely it would be only seconds before the wheels from the fixed undercarriage sank safely on to the earth. *Two-hundred and fifty feet...* Captain Leleu was seen to be standing up in the cockpit, exerting all his strength in an effort to wrench response from his controls. Suddenly there was a strange and seemingly irrelevant sound like two enormous pistol shots. There followed a sight so terrible that those who saw it no doubt never forgot it. As if it had been a stick in the hands of a destructive child the Argosy snapped in two, the pieces separating completely. As the front section hit the ground the fuel tanks caught fire, the flames spreading instantly to the passenger cabin which had hitherto been unscathed. A woman passenger was seen to be thrown clear as the aircraft broke up, her clothes billowing parachute-like as she fell, baggage erupting from the freight compartment and cascading around her. Some pieces of luggage were to be found hundreds of yards from the main scene of the crash.

It was the worst disaster in the 14-year-old history of British civil aviation, with no precedents to suggest immediately what had caused it. The fore part of the aircraft burned furiously after the crash had burst the fuel tanks; yet eyewitnesses maintained that there had been no fire in that part before the impact. Experts sought to confirm this by examination of the wreckage. The crash had been so violent that some of the aircraft's structure and items of baggage were forced into the ground, shielding them from the post-crash fire. When they were recovered they were found to be unscorched, proving that no fire had touched them before the disaster as well as after. By process of elimination the British and Belgian salvage experts narrowed down the probable source of the fire to a tiny area at the rear of the passenger cabin. It suggested sabotage; its likeliest point of origin would seem to have been in either the lavatory or the luggage rack. Both had been destroyed utterly. It seemed certain therefore that the fire had not started as a result of any fault pertaining to the aircraft itself, but must have been caused, inadvertently or deliberately, by a passenger. Perhaps something inflammable had been contained in a suitcase and had ignited spontaneously or through contact with something else. Perhaps someone had been careless with a cigarette.

Perhaps someone had been fiendishly successful with a bomb.

No one survived the disaster to the *City of Liverpool* — but one passenger, it was established, had died before the rest. That passenger was Albert Voss. Belgian witnesses testified that, at the time of the aircraft's initial dive, they had spotted a black object, thought to have been an item of luggage, falling away from the fuselage. It fell at a point a good mile before the place the aircraft finally crashed. Searchers found that it was no piece of luggage, but a body which subsequent inquiries revealed to be that of Albert Voss, a 68-year-old German Jew, naturalized in Britain and practising as a dentist in Manchester.

A dapper, prosperous-looking person whom anyone might have been forgiven for believing to be ten years younger, Voss was a manic depressive type, temperamental to the point at times of hysteria. He had been known to threaten suicide over a relatively small matter. He lived in a style above that of most dentists, making many trips abroad on business. Actually, Voss was constantly in financial difficulty and dabbled in a number of money-raising schemes, perhaps the most substantial of which was buying and selling dental equipment, which took him often to the Continent and Germany. There was nothing disreputable about this, but Voss's business integrity was, to say the least, questionable. There were rumours of less reputable enterprises. He was an undischarged bankrupt, a fact he may have been a little too secretive about for his own good, which may in turn have accounted for some of Scotland Yard's interest in his dealings.

Lately, he had been even more short of money than usual. As a Jew, the formation of a Nazi government in Germany had not suited his book at all; in addition to which it was hinted that the civil police in Berlin had quite a substantial fraud dossier on him. Nearly desperate, the man had to find new outlets for his activities; hence the trip to Brussels, in the company of a young man named Dearden, of whom much was said (none of it to his credit) but little known.

There seemed nothing shady about this particular business trip. Voss and Dearden had flown to Brussels on 24 March, but it was not until three days later that they actually got down to the real purpose of their visit. Before discussing business they gambled heavily in the casino at Spa, a piece of intelligence which might suggest that Albert Voss was a spendthrift and gambler, rather than an habitual criminal. On 27 March the two businessmen visited the head of a firm of dental appliance manufacturers. Seeking to buy at the smallest price so that he could resell in England at the highest profit, Voss bargained hard and at length placed an order to the value of £1,250. He said he and his companion would return the following day to discuss packing and delivery.

Voss and Dearden duly turned up the next day, only to tell the seller, Mr Bogaert, that they had been called home unexpectedly, but would return as soon as they could. As an earnest of good faith Voss left a cheque for £400.

The departure of Voss and Dearden from Brussels was twenty-four hours in advance of their original air booking. At eleven o'clock on that fateful day, the two men took a taxi from their hotel to the airport. Both bought 35-franc insurance policies which covered their dependants for the sum of £500 in case of death through air accident in the following twenty-four hours. Voss had told Mr Bogaert that the summons back to England had come by cable. What was contained in the cable, what was so serious that everything had to be dropped in favour of an immediate return, is not known. It has never been established whether or not that cable ever existed. Whatever his reasons for leaving Brussels, Voss was certainly in a hurry.

Voss elected to sit alone aboard *City of Liverpool* and deliberately took the rear seat on the starboard side. What he did between then and meeting his violent death is also not known, for no one survived to tell. His body, with those of the other victims, was flown home two days after the accident. Voss was to be buried in the Jewish cemetery outside Manchester.

To the horror of his bereaved family, Voss's body was seized by detectives as soon as it reached Manchester from Croydon the day before, for examination by experts in forensic medicine. The funeral, Voss's widow was told, must wait.

There was certainly enough that was strange about the death of Albert Voss to merit investigation. The fire had evidently started either in luggage rack or lavatory and Voss had been sitting within easy reach of both. Moreover, he had been sitting alone, with less chance of anyone seeing what he was up to. As a dentist he had had access to all sorts of inflammable substances, including anaesthetics. The man was known to have been in debt and subject to periodic bouts of depression. He had talked of suicide. It seemed a far-fetched theory that anyone would attempt to kill himself by setting fire to the aircraft in which he was travelling and then proceed to hurl himself out of it — a needlessly complicated, difficult and painful way of going voluntarily to one's death.

But supposing Voss had not wanted to kill himself, but simply to disappear? It would be difficult to find a better way. An aircraft is blown to smithereens, and its passengers and crew with it. No one would be suspicious if it proved impossible to find the remains of one missing businessman.

This theory was popular in England, reminiscent as it was of a murder case that had taken place only in the previous year, the *cause célèbre* which has gone down in criminal history as "the blazing-car murder". It had resulted in a 36-year-old commercial traveller named Alfred Arthur Rouse being convicted and hanged for staging his "disappearance" by setting fire to his car and placing in it the body of a man he had murdered, hoping that the corpse would be identified as his. A married man who had fathered many illegitimate children, Rouse had found his various amours catching up with him and had decided to stage-manage his own death, and disappear. If he had not been noticed by two youths near the scene of the crime he might well have succeeded.

There had been — and have been since — innumerable cases of men trying to "disappear" in order to escape financial and amorous embarrassments. Few have succeeded — and fewer have chosen such dramatic means as Voss may have done. If Voss had taken a leaf out of Rouse's book, and planned to disappear from the doomed airliner before she crashed, how had he tried to do it? No one had reported seeing him attempt to open a parachute as he fell from the *City of Liverpool*. No trace of one was ever found in the vicinity. Had he been wearing a parachute which had failed to open, the body would have carried at least some marks of shoulder straps; and these were not present. A theory was advanced that Voss had planned to get hold of a parachute situated conveniently near him, but had been prevented by the fire which had spread quicker than intended. In a blind panic he had thrown himself out of the aircraft.

If this were true, the whole plan would appear the product of a mind unhinged, of someone single-minded enough to be prepared to take the most incredible risks to preserve his own life while sacrificing innocent people. There had been whispers that Voss had been trafficking in drugs. The suggestion that he had been under their influence at the time of his death was disproved by the pathologist's report which showed quite clearly that Voss was not a drug addict and had not taken any drug on the day he died. As to the suggestion that he might have set fire to the aircraft with some inflammable liquid, an examination of the wreckage failed to bear this out.

The existence or otherwise of the cable summoning him home remains problematical; but there is another curious fact in the Voss story. One of the passengers from Cologne aboard *City of Liverpool* was a 16-year-old schoolgirl bound for a Wimbledon finishing school. Her name was Fräulein Lotte Voss. At Voss's inquest there was a suggestion that possibly the girl was a relation about whose existence none of the dead man's family in England had known. There was even an inference which was seized upon eagerly in some quarters where the scent of scandal reaches most potently, that Fräulein Lotte was no relation at all. Nothing, either way, was ever proved. Voss is a common enough German name.

The truth is that there is simply not enough evidence to connect Voss with sabotage, even if sabotage had been the cause of the crash. The latter seems likely, for this was a strange sort of accident. If indeed there was a saboteur, it seems probable that he had not banked on *City of Liverpool* being overdue. If it had flown to schedule, it would have reached mid-Channel before crashing and the accident would have been put down to an inexplicable mechanical failure or human error.

The jury returned an open verdict on Albert Voss. It still stands.

20: THE ECCENTRIC AVIATOR OF WOBURN ABBEY

The time is decidedly out of joint for aviation eccentrics. Most of the romantic figures have vanished. A Sheila Scott is produced once in a generation, and one would not apply the term "eccentric" to her. In the jet age, flying becomes a colourless procedure, shorn of most of its pioneering mystique. To be a passenger over even the longest distances is merely to exchange one clinical airport lounge for another. In between are little but dull woolly clouds. Neither is there so much fun these days in holding a private licence. The airlines get busier and busier. The Sunday flier becomes, not an aviator, but a dodger of always increasing obstacles. In any case, the planes have changed. You no longer fly with your head stuck out into the air, feeling the slipstream and knowing that you really *are* flying.

Once upon a time, the air was a novel and challenging element and the private flier something of a rarity. There was a good deal of fun to be had and shared with some ripe characters. Towering above them all in superbly confident eccentricity was Mary, Duchess of Bedford, who in the 1920s and 1930s became a national figure through her flying exploits.

In 1935 this game old aristocrat who scandalized husband and family with a succession of unladylike flips all over the world took to the air one day and simply vanished. She was 71 years old. The truth of her disappearance has defied every attempt at investigation; and that, one feels, is precisely how this fiercely independent spirit, this "Flying Duchess", would have been pleased to leave things.

Mary du Caurroy Tribe, high-spirited daughter of a West Sussex clergyman, was a rebel right from the moment she married Lord Herbrand Russell, a lieutenant in the Grenadier Guards. He was later to become Duke of Bedford. It was not, by the social standards of the time, an ideal match. Queen Victoria had once expressed her profound disfavour when one of her ladies-in-waiting wished to marry a clergyman: the Church was not a profession for gentry. The noble families of England, of which the Bedfords were fairly representative, followed the lead.

A duke was never meant for a clergyman's daughter. The Bedfords had underestimated Mary Tribe. She scorned the rigorously prescribed social niceties of the late Victorians. The social round of the great houses bored her — she preferred bird-watching in the Outer Hebrides. During the summer of 1907, for example, she declined to attend an evening party given at Buckingham Palace by King Edward VII, choosing instead to wander in the Orkneys, looking for the vastly more interesting white-tailed eagle.

The greatest passion of her earlier life was the cottage hospital she ran at Woburn, the Bedfords' magnificent country home. To indulge in good works was in those days permissible in the aristocracy, but it seldom went beyond a few genteel visits with baskets of food to the tenantry or the yearly subscription to carefully chosen charities. As in other things, the Duchess of Bedford had her own ideas of what was permissible. The Bedfords were one of the richest families in England. Mary could have lived in luxury and it would have been thought entirely right that she should do so. Instead, she took her hospital work immensely seriously. She became an excellent radiologist conducting her own X-ray examinations and developing the plates herself. Some of the country's leading surgeons were proud to have her as an assistant. As a trained theatre sister, she even conducted some operations. She was in her element on the outbreak of war in 1914. To the intense annoyance of the Duke, who disliked his wife's abundant energy, more and more of Woburn's 3,000 acres were commandeered for the wartime hospital where the Duchess and a hand-picked staff were coping with wounded from the Front.

As well as running the hospital the Duchess developed, as time went on, another passion. She did nothing by half-measures and when she became interested in flying refused to let it alone. It began, as it happened, by accident. As she grew older, she became critically deaf and suffered from a tiresome buzzing in the ears. A friend suggested that flying might help and that high altitudes could lessen the affliction. Once the idea took root, there was no holding Mary.

One would have given a great deal to be at Woburn one particular afternoon in the 1920s. Deer grazing placidly in the park looked up in mild astonishment as a frail Gipsy Moth biplane dipped towards them. Behind the windows of the servants' quarters, the Woburn staff watched with considerable apprehension. A noticeably tense pilot crouched over his controls while, in the cockpit behind him, a female passenger of commanding mien harangued him endlessly. It looked as if she was frightened and begging the pilot to land the machine.

Quite the reverse. The Duchess, as it turned out, had not been afraid at all and the last thing she had wanted was to land at Woburn or anywhere else. She had made her first flight. Her love affair with the air had begun.

It was far from being an eccentric fancy which encouraged the Duchess to take up flying. It was a genuine enthusiasm that grew into something like an obsession. She was one of those women to whom inactivity was a kind of death. She found an outlet for her bursting energies in a series of strenuous flights that a woman half her age would have hesitated to embark upon; yet it was not until she was 61 that she had set foot in an aircraft at all.

To her husband, all flying-machines and aviators were in league with the devil. No good could possibly come of them. But his redoubtable Duchess made it abundantly clear that she would have her way. Although she was a plucky woman she was not reckless, and certainly no fool. She realized that flying had to be learnt, so for two years was content to be purely a passenger in a hired de Havilland Moth. She found a kindred spirit in Captain C. D. Barnard. She badgered him into teaching her to fly, and, seasoned veteran that he was, he expressed himself astonished at the aptitude of a pupil who until well into middle age had not known one end of an aircraft from the other. He must have been more than a little doubtful, however, when the Duchess announced, with a casualness better suited to the discussion of a flip over Woburn, that she wished to reach India — by air. Furthermore, she made it clear that she had outgrown the little Moth and had her eyes on a big Fokker monoplane — and that she took it that Barnard would be going with her. As always, her will prevailed.

Her flight began at 4 a.m. at Lympne, near Hythe, in Kent, on 10 June 1928. An intimidating wind swept across the airfield. The Fokker buffeted its way through the skies; on take-off it took with it a number of telephone wires. Across the Channel the bad weather persisted and only cleared when the aircraft reached Sofia, Bulgaria, after an initial leg of 1,200 miles.

The Duchess was never one to waste valuable time on sleep and it is not difficult to imagine Captain Barnard's inner reaction when his partner, before going to her lodgings at 10 p.m., announced that she proposed continuing the flight six hours later. The Fokker took off again at 4.30 the following morning, Her Grace having breakfasted on lime juice. The most experienced of today's pilots would have broken out in a cold sweat on learning of pilot's and passenger's methods of navigation. Above the drone of the Fokker, Barnard bawled directions to the Duchess who scribbled on a scrap of paper, for ever threatened with loss by the wind. Over Babylon, they became enmeshed in a swirling sandstorm. Matters were not helped by the lady's voluble insistence on taking over the controls from time to time, a hazardous procedure for somebody who had done only the shortest "solos" on a Gipsy Moth.

Troubles of an unforeseen kind awaited the pair at Bushire aerodrome in Persia. The staff were understandably puzzled by the sudden appearance of a strange pilot and an untidily attired woman passenger of noticeably dominating manner. Permission to land had evidently been obtained in advance, but communications had broken down. The Persians appropriated the Fokker and threatened to shoot anyone who came near it. However, the misunderstanding was sorted out and, in a mood of triumph, the Duchess continued her progress. But not for long. Over the sea, the cabin of the aircraft began to fill with smoke and the windscreen became clouded with black oil. There was nothing for it but to turn back. The oil supply had become hopelessly choked. Examination showed that the Fokker needed a complete new engine — and that could only be obtained from England. It meant a six weeks' delay, much to the chagrin of the Duchess who had hoped to do the flight from Lympne to Karachi in four days. She had to kick her heels until the engine arrived, after which the rest of the journey passed off without serious incident and Karachi was reached.

This member of one of England's noblest families presented a truly remarkable spectacle as she set foot in the country that had been termed the brightest jewel in the Empire's crown. The Duchess wore Czechoslovakian shoes bought in Ispahan. She had on artificial silk stockings from Abadan and silk knickers from Bushire, plus a shirt copied in Persia from the upper part of a pyjama suit. She had just flown 13 hours without a break. She said that she was not at all tired, but wanted a meal. A delighted crowd whisked her off to Government House where, without being in any way conscious of incongruity, she forthwith slipped into the easy, well-ordered existence of a guest at a country house. For all the world she might have been back at Woburn.

It was a brave individual who suggested that the Duchess should do one thing when she had quite made up her mind to do another, but someone was bold enough to suggest, with infinite tact, that it might be wise of her to return to England by sea. The cunning old lady had the last laugh. She agreed to go to Marseilles by boat and arrived there on 8 September. But she flew the last stage home in her beloved Moth which had been sent to meet her.

The newspapers of two decades had every reason to be grateful to the Duchess of Bedford. Each of her flights brought its fair share of drama. In 1930 she and her pilot flew to the Cape and back in a new Puss Moth, a journey that took seventeen days. On this flight, as in all others, the Duchess was by no means content to sit back and let anyone else do all the work. One of her duties on the Cape flight was to pump petrol into the wing tanks, a particularly exhausting task, especially when undertaken in very cramped quarters. Her deafness had grown even more acute since the India trip, so shouting between pilot and co-pilot — the Duchess was by now doing her share of the flying — became out of the question. Since the passing of notes was scarcely an ideal method of communication, a complicated system of speaking tubes was set up. The Duchess used them with relish, but she confessed that the arrangement had its drawbacks — at critical moments she was apt to put the tube to her deafer ear.

Over a remote part of Uganda, storms and bad visibility forced down the Moth in a part of jungle that was lion-infested. An imposing collection of natives escorted the two pilots to a candlelit hut where they spent the night, but dared not sleep for fear of the lions. The journey continued next day, with the Duchess flying like a veteran over vast expanses of desert on the way to Khartoum.

On 16 May 1933 the Duchess of Bedford was, to her own astonishment, passed fit by the Air Ministry Medical Board and granted a Pilot's "A" Licence. It meant she could fly solo. She commented to a friend: "Two years ago they turned me down because of deafness. I'm even deafer now. It doesn't make sense." She was 67 years old and had done 53 hours solo.

The Duchess's highly colourful flying adventures had to be sandwiched in between her hospital work. Flying was still an obsession, but it took second place to nursing. No one, and certainly none of the pilots whom she employed over the years, ever knew precisely at what moment of the day she would take it into her head to fly off wherever she fancied. Her deafness precluded her from doing all the solo flying she wanted, despite her certificate. A co-pilot was expected to be on hand at any time, day or night. It required a special dedication, but the Duchess for all her grim exterior had a kindness which commanded loyalty from anyone she employed. Hard-bitten aviators respected her, recognizing a fellow professional.

The Flying Duchess celebrated her seventieth birthday on 26 September 1935. All her life she had had a great impatience with anyone or anything that threatened to obstruct her plans and she possessed enough strength of character to overcome most of them. But she could do nothing to stem old age and encroaching deafness. She had planned to fly to Africa this year, but her health was failing and preparations were interrupted by the death of King George V whose funeral she was obliged to attend. Then came a fresh blow. Ever since the Great War, the fortunes of even the richest families had been steadily eroded by rising living costs and taxes.

The Bedfords, although still remarkably wealthy, were to prove no exception. It became obvious that her beloved hospital was a serious drain on family resources. The search for funds became harder. In any case, the Duke had never approved of the enterprise and refused to foot any more of the bills. The place had to be closed.

For the Duchess it was like losing a child. During the war, she had taken over the Riding School at Woburn and it had been completely refurbished for its new purpose. In those days money had seemed no object. But funds were no longer forthcoming. All this happened a short time before her disappearance. Frequently, in times of stress, such as when her deafness had become too great to bear, she had flown away from Woburn alone. In the sky she found an escape and freedom of the spirit that eluded her elsewhere. It has been suggested that this is what caused her to take to the air on the afternoon of 22 March 1937. On the other hand, she had been looking for an opportunity to complete her 200 hours of solo flying and required another fifty-five minutes to do it. A flight mapped out for her previously by her then pilot, Flight-Lieutenant Preston, and adopted on this occasion covered 88 miles, from Woburn to Buntingford in Hertfordshire and over Girton College before turning for home. For a pilot of the Duchess's experience it was a mere flip. She took off. Until 4 p.m. the weather was perfect. Then a snowstorm set in. Mary, Duchess of Bedford, never returned.

A full-scale search was soon under way, spearheaded by the R.A.F. On 2 April came a discovery, though it only served to deepen the mystery — a strut was washed up at Yarmouth and other wreckage was identified at points along the East Coast. What could have possessed the Duchess to change course for the sea? One favourite theory is that her age had made her senile and incapable of knowing what she was doing. There is no evidence of this. She was an experienced pilot with a current licence and had undergone the usual strenuous medical test each year. Had the crushing news of the closure of her hospital depressed her unduly? In his book *The Flying Duchess*, based largely on his grandmother's letters and diaries, the 13th Duke of Bedford presents evidence that she was very depressed and more than usually tired when she took off for the last time.

As the Duke comments, it was an end such as she would have chosen.

The Flying Duchess was a product of the Victorian Age, so many of whose notable figures combined a pioneering spirit with an eccentricity notably at odds with the straitlaced conformity of the time. Her sort are rare enough on the earth now, let alone in the air.

21: COLLISION COURSE

There is no mystery about what happens when two aircraft collide: the question — sometimes unanswered and unanswerable — is why did they?

Ships collide, trains collide, cars collide. Even when those supposedly in control of them see the crunch coming the amount they can do about it is limited by the angle at which the two vehicles are converging on their "collision course", and the speed at which each is travelling. Inevitably, head-on crashes cause the most damage and injury. If a car moving at 50 miles per hour smashes head-on into another travelling at 70, the impact upon each is the equivalent of its having been driven into a solid wall at 120 miles per hour. Even two pedestrians, with the ability to skip aside or stop dead in a split second rather than crash into one another, can, if they do neither, damage themselves quite nastily by meeting in full stride. How much more terrifying, then, is the thought of two jet airliners meeting at a combined speed in four figures.

Just as alert pedestrians have the ability to manoeuvre pretty well unrestrictedly in a way that is not possible for drivers of fast-moving cars, wrongly-switched trains, or ships meeting in thick fog, it might be thought that aircraft, with so much space in which to fly, ought to be able to keep so far out of each other's way that there could be little or no chance of colliding. Even in cities with airports one does not see aeroplanes streaming back and forth like cars on a two-way road, overtaking, braking, accelerating, weaving in and out of the traffic pattern. They pass over, almost always in just one direction — depending on the direction of the wind that day

— at intervals of several minutes, which means a spacing of many miles. They have the additional dimension of height in which to separate farther from one another's course. Yet aircraft have collided, and many more have only just avoided doing so; and aircraft do not need to meet head-on to suffer total disaster. A mere touch together can send one or both plunging out of control.

In early flying days it was up to pilots alone to ensure they did not run into one another. In some ways their task was easier than today. Flying small aircraft and seated in open cockpits, with their begoggled heads stuck out in the air, they enjoyed a quite advantageous field of view — not to mention the assurance that there were not all that many other aircraft in the world, let alone in their own vicinity. Every aircraft had, and still has, its blind spots, as the fliers of the First World War soon learned to recognize in terms of both offensive and defensive tactics; but by twisting and turning his head, a pilot could see all round him and above, and by craning over his cockpit's sides he could keep a watch below. Wartime airmen on patrol in seemingly empty skies knew all too well the need for constant scrutiny of this kind if they were not to be jerked from complacency by a stream of bullets hammering into their machines. The more sophisticated airmen of the Second World War shared this habit of unceasing vigilance against the attacker's sudden swoop out of the sun's glare or the cloud's concealment, or from some quarter a pilot could not keep constantly observed, such as behind and below his tail. Those who did not fly in perpetual mistrust of a sky whose sole occupant they appeared to be, died, or were sometimes lucky not to.

So it was in civil flying, especially close to airports where aircraft converged in growing numbers as flying boomed. As

275

the free-for-all 1930s approached their end it had become more than ever obvious that the boundless skies could no longer be at the haphazard disposal of aircraft. They would have to be marshalled on to defined channels, and kept there by rigid compulsion.

Those invisible highways of the sky are there above us now: intangible, unmarked by any signposts, yet exactly mapped out in terms of compass bearings and altitudes. They form a pattern which might be compared with those of the most up-to-date land roads, with fast lanes, intersections, "clover-leaf" entry and exit points, and all the rest of it. Like roads, they have their individual numbers. They have their highway code too; but unlike road users, aeroplane pilots are totally disciplined — at least, those of them who fly for the airlines. So are the majority of Service fliers, though the nature of their operations does not restrict them to the skyways. And so are most of the growing band of private pilots, flying their own small machines on business or pleasure, though they, too, cannot be disciplined like their commercial counterparts.

If the demands of modern flying have planted more responsibility on the airline pilot's shoulders, they have also relieved him of some. It was once his duty, by keeping that constant visual watch, to spot any other aircraft flying nearby and keep well out of its way. This is no longer so. With airliners flying at such high speeds and in such numbers in every part of the world, it has long been recognized that a man seated at a control room desk, hundreds of miles from an aircraft's location, is generally better placed to serve as its "lookout" than anyone aboard it.

Before taking off every airliner captain files their flight plan, detailing their intentions in the light of timetable, load, weather forecast, and so forth. They are allocated an "airway" along which to fly and must not deviate from it except if ordered by radio during flight or if granted permission in response to their own radioed request. Thus, controllers on the ground know where their aircraft are expected to be at every stage of the flight, and how they relate to other planes in the vicinity. During flight a stream of radioed reports from the aeroplane confirms progress and conditions; and when land is below or near, each aircraft is watched on radar. So the person on the ground has the overall picture, even at night or when the aircraft is "blind" in cloud or fog.

None of this means that a pilot is no longer required to look out of their windows; that if they see another aircraft converging with theirs they can shrug their shoulders and leave it to ground control to avert a collision. What it does mean is that a plane, seemingly alone in the vastness of sky, is nothing of the sort: it is in a sense a piece on a mighty chessboard. But while a game of chess starts with a certain number of pieces, limited in size and spheres of movement according to the game's ancient rules and bound to become less in number as it proceeds, the skyways of the world are year by year having to accommodate more and more aircraft of bigger and faster types. The outcome is seen at the bigger airports in terms of queues of aircraft waiting to take off, and land, for planes can queue in the air as well as at the end of the runway, and it is the growing headache of the ground controllers to find space in which to "stack" incoming aircraft, keeping them circuiting at different altitudes until, one by one, they can be called in to the ground.

At the end of a safe, comfortable flight passengers disembark feeling gratitude towards the captain who has set them down so gently, the cabin crew who have served them so deftly and cheerfully with their food, drinks and duty-free goods, and, perhaps, those briefly glimpsed other occupants of the flight deck whose concern is vaguely supposed to be to do with radio and navigation. It is doubtful whether one passenger in a thousand gives a thought to the ground controller, with their flickering screens, their microphones and telephones, their concentration and tension in the claustrophobic atmosphere of the tower.

The complex ground-control organization, more or less standardized throughout the world, has evolved rather than been created; and, like much else in aviation, disaster has contributed to development. Collision has played its part. Aircraft collide much less often than trains or ships, infinitely less often than cars, and those unlucky enough to be the exceptions to this are mostly Service machines or light civilian ones, rather than airliners.

One of the worst of air disasters, in 1955, involved collision between two big U.S. Army troop carriers. They had just taken off from an aerodrome in Germany together with a third plane and were settling into formation for a training flight when one seemingly began to suffer engine trouble. Seeking to correct loss of height, the pilot brought it into the path of one of the other machines, which hit it. Both fell to the ground and burst into flames too fierce to let would-be rescuers get near. Sixty-six passengers and crew were killed. No ground-control organization could have averted such a disaster, but it will never be known why either of the pilots could not have done, for neither survived to testify. Perhaps each simply happened to be looking the other way as their aircraft came together and never knew their danger until too late.

A salutary instance of what could happen to two converging aircraft whose pilots did not happen to be looking at the time belongs to September 1956. It happened in America, over the town of Bartlesville, Oklahoma. A DC-3 (Dakota) of Continental Airlines en route from Tulsa to Kansas City, carrying two pilots, a stewardess and 14 passengers, was approaching the town at about 2.30 p.m. in good visibility. It was in touch with the local airport where it was due to land in a few minutes' time. In preparation for this the pilot and co-pilot began their routine catechism, a cockpit check which required the co-pilot to read aloud a list of seven instrument readings, to which the captain had to respond. The familiar check would take some thirty seconds, during which the co-pilot's eyes would be on his list, the captain's on the instruments — and no one's eyes, except the passengers', looking out of the windows as the aircraft approached the built-up area of the small town.

Also approaching Bartlesville at that moment was a single-engined Cessna monoplane, a small, privately owned aircraft piloted by a visitor to the town who was giving four local children a pleasure flight rounded off by a bird's-eye view of their home. This pilot and all four children were peering groundwards, trying to pick out the children's house — and the Cessna was flying on a course at exact right-angles to the airliner's.

The two aircraft were three miles apart, then two, then one. There was no ground radar on which their convergence could be seen and they were across the town from the airport, so that there was no chance for the situation to be realized by anyone with access to them by radio. In any case, although the Dakota's radio was active, the Cessna's was switched off. Townspeople in Bartlesville who had bothered to look up on hearing the everyday sound of aircraft engines could only watch horrified at the planes, doomed to meet unless either pilot took the evasive action which seemed to be agonizingly delayed.

By a quirk of fate, neither had seen the other. The Cessna pilot's eyes were on the ground, the Dakota captain's on his instruments. Even so, it only needed the merest glance from the airliner's cabin window for the corner of either of its two pilots' eyes to catch the little monoplane streaking towards them on the starboard bow. They were half a mile apart and closing rapidly; a quarter of a mile, a few hundred yards. The cockpit check all but completed, the Dakota captain raised his head — but at the same time turned away from the window, in order to read the hydraulic fuel indicator behind him.

Fortunately for twenty-two people, at that very moment the Cessna pilot, still without having seen the airliner, began a turn to starboard. The children had excitedly pointed out their house; they had passed over it, and now the pilot was preparing to cross the town and make for the airport. The turn started to bring the Cessna into the same path as the Dakota — and as it did, they met. There was a grinding crash. Both aircraft lurched and shuddered. Their passengers screamed as their startled pilots clutched their controls and gave split-second thought to what must have happened and what might be going to happen next.

Minutes later the two aircraft were safely on the runway at Bartlesville airport. Thankfully, their pilots had found them still responsive to the controls and had gingerly nursed them in to safe landings. The last-moment turn of the Cessna had saved them. Instead of crashing into the Dakota broadside on, with inevitably fatal consequences for both aircraft and all aboard them, the two at the moment of impact had been flying in the same direction, with the result that their collision had had little more violence than that of an overtaking car brushing the slower one. The damage had been slight enough to allow both pilots to remain in control, and twenty-two badly shaken people could at least give thanks as they might have been dead.

So, we have instances of collisions between two Service aircraft, and an airliner and a private machine; and, as has already been discussed, the discipline of the skies today, let alone in the mid-1950s, is less stringent for Service and private planes than for airliners. Yet, though very rarely, even airliners have been known to collide — that they have managed to do so in spite of all the discipline and safeguards earlier described is mystery indeed. Perhaps the most celebrated case, leading to the most searching investigation into existing standards of safety, which were duly changed after it, happened over one of earth's most spectacular showplaces, the Grand Canyon in Arizona.

The world has no more remarkable natural piece of sculpture to show than the Grand Canyon; to see it is to marvel and never to forget its immensity, its strange-hewn outlines and its vivid colouring. It begins at Marble Gorge, near Arizona's northern boundary, and extends some 280 miles — little less than the equivalent distance from London to Carlisle — to end at Grand Wash Cliffs, near the Nevada State line. At its narrowest it is some four miles wide; at its broadest the best part of twenty. In a plateau between 5,000 and 9,000 feet above sea-level the canyon is a great, jagged cut, up to a mile deep in parts, carved over the course of millions of years by the Colorado river and the effects of heat, rain, frost, wind and, in more "recent" times, the gradual rising of the surrounding land.

In fact, for all its ancient origins — and impressions and fossils of animals, fishes and shells long extinct are found at many parts of it — the Grand Canyon is, geologically speaking, something quite new, and it is only just over a century since a person first traversed its depths.

What makes the Canyon most indelibly memorable is not so much its grandeur as its colours. The many differing layers of rock, stone, lava and ancient wind-blown sand that the carving-out of its sides has revealed each have their own colours — from pastel greens and pinks, to sombre browns and greys, to vivid yellows and, most prominent of all, a subdued red which comes to glowing life when the sun is on it. Add to these the green of the cattle- and deer-pastures and pine forests, the prevalent misty purple haze and the intense hot blue of the Arizona sky, and you have an unmatched spectacle which many people have journeyed from distant parts of the world to see and have come away not begrudging one cent of the expense.

You can see the Grand Canyon by car or train; but one of the most rewarding ways of doing so is by air, when the whole great natural scheme is perhaps at its most awe-inspiring. Airliners passing over that part of Arizona used, if time and conditions allowed, to detour a little to give their passengers a high-altitude view of the Canyon, and the possibility of such a treat would be pleasurably anticipated by anyone due to fly that way in daylight, especially during those hours when the sun would be giving the prospect the semblance of an artist's freshly-daubed palette.

No doubt the passengers who left Los Angeles International Airport in the two big airliners which took-off a few minutes apart in the morning of 30 June 1956 were hoping for the bonus of a Grand Canyon view. Although the Californian sky was heavily overcast as they left, there was a long way to go and conditions might be much clearer over inland Arizona. Their aircraft, both four-engined and of similar performance, were a Lockheed Super Constellation of Trans-World Airlines, with 70 passengers and crew bound for Kansas City, and a United Airlines Douglas DC-7, heading for Chicago with 58 passengers and crew.

Each aircraft had been assigned to a routing along a series of those invisible highways of the sky: the Constellation to Green Airway 5, Amber 2 and Victor 10; the DC-7 to Green Airway 5, Victor 116 and Victor 84. These courses would keep them widely apart for most of the flight until they were due to converge and cross paths at a point over the Grand Canyon. Even here they would not come too near to one another for any danger: the DC-7, flying slightly the faster, would pass northward of the Constellation, and would be cruising at 21,000 feet which gave it a vertical clearance of 2,000 feet over the Constellation at 19,000 feet.

Radar would watch the two aircraft on the first stages of their flight. In 1956 its coverage did not extend as far as the Grand Canyon itself, so that it would be up to the two pilots, checked upon by the ground controllers to whom they would radio regular position reports, to accomplish what were in every sense routine flights which each had made very many times before.

Because of the cloud conditions over California both Captain Jack Gandy of TWA and Robert Shirley of UA had elected, in their flight plans, to fly by IFR — Instrument Flight Rules; but it was not long after take-off before Gandy found himself beyond the coastal cloud and in clear but rather turbulent air. He called Los Angeles Flight Control for permission to change to VFR — Visual Flight Rules — under which it would be his and his crew's responsibility to "see or be seen by" any other aircraft, and to climb to 21,000 feet. The first part of this request was granted; the second, no doubt because of the presence of the DC-7 on that same first leg, Green Airway 5, at 21,000 feet, was firmly refused.

Captain Shirley in the DC-7 also asked to switch to Visual Flight Rules but made no request to change height. The permission was granted.

As the two airliners passed on inland they found conditions of generally scattered cloud with some of those towering banks of cumulus which appear beautiful to aircraft passengers but are not so admired by the men who are flying the aircraft. Captain Gandy again asked permission to change height, this time to fly 1,000 feet over the cloudbanks rather than subject his passengers to the discomfort of passing through the turbulence they concealed. His request was allowed. He would be constantly in clear sky, able to keep a far-ranging lookout for any other aircraft. He was reminded of the DC-7's path and acknowledged the caution.

Gandy and Shirley both radioed Control their reports of passing over their respective stipulated checkpoints at the expected times. As the controller logged their reports he could see how their courses were beginning to converge. Eventually came each pilot's estimated time of passing a point over the Painted Desert, near the Grand Canyon, where the charts showed their paths would cross. Gandy estimated 10.31, Shirley 10.34, three and a half minutes behind his schedule. Though flying at 288 knots against the Constellation's 270, the DC-7 had had a longer course to pursue. The differentials had brought them back to just that same three-minute margin that had separated their take-offs from Los Angeles.

Los Angeles Control was no longer monitoring their progress. They were out of its area and over one administered by Salt Lake City Control. In any case, both were flying VFR, keeping their own lookout without reliance upon the ground.

At 10.30 a third aircraft, flying lower, reported to Salt Lake City that the scattered cloud was beginning to consolidate into a general overcast, with some pillars of cumulus rearing up to an estimated 25,000 feet. Within a minute the men on duty at Salt Lake City heard something which contrasted dramatically and chillingly with this laconic report. Two voices, pitched high with alarm, came indistinctly over the radio, "Salt Lake. United 718..." and "Up! Up!" Immediately after, the first voice cried, "We're going in!" Then came silence.

United 718 was the United Airlines DC-7. Control called it up — in vain. They called the TWA Constellation. Again there was only silence.

The conclusion was obvious. Within minutes, summonses were going out to investigators of the Civil Aeronautics Board, calling them from many points to converge on the Grand Canyon.

By the time they got there, small aircraft had located the wreckage of both planes. They lay about a mile apart. The Constellation, readily recognizable by its triple tail, lay shattered on Temple Butte, a high knob of rock with steep walls deep in the mighty canyon. The other aircraft lay on another of these buttes so characteristic of the arid plateau country.

Clearly, there was going to be a rescue difficulty in such a region — if anyone had survived. A doctor, landed by helicopter at each site in turn, soon confirmed that the problem did not arise: 128 people had perished.

Finding out why was going to be the next difficulty. The CAB officials set about the task with typical energy and thoroughness. While some toured the sparsely inhabited district seeking eyewitnesses to the disaster, others tried to clamber to the scenes of the two crashes to bring out bodies and examine wreckage for clues to what had happened. They were helped by locals, but even so the rugged Canyon was against them. Expert climbers would be needed to tackle some of the rocky slopes. Again it is characteristic of the CAB that there was no hesitation or sparing of expense to send for and fly to Arizona a team of mountain guides from Switzerland, 9,000 miles away. Even these experts found gruelling days before them.

The agents seeking witnesses were also hampered by the nature of the terrain — it was too rugged to support many homesteads, and these few were widely scattered. One after another was visited, but no one seemed to have watched the two high-flying airliners. Tourists who had been in the area were traced and questioned equally fruitlessly. The usual sprinkling of people capable of deluding themselves into thinking they had seen the disaster emerged. None could have done, as the anomalies in their evidence proved, but each contention needed investigating closely before rejection.

In the early stages there was no conclusive evidence as to how the aircraft had met their simultaneous end. Collision was the obvious explanation but needed proving and accounting for. Some natural phenomenon could perhaps have dashed them from the sky at the same instant, to fall a mile apart, but it was monumentally unlikely. By all the rules the airliners should not have arrived at the same point at the same time, flying at the same altitude. Enough precautions had been taken to keep them well apart and their last position reports had confirmed that these had been working. Yet by the time enough pieces of wreckage had been retrieved from the deep Canyon, and marks on them compared, no room was left for doubt that there had, indeed, been a collision.

Deducing from those marks of damage, the CAB "detectives" were even able to say in what manner the big planes had come together so fatally. Seconds before, it appeared, the Constellation must have been just ahead of the DC-7 and slightly below it. Both aircraft were presumed to have been in cloud at the time — but cloud is seldom so consistently dense that the crew of an aircraft overhauling another one in it could not have caught even a momentary glimpse of it in time to take violent avoiding action.

The decisive clue to this disaster is no doubt the relative positions of the aircraft. The DC-7 pilot and co-pilot would not have seen the Constellation because it was just lower than they, and therefore hidden by their own aircraft's nose. The Constellation crew could not, unless they had happened to look back and upward, have seen the DC-7 above and behind them, as it would have been hidden by their cockpit roof. In the collision between the DC-3 and the Cessna over Bartlesville, as we have seen, the chance that the two were flying in the same direction at the time lessened the impact and saved a fatal accident. The two big airliners over the Grand Canyon did not have this luck.

Had they been under the control of someone far away equipped with radar, their convergence must have been seen and averted. They had not been and had flown through a gap in the control system, to meet and collide.

Investigation into the case went on for nearly a year and brought beneficial changes including improvement to flightdeck range of vision in airliners, the insistence upon Instrument Flight Rules being observed at all heights, the speeding-up of the extension of radar coverage, and other new regulations. Airline operators and their passengers throughout the world benefited from the tragedy over Grand Canyon.

Despite its long and painstaking deliberations the inquiry had to leave one important question open — how had the two airliners which should have crossed each other's path with a safe margin of distance and height come to be flying a parallel course at identical altitude? It can never be known. The answer probably lies in the paragraph or two of travelogue at the beginning of this account. Wanting to give their passengers a treat, either or both pilots had made a slight detour from course in order to take in the spectacular view of the Grand Canyon, in which, moments later, they, their aircraft and all aboard them would lie dead.

There had been a good deal of cloud about at the time of this disaster, and no doubt this played its part in causing it. Given a completely clear sky, Captain Shirley might have seen the other aircraft before that last split moment when it was already too late to take effective avoiding action. Yet, it does not follow that he would. Ironically enough, there have been perhaps more collisions between aircraft in conditions of perfect visibility than in any others. One might expect them to occur at dark of night, in dense cloud, or fog, or driving rain or snow; but it is in just such conditions that the pilot's whole reliance is upon his instruments and the judgment of his distant controller. In clear conditions he may assume the responsibility himself; and no human being can, as it were, stand outside himself and see his situation in relation to others.

Airlines have done their best to turn their pilots into computers. They are trained to a sort of mechanical perfection as operators of the aircraft; taught to recognize swiftly the cause of any defect that might arise in the performance of the machine, and to take the necessary corrective action. They must have the utmost familiarity with the characteristics, physical and weatherwise, of every part of the route they are to fly and of every airport they will use. The route manuals they must study and memorize incorporate details of the terrain, prevailing winds, landmarks likely to aid or confuse, and man-made obstructions, such as towers, tall chimneys and cable-carrying lines of electricity pylons. They themselves must be of stable character, mature judgment and peak physical fitness: their profession may be one of the "glamorous" ones, as viewed from the outside, but there is very little of the swashbuckler of pioneering days about the modern airline pilot.

But those who fly aircraft are *not* computers. They are subject to physical limitations, one of which is that they cannot necessarily be doing two jobs at once. Another, undoubtedly, is that they do not have eyes in the back or sides of their heads. If they had, a collision mysterious only in its relentless inevitability against all the odds would not have occurred over New York in perfect visibility one afternoon in 1949.

A Constellation airliner of Pan American left La Guardia Airport, New York, that January afternoon, bound for Ireland with ten crew and twenty-three passengers. Authorized to climb to a cruising altitude of 17,000 feet under Visual Flight Rules, the captain took his aircraft off and began the long haul upward.

An hour earlier, a Cessna light aircraft had left a small airfield in Connecticut, some eighty miles away. In it were two private pilots who had decided to get in some flying time by taking a trip to New York and back without landing. They had duly arrived over the great metropolis, flown around for a little while pointing out landmarks to one another, and had then turned for home, a few hundred feet higher than their authorized altitude of 3,000 feet. For all their observing of what was below them, they appear to have been singularly blind to the one thing which it was imperative they should see that day — the Constellation, coming up at them from the direction of La Guardia, on a collision course with their plane.

The Constellation was approaching from the west and the Cessna from the south-west, so that both had the sinking winter sun more or less behind them and not in a quarter where its glare could dazzle or distract either pilot. However good a lookout the occupants of an aircraft keep, there are limitations to their field of vision, due to the construction of the cockpit. This could have had little bearing on this occasion. The airliner pilot, seated on the left, would not have had much chance of seeing the small aircraft above to starboard; but his co-pilot might, had he not been busy with post-take-off duties which kept his eyes down and his attention concentrated.

The real onus to keep a watch was on the pilot of the Cessna. He knew he was in the vicinity of La Guardia and should have kept himself and his passenger alert to the possibility of big aircraft approaching from take-off or to land. Perhaps both men were too busy still sightseeing: at all events, they did not see the Constellation coming. Perhaps they never knew what hit them.

The Constellation captain saw the small aircraft just before they met at 3,500 feet. With a desperate thrust on the control yoke he jerked the nose of the airliner down. It was too late. The big plane ploughed into the small one at 175mph, smashing it to bits which scattered dangerously over the built-up area below. The Cessna's engine, landing gear and propeller were left sticking in the airliner's fuselage.

The two men in the Cessna had been killed outright. By the pilot's immense skill, the greater tragedy was averted. Not daring to risk trying to get back to La Guardia, he nursed his plane to a United States Air Force field some miles away and managed to land safely with a full load of fuel.

Not a very mysterious affair, perhaps; but in any circumstance where events or human behaviour seem inexplicably to have defied all odds we tend to shake our heads wonderingly and mutter, "How on earth...?" Perhaps "How in the air...?" would be more appropriate to the cases recounted in this book. The meaning is the same.

ACKNOWLEDGEMENTS

This book has been compiled from a wide variety of sources, from personal interviews to published books and newspapers of several countries.

I am especially obliged to Mr Ralph Barker for his co-operation and permission to draw upon his excellent book *Great Mysteries of the Air* (Chatto & Windus, 1966) for the main facts of the following chapters: "Two Stars Fall", "A Royal Tragedy at Eagle's Rock", "The Lost Tycoon", "Exit a Heroine", "Suicide Behind Schedule", and part of "Flight Into Mystery". Enthusiasts for air mysteries will find several more in Mr Barker's book that I have not used.

Messrs Roger Stanway and Anthony Pace have kindly permitted me to draw upon and quote from their interesting document of first-hand investigation into Unidentified Flying Objects, *Flying Saucer Report*, published by them in 1968 from Newchapel Observatory, Newchapel, Stoke-on-Trent, Staffordshire.

The Royal Aircraft Establishment, Farnborough, Dr Christopher Dowling and the library staff of the Imperial War Museum, and the Ministry of Defence have been of much assistance, as has Mr Ronald Howard, son of the late Leslie Howard. Special acknowledgement is due to Mr Rupert Butler for research and editorial assistance.

The bibliography is not intended to be a list of books used — I have not used them all, and did refer to some others not mentioned here — but rather a reading guide for anyone wishing to pursue these mysteries in greater detail than I have had space to give.

BIBLIOGRAPHY

Barker, Ralph, *Great Mysteries of the Air*, Chatto & Windus, 1966

Carter, I. R., *Southern Cloud*, Angus & Robertson, 1964

Chapman, Robert, *Unidentified Flying Objects*, Arthur Barker, 1969

Colvin, Ian, *Flight 777*, Evans, 1957

Cramp, Leonard G., *Space, Gravity and the Flying Saucer*, Werner Laurie, 1954

De la Croix, Robert, *Mysteries of the North Pole*, Muller, 1954

Goerner, Fred, *The Search for Amelia Earhart*, Bodley Head, 1966

Hewal, Timothy & Waterton, W. A., *The Comet Riddle*, Muller, 1955

Higham, Robin, *The British Rigid Airship 1908–1931*, G. T. Foulis, 1961

Hogg, Garry, *Airship Over the Pole*, Abelard-Schuman, 1969

Knight, Clayton & K. S., *Plane Crash*, Elek, 1958

Launay, André, *Historic Air Disasters*, Ian Allan, 1967

Leasor, James, *The Millionth Chance*, Hamish Hamilton, 1957

Leslie, Desmond & Adamski, George, *Flying Saucers Have Landed*, Werner Laurie, 1953

Lipscomb, Cmdr. Frank W., O.B.E., R.N. & Davies, John, *"Up She Rises"*, Hutchinson, 1966

Stanway, Roger & Pace, Anthony, *Flying Saucer Report*, Newchapel Observatory, 1968

Stewart, Oliver, *Danger in the Air*, Routledge & Kegan Paul, 1958

A NOTE TO THE READER

If you have enjoyed this book enough to leave a review on **Amazon** and **Goodreads**, then we would be truly grateful.
The Estate of Michael Hardwick

Sapere Books is an exciting new publisher of brilliant fiction and popular history.

To find out more about our latest releases and our monthly bargain books visit our website:
saperebooks.com

Made in the USA
Middletown, DE
27 November 2022

16129237R00166